The Tripersonal God

Other Titles by Gerald O'Collins, S.J.

The Case Against Dogma (1975)
The Cross Today (1977)
What Are They Saying About Jesus? (1977)
The Second Journey (1978)
What Are They Saying About the Resurrection? (1978)
Fundamental Theology (1981)
Problems and Perspectives of Fundamental Theology (1982)
Finding Jesus (1983)
Interpreting Jesus (1983; reissued 1999 by Cassell)
The People's Christmas (1984)
Jesus Today (1986)
Jesus Risen (1987)
Interpreting the Resurrection (1987)
Friends in Faith (1989)
A Concise Dictionary of Theology (1991)*
Believing (1991)
Luke and Acts (1993)*
Retrieving Fundamental Theology (1993)*
Experiencing Jesus (1994)
Faith and the Future (1994)
The Bible for Theology (1997)*
All Things New (1998)*

*Available from Paulist Press, Mahwah, New Jersey, USA.

THE TRIPERSONAL GOD

Understanding and Interpreting the Trinity

by

Gerald O'Collins, S.J.

PAULIST PRESS
New York/Mahwah, N.J.

Scripture quotations are taken from the New Revised Standard Version.

Cover design by Cindy Dunne

Library of Congress Cataloging-in-Publication Data

O'Collins, Gerald.
The tripersonal God : understanding and interpreting the Trinity / by Gerald O'Collins.
p. cm.
Includes bibliographical references and index.
ISBN 0-8091-3887-5 (alk. paper)
1. Trinity. 2. Catholic Church—Doctrines. I. Title.
BT111.2.035 1999
231´.044—dc21 99-33448
CIP

Distributed in Australia by
Rainbow Book Agencies Pty.Ltd/
Word of Life Distributors
303 Arthur Street
Fairfield, VIC 3078

Published by Paulist Press
997 Macarthur Boulevard
Mahwah, New Jersey 07430

www.paulistpress.com

Printed and bound in the
United States of America

CONTENTS

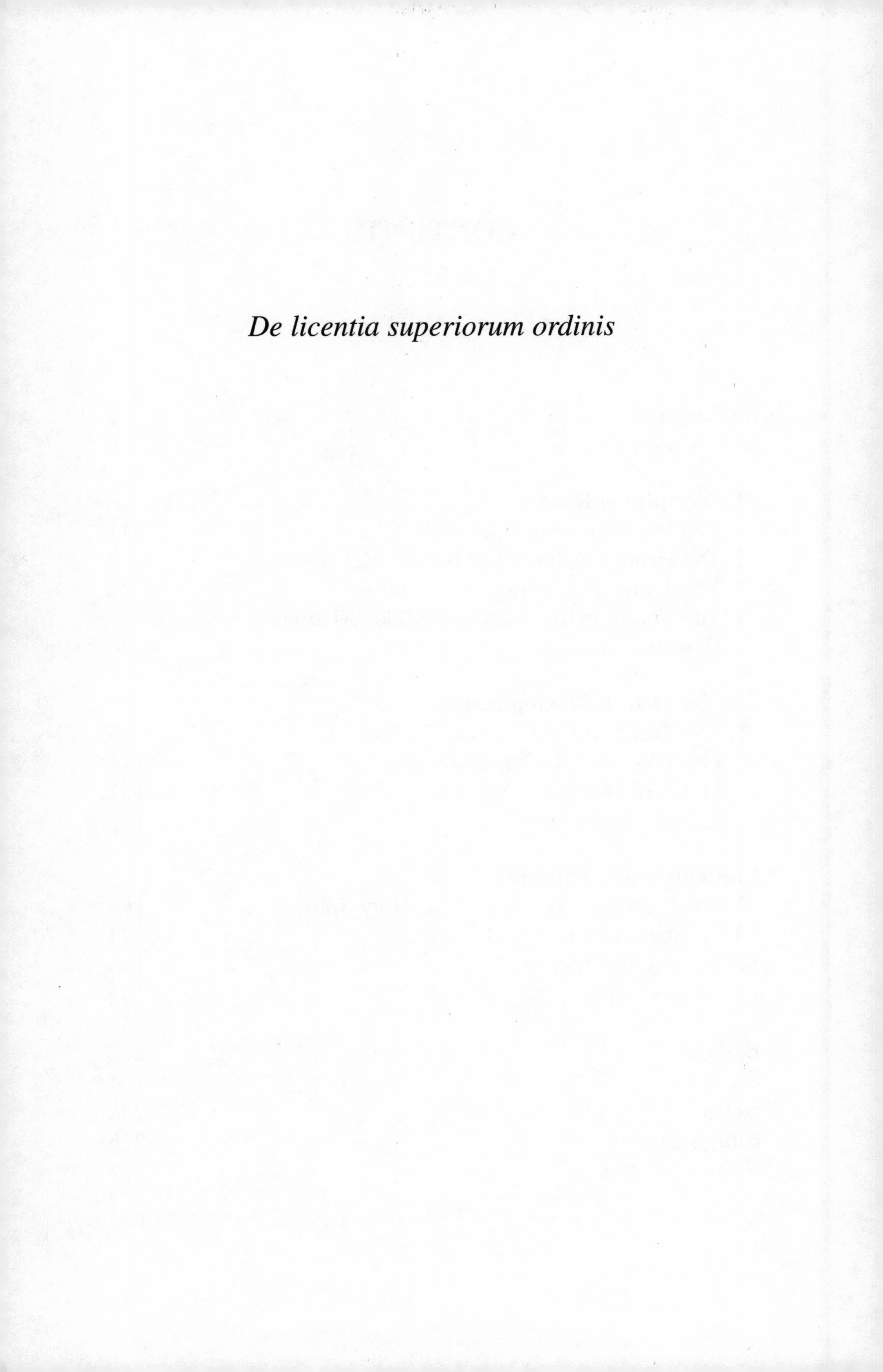

De licentia superiorum ordinis

INTRODUCTION

"This Jesus God raised up, and of that we all are witnesses. Being therefore exalted at the right hand of God, and having received from the Father the promise of the Holy Spirit, he has poured out this which you see and hear."

Acts of the Apostles 2:32–33

"Any doctrine of God which has ceased to be trinitarian in character has thereby ceased to be Christian."

Nicholas Lash, *"Considering the Trinity"*

"Three does not mean three, one does not mean one, and person does not mean person."

Bishop David Jenkins, an Oxford sermon on the Trinity

To be a Christian is to believe in, experience, and worship God in a trinitarian way. But what should Christians believe about the Trinity? Why should they believe what they do about the Trinity? These questions about the "what?" and the "why?" obviously interlock, with the answer to the latter determining our answer to the former. We hold—and rightly hold—this or that belief about God by truly answering the question: "Why and how do we know and experience in faith the tripersonal God?" Answering this question can justify what we hold to be the case about God.

In reflecting on their trinitarian faith, Christian believers have the task of looking at and drawing on three distinct, if interrelated, areas:

(1) the historical experience of salvation which the scriptures record and which teachers in the church have interpreted through the centuries; (2) the testimony of public worship; and (3) the experience of practicing discipleship today.

Three Tasks

The first task entails pursuing the meaning and truth of what was revealed about God in the events that climaxed with the whole story of Jesus Christ and his original followers. This way of doing trinitarian theology characteristically finds its sources in writings from the past: in the Bible; in the works of Greek, Latin and Syriac writers; in church documents; in the books of Eastern and Western theologians; and in other traditional texts that indicate how Christians, with varying degrees of wisdom and authority, understood and interpreted what they believed about the tripersonal God and why they believed what they did. Which events supported their trinitarian faith and why did these events do just that? How did they come to recognize in their religious history a trinitarian pattern or the tripersonal God's way of being with them, and how did they do so in such a way as to correlate this salvific experience with the eternal being of God?

Public prayer and worship form the source and setting for a second way of developing trinitarian theology. How do liturgical celebrations in the Eastern and the Western churches bear witness to and prompt experience of the tripersonal God? What does the glory of Orthodoxy's iconographic tradition show us? What do we hear if we consult worshipers in matters of trinitarian faith and doctrine? In eucharistic worship, both the *anamnesis* and the *epiclesis* have, for example, their inseparable but distinct place in leading up to the doxology. The *anamnesis* (as "remembering") involves bringing to mind God's saving actions in history—especially in Christ's passion, death, resurrection, and glorification—for the assembly that seeks to appropriate the salvation that the Son of God has effected once and for all. As "anticipation," *anamnesis* means looking forward to the end time of final fulfillment and doing so with an expectation that already receives and perceives something of that ultimate future. In the eucharistic prayers the *epiclesis* (or "invocation") normally asks that the Holy Spirit descend upon the gifts to change them into the body and blood of Christ for the spiritual profit of those who receive them. In the new eucharistic prayers introduced for the Roman Catholic Church after the Second Vatican Council, the *epiclesis* before the consecration prays that the gifts be changed, while the *epiclesis* after the consecration prays that the communicants be changed. In *epiclesis* the Spirit is invoked, and in *anamnesis* Christ is remembered and anticipated; through the presence of the Spirit, the eucharistic presence of Christ is actualized. Then the *doxology* (or "giving glory" to God) completes the eucharistic prayer, by directing "all glory and honor" to God the Father "through, with, and in" Christ "in the unity" effected by the Holy Spirit. The eucharistic worship of Christian believers is unthinkable without its trinitarian *anamnesis, epiclesis,* and *doxology.*

Anamnesis, epiclesis, and *doxology* would obviously need to be supplemented by those who aim at constructing an adequate approach to trinitarian doctrine through worship. Further liturgical texts, scriptural readings, and images, a whole range of visual icons, and musical settings for the Creed (with its celebration of the Trinity) show us much more richly how the tripersonal God is experienced, rather than described, in Christian worship of all kinds and rites.

A third approach to the tripersonal God typically asks: What does trinitarian faith lead Christ's followers to do or leave undone in the world? Does it bring something special, even unique, to the struggle for promoting the common good and relieving the massive injustice of human society? What could faith in the tripersonal God mean for the poor and suffering victims of our world? This third approach will develop its trinitarian doctrine with an eye on and for the sake of the millions of victimized nonpersons who surround us.

Trinitarian faith and theology express themselves, then, as knowledge, worship, and action. Hence, apropos of the Trinity, we can distinguish (1) faith seeking "scientific" understanding, or *fides quaerens intellectum scientificum,* (2) faith seeking worship, or *fides quaerens adorationem,* and (3) faith seeking social justice, or *fides quaerens iustitiam socialem* In all three descriptions, the word *seeking* (*quaerens*) has a significant function. Trinitarian faith seeks a knowledge and understanding that in this life will never be conclusive or exhaustive. It seeks to worship the tripersonal God with an adoration that will be fully realized only in the final kingdom. It seeks a just society that can never completely come in this world. A proper attention to the force of "seeking" will thus ensure that we respect the future implications in all three ways of "doing" trinitarian theology.

Rather than to adopt one way and then another artificially, this book will aim to do justice to all three approaches. It will attend to the truth (the first way), the beauty (the second way), and the justice (the third way) of full trinitarian faith. Such an integral approach to the Trinity means using our heads (the first way), our hearts (the second way), and our hands (the third way). Any such integral trinitarian theology entails searching for the truth, lifting our hearts in worship, and putting ourselves to work for a transformed world that faith in the tripersonal God requires. Obviously one or other concern will be more to the fore at different stages of this book, but the challenge is to honor all three concerns and respond to three questions. Is this trinitarian doctrine true to the foundational story of the divine self-revelation in Jesus Christ? How can you pray it, above all in eucharistic worship? Can you live it, and how can you put it into practice? Knowledge of the Trinity is closely connected with the worship of the Trinity and the practice of a trinitarian life.

The Bible and Beyond

We begin from the scriptures and their testimony to the tripersonal God. First-century Christians proposed a trinitarian interpretation of the events of Good Friday and Easter Sunday. In those events, along with the outpouring of the Spirit, they experienced the unique high point of God's revelatory activity for our salvation. This saving revelation was experienced as threefold. Undoubtedly, we should be careful not to be anachronistic here and use the language of a later time. Christians had to pursue matters for several centuries before they could come to a clearer position on the divinity of Christ and the personal identity of the Holy Spirit. All the same, we find at the origin of Christianity a certain sense that the Father, the Son, and the Holy Spirit were revealed as acting in our human history, above all in the events of Good Friday and Easter Sunday and their aftermath. The fully deployed doctrine of the Trinity points to and develops the self-revelation of the tripersonal God communicated through the whole Easter mystery. To use the technical expression, this means beginning with the "economic" Trinity, the tripersonal God actively disclosed in the whole history Jesus enacted through his life, death, and new life as risen from the grave. The perennial custom of invoking the names of the Father, the Son, and the Holy Spirit when making the sign of the cross testifies to the essential link Christians felt from the start between Jesus' crucifixion (and resurrection) and their faith in the tripersonal God.

After examining the biblical testimony, we will move to patristic and subsequent elaboration of trinitarian teaching. For earlier and later Christian thinkers, pressing issues emerged. What could they know about the absolute mystery of the Godhead in its eternal, divine life? Through the "economy" or history of salvation, initiated in the OT and fulfilled in the NT with the mission of the Son and the sending of the Holy Spirit, they held the tripersonal God to be revealed in such a way as to be accessible to their thought. From describing the "economic" Trinity as experienced in the history of salvation, they moved to say something about the "immanent" Trinity or the life of the tripersonal God in itself. But did such a move defy the divine incomprehensibility and illegitimately eliminate elements of mystery? In other words, should they have practiced apophatic or negative theology and recognized the wisdom of saying more what God is not rather than what God is? St. Augustine of Hippo and others asked themselves: How far is trinitarian faith a fit subject for probing by reason? Should we humbly remain dependent on revelation and refuse all attempts at developing models of the Trinity drawn from our human experience and the created world? Modern emancipation has brought further questions: Is there, for example, an inherent sexism in the way the Trinity has been traditionally understood and named with two gender-specific names as "the Father, the Son, and the Holy Spirit"? Does such naming continue to encourage androcentric patriarchy, or—if properly understood—does it subvert an oppressive, male-dominated patriarchy? All those who accept the scriptures as *the* foundational record and interpretation of divine revelation face here the question: What naming of God is required by fidelity to the original witness? A further issue concerns modern, Western atheism—at least in the form of autonomous individualism and a secularized indifference toward the question of God and even toward the question of the divine identity. How can trinitarian faith respond to this situation?

After eight chapters on the biblical and historical side, in the third and final part of the book, I will single out for discussion several systematic issues: the personal existence of the Holy Spirit (Chapter 9), applying the language of persons and actions to the Trinity (Chapter 10), naming the Trinity as the Father, the Son, and the Holy Spirit (Chapter 11), and images of the Trinity (Chapter 12). This book is written out of a faith that "God" is not merely the chief player in some language game and that the "tripersonal God" is not just some expression of our individual or collective psyche. Christianity stands or falls with trinitarian faith. This divine truth calls for our faith and worship—in life and in death. Right from the birth of Christianity, trinitarian faith has been the faith of martyrs.

For various kinds of help with this book, I wish to thank Donald Buggert, John Farrelly, Earl Muller, Aidan O'Boyle, Steven Olds, Gregory Sterling, Frank Sullivan, Kathleen Walsh, the men and women who attended three courses I taught at the University of Notre Dame, the members of a first-cycle seminar at the Gregorian University, those who contributed to the Trinity Summit (held in New York at Easter 1998), the members of a study circle who met at the Augustinianum in Rome, the community of the Jesuit Theological College, Melbourne (Australia), where almost half of this book was first written, and Marquette University (Wisconsin) for making me once again the Wade Distinguished Professor of Theology (fall semester of 1998/99), an appointment that provided the opportunity to complete this book. For the translation of biblical texts, I normally follow the New Revised Standard Version. With much affection this book is dedicated to Martin and Tessa de Bertodano and all their family.

Gerald O'Collins, S.J.
Marquette University, Milwaukee
October 13, 1998

ABBREVIATIONS

ABD	D. N. Freedman (ed.), *Anchor Bible Dictionary,* 6 vols. (New York: Doubleday, 1992).
DH	P. Hünermann (ed.), *Enchiridion Symbolorum, Definitionum et Declarationum de Rebus Fidei et Morum* (Freiburg im Breisgau: Herder, 37th ed., 1991).
ND	J. Neuner and J. Dupuis (eds.), *The Christian Faith* (New York: Alba House, 6th ed., 1996).
NT	New Testament.
OT	Old Testament.
par(r).	and parallel(s) in other gospel(s).
ST	St. Thomas Aquinas, *Summa theologiae.*

Note: references to DH, ND, and ST will be given in parentheses in the running text, as will happen also in the case of ancient Christian sources. For the works of St. Justin, St. Irenaeus, Tertullian, St. Augustine, other ancient writers, and St. Thomas Aquinas's *Summa theologiae,* readers can choose from the range of editions and translations available in any adequate theological library. Readers will find that various translations of these ancient texts are available in any decent library; this book provides its own translation or follows in places the translation provided by H. Bettenson, and so on.

The Scriptural Roots

1.
THE OLD TESTAMENT BACKGROUND

"What is needed is a loving confession of ignorance rather than a rash profession of knowledge. To reach out a little toward God with the mind is a great blessedness; yet to understand is wholly impossible."
St. Augustine of Hippo, Sermones, *117*

A famous and widely reproduced image of the Trinity by St. Andrew Roublev (ca. 1360–1430) represents the scene of the hospitality offered by Abraham and Sarah to three angels seated around their table (Gn 18:1–15), a scene that has encouraged many Christians to think of the Blessed Trinity. A chalice on the table links the scene with the Eucharist, and hence with the saving and revealing story of Christ's passion, death, and resurrection. The icon should also make us think of ways in which the OT faith and its scriptures helped the early followers of Jesus to interpret and proclaim the central mystery of the Blessed Trinity that they had experienced and responded to. Some knowledge of the OT is indispensable for grasping the NT trinitarian message and its specifics. The OT contains, in anticipation, categories used to express and elaborate the Trinity. To put this point negatively, a theology of the Trinity that ignores or plays down the OT can only be radically deficient. Something essential will be missing from what we mean by *the Trinity* if we ignore the Jewish roots of Jesus and those of his first followers. Several notions and images are peculiarly relevant here: God as Father, the divine Wisdom and Word, and the Spirit of God. This chapter will examine them in turn.

God as Father

Some or even many argue nowadays that by naming the first person of the Trinity *Father,* Christian preaching, theology, and worship have underwritten the oppression of women and helped to maintain a patriarchal system in society and church. A later chapter will address this issue directly. The present chapter will examine the earliest biblical roots for this name, which has obviously left its central mark on the creed, liturgy, life, and art of Christians.

To introduce our examination of particular data from the OT, it is as well to recall the relative absence of feminine language and images for God in Judaism, Christianity, and Islam. This feature of these monotheistic religions[1] distinguishes them from the ancient cultures that expressed the divine through such language: as the goddess Tiamat in the Babylonian *Enuma Elish* cycles, Asherah in the Canaanite religion, Fricka in the Scandinavian epics, and Hera who was the sister and consort of Zeus for the Greeks and was identified as the goddess Juno by the Romans. In the OT scriptures, God exercises no sexuality and is utterly transcendent. Even if male and sometimes female images are applied to the deity, the sense that God is literally neither male nor female and transcends creaturely representations comes through the official OT prohibition of divine images. The prophet Hosea witnesses to this sense of the divine transcendence when God speaks through him: "I am God and not man, the Holy One in your midst" (Hos 11:9). This sense of YHWH's being utterly holy and different from human beings backs the prohibition of material images for God and affects the language the OT uses for the divinity.

Before examining the OT use of metaphorical "Father" language for God, we should note that even if the OT neither speaks of nor addresses God as anyone's "Mother," it does use maternal *similes* in this context. God is graphically compared with a woman who suffers in childbirth (Is 42:14), as well as with a midwife (Ps 22:9–10). Comparisons with maternal conception and begetting are also pressed into service by the Pentateuch (Nm 11:12; Dt 32:18). As a mother does, God wishes to comfort the suffering people (Is 66:13). The divine love goes beyond even that of a woman for her children: "Can a woman forget her nursing child, or show no compassion for the child of her womb? Even these may forget, yet I will not forget you" (Is 49:15). A tenderness beyond that of a mother is highlighted by Sirach 4:10: "The Most High will be more tender to you than a mother."

At the outset it is worth recalling how simile differs from metaphor.[2] In a particular context that clarifies matters, a simile uses language in its customary sense to compare an aspect of something (or someone) with that of something (or someone) else. In the case of Isaiah 42:14, God's "loud" intervention is likened to a woman gasping and panting in labor. Metaphor extends the use of language beyond its "ordinary" meaning(s) to generate new perspectives on reality by asserting an identity between two subjects (and not merely by comparing two aspects): "Nigel spends his evenings surfing the World Wide Web"; "Sally is the lioness of her netball team"; "God is Father to the people." This latter statement contains some crucial information about God that emerges in the OT and is then developed in the history of Jesus and the founding generation of Christianity.

In the OT scriptures, God is known through many names, above all through the personal name of YHWH (e.g., Ex 3:14; 6:6–8), the most sacred of names that is used about 6,800 times in the OT, both by itself or in compounds like *YHWH Malak* ("King": e.g., Ps 93:1). God is also generically known as *El* ("divinity"), as in *El Shaddai* ("God, the One of the Mountain(s)": e.g., Ex 6:3; Nm 24:4,16), the intensified plural *Elohim* ("divine God"; e.g., Gn 1:1), and *El Elyon* ("God Most High").[3] In *God Is King: Understanding an Israelite Metaphor*[4] Marc Zvi Brettler points out that "God is King" is the "predominant metaphor for God in the OT, appearing much more frequently than metaphors such as 'God is lover/husband' (e.g., Jer 3, Ez 16, and Hos 2) or 'God is a father' (Dt 32:6; Is 63:16; Jer 3:19)." But what do we find about the last metaphor, the one that particularly interests us here?

A little more than 20 times, God is named (or addressed) as *Father* in the OT. Let us look first at the cases in the protocanonical books (those 39 books accepted by all as inspired and canonical) and then at those in the (later) deuterocanonical works (or the six books and further portions of the protocanonical books found in the Greek but not in the Hebrew canon of scriptures).

(a) Father in the Proto-Canonical Books

One of the oldest texts in which God is called *Father* comes from a song attributed to Moses: "Do you thus repay the Lord, O foolish and senseless people? Is he not your Father, who formed you, who made you and established you?" (Dt 32:6). Here and elsewhere in these closing chapters of Deuteronomy, Moses is pictured as recalling the intimate covenant bond between God and the people. By flirting with other religions, the people deny their true parentage and behave like ungrateful children. God's nurturing fidelity and mercy are contrasted with the perverse infidelity of Israel. This text from Deuteronomy indicates how *Father*, when used of God, usually refers to the special covenantal relationship with God of the people who have been delivered from captivity and called God's (firstborn) son (e.g., Ex 4:22–23; Hos 11:1) or God's "sons and daughters" (e.g., Dt 32:19; Is 1:2; 30:1). God gave them birth (Dt 32:18) by electing and adopting them. An historical divine choice, and not any kind of sexual activity and physical generation (as in the case of the gendered gods of surrounding nations), made God their Father.

A later passage recalls God's covenantal promise, conveyed in an oracle through the prophet Nathan to King David: "I will raise up your offspring after you…and will establish the throne of his kingdom forever. I will be a father to him, and he shall be a son to me. When he commits iniquity, I will punish him with a rod such as mortals use…But I will not take my steadfast love from him" (2 Sm 7:12–15). In ancient Egypt and elsewhere in the Middle East, rulers were styled "sons of God." Hence it is not surprising to find God's promise in 2 Samuel about an everlasting Davidic dynasty mentioning Solomon, David's son and successor, in these terms. The royal psalms reflect the belief that the anointed king was divinely chosen and was deemed to be God's adopted son: "You are my son; today I have begotten you" (Ps 2:7). This psalm refers to the day when the king was installed as the people's God-given leader.

The king was understood to rule by divine choice, through God's power, and in fulfillment of God's purpose. Being enthroned on Mount Zion where God was believed to "dwell" (Ps 2:6), the royal son of David was legitimated by God his Father—God's son in that sense but not in the sense of physical sonship (as being literally God's offspring), nor in the sense of being divinized or literally made divine. By naming God as *Father*, the oracle delivered by Nathan in 2 Samuel 7 brings out the unconditional nature of the promise and relationship. No matter what happens, God's choice of the Davidic dynasty, like the divine election of the whole people, has established a permanent relationship: God is and will remain faithful Father to the people and its king. God disciplines the people and its monarch but will do so with steadfast love. After the Babylonian Exile the failure of efforts to reestablish the Davidic dynasty will create problems for the promise communicated by Nathan.

We find parallels to 2 Samuel 7:12–15 in 1 Chronicles 17:11–15; 22:9–10; 28:5–6, a work which comes into existence between 350 and 300 B.C. and which draws, sometimes verbatim, on the books of Samuel and Kings but without mentioning them by name. All three texts from 1 Chronicles repeat Nathan's oracle and God's promise to be Father to the king as the divinely adopted son. The intimacy of the God–king relationship is implied by an interesting omission when the redactor reworks the material in all three passages of 1 Chronicles. In the first passage, any reference to discipline is simply dropped. The second passage goes on to encourage Solomon to observe God's law, implying a warning about what might happen if he fails to do so: "May the Lord grant you discretion and understanding, so that when he gives you charge over Israel you may keep the law of the Lord your God. Then you will prosper if you are careful to observe the statutes and the ordinances that the Lord commanded Moses for Israel" (1 Chr 22:12–13). The third passage also adds some words from God, who requires fidelity to the law: "I will establish his kingdom forever if he continues resolute in keeping my commandments and my ordinances, as he is today" (1 Chr 28:7). There is a hint here of bad consequences if the king fails in such resolution, but no straightforward reference to the discipline that will follow iniquity that we find in 2 Samuel and its version of Nathan's oracle. When 1 Chronicles plays down the disciplinary element in the fathering metaphor, the result is to highlight even more how God is and will be a tender, caring Father.

The Psalms yield at least two passages that speak directly, and not merely indirectly (as in Psalm 2), of the divine fatherhood. Evidently the product of a long history, Psalm 68 praises the God of heaven who is also named as Father to the defenseless:

> Sing to God, sing praises to his name;
> lift up a song to him who rides upon the clouds—
> his name is the Lord—
> be exultant before him.
> *Father* of orphans and protector of widows
> is God in his holy habitation.
> God gives the desolate a home to live in;
> he leads out the prisoners to prosperity,
> but the rebellious live in a parched land. (Ps 68:4–6)

The God whose strength is expressed by the standard image of "riding upon the clouds" places his power at the service of the powerless, the forsaken, and the imprisoned. God acts as Father toward them all.

A royal prayer for deliverance, Psalm 89 is unusual in that someone (here the king) addresses God as *Father,* albeit that the address is placed by God in the mouth of the king. God speaks of his "faithful one" (David):

> He shall cry to me, 'You are my *Father,*
> my God, and the Rock of my salvation!'
> I will make him the first-born,
> the highest of the kings of the earth.
> Forever I will keep my steadfast love for him,

> and my covenant with him will stand firm.
> I will establish his line forever. (Ps 89: 26–29)

The Davidic king will address God as *Father,* the God whose strong fidelity to his covenanted love allows God to be also named as *Rock of salvation.* With language that recalls 2 Samuel 7:14–15, the psalm also warns that, while violation of the divine law will bring punishment, God's steadfast love will never be withdrawn (Ps 89:30–33).

Turning to the prophetic literature, we can start with Jeremiah and oracular material from the late seventh century, when Judah was threatened by both external forces and internal infidelity. In the first passage, YHWH is presented as both Father and Bridegroom (or Friend), in the second as Father to his children; in both passages the people are movingly encouraged to address God as *my Father.* In the first passage, YHWH exhorts the people to repent of their infidelity: "Have you not just now called to me, '*My Father,* you are the Friend [or Bridegroom] of my youth—will he be angry forever, will he be indignant to the end?' This is how you have spoken, but you have done all the evil that you could" (Jer 3:4–5). In the second passage, God explains how Judah's infidelity blocked the divine hopes for them: "I thought how I would set you among my children, and give you a pleasant land, the most beautiful heritage of all the nations. And I thought you would call me *My Father,* and would not turn from following me" (Jer 3:19).

A sharp contrast comes through these two passages. God follows his people with a father's love and fidelity, but they fall into infidelity and indulge idolatrous attitudes, even saying to a tree, "You are my father" (Jer 2:27). God does not sustain grudges against the people but expects a loyal love that will not only address him as *My Father* but also act accordingly. The first passage seems to interweave father and friend imagery because paternal and marital love express the covenantal partnership that God maintains with the people. The latter image, with God as Husband to the people, recurs in the prophetic literature (e.g., Is 54:4–8; Jer 2:2; Ez 16:1–63; Hos 2:7, 19) and probably helped to keep talk of YHWH as Father to a minimum. Another obvious reason for the OT rarely applying to God the metaphor of Father (and never that of Mother) was that such usage could suggest the "natural," procreative activity attributed to Baal, Asherah, and other gods and goddesses of the Near East. Far from being that kind of biological or physical parent, YHWH had no consort. The divine fatherhood (and the Israelites' corresponding status as God's sons and daughters) was understood, as we have seen, to result from the free divine choice and activity in the history of salvation.

Despite any inhibition about calling God *Father,* the name turns up several more times in Jeremiah and other prophetic books. God's paternal power will bring home the scattered exiles: "With weeping they shall come, and with consolations [or supplications] I will lead them back. I will let them walk by brooks of water, in a straight path in which they shall not stumble; for I have become *a father* to Israel, and Ephraim is my *firstborn*" (Jer 31:9). Acting as a loving father, YHWH will gather and guide the people on a new exodus, which is described with language ("brooks of water" and "a straight path") that evokes the better-known passages of Deutero-Isaiah (e.g., Is 40:3–4; 42:16; 43:19–20).

The closing chapters of Isaiah yield two further examples for our study. At least some of the exiles have returned from Babylon to Jerusalem, when the prophet voices the community's laments in one of the very few passages in which God is addressed as *Father* and, in fact, addressed as *our Father:* "For you are *our Father,* though Abraham does not know us and Israel does not acknowledge us; you, O Lord, are *our Father;* our Redeemer from of old is your name" (Is 63:16). The patriarchs, Abraham and Israel (i.e., Jacob), have died and are of no help. God, the people's Redeemer from of old, is immortal and as "our Father" revives hopes for salvation. In a prayer that God will reveal himself and act again with power, the prophet confesses not only the people's sin and helplessness but also their trust in the Father who has made them: "You have hidden your face from us, and have delivered us up to our iniquity. Yet, O Lord, you are *our Father,* we are the clay, and you are our potter; we are all the work of your hands" (Is 64:6–8). The Book of Isaiah began by calling God "our God" (Is 1:10); it ends by addressing YHWH as "our Father," the people's God who will care for them in their distress and patiently mold them as a potter does with clay.

A divine oracle from Malachi uses the image of *father* to illustrate the people's infidelity: "A son honors his father and servants their master. If then I am a father, where is the honor due to me? And if I am a master, where is the respect due to me?" (Mal 1:6).[5] *Father* is associated here with *master* to evoke the authority of the divine Master whom Israel should serve. But the context puts the primary emphasis on God as the loving Father who has adopted the people into a covenant relationship which they have failed to live up to: "'I have loved you,' says the Lord" (Mal 1:2). Malachi's imagery recalls what one psalm says of the people's humble submission as God's male and female servants, with God pictured as both master and mistress: "As the eyes of the servants look to the hand of their master, as the eyes of a maid to the hand of her mistress, so our eyes look to the Lord our God, until he has mercy upon us" (Ps 123:2).

A further passage in Malachi is directed against marriage with foreigners, a practice that damages the religious unity of the people: "Have we [the people] not all one *Father*? Has not one God created us? Why then are we faithless to one another, profaning the covenant of our ancestors?" (Mal 2:10). The law forbids intermarriage with foreigners (Dt 7:1–4; see Ex 34:10–17). Violations of the ancient covenant such as divorcing faithful Jewish wives and contracting new marriages with foreign women are incompatible with loyalty toward the extended family of faith; the Israelites are all children of one Father who is their God, as Malachi 1:6 has already said (see Jn 8:41–42). Intermarriage not only means social disloyalty but also threatens the religious unity of the nation. Here it should be noted, however, that the "one Father" may refer to Abraham, who at the human level provides the nation with its unity (see Mt 3:9, see also Lk 3:8; Jn 8:33, 37, 39). Possibly "the covenant of our ancestors" recalls the covenant made with Abraham, or it may indicate in a general way an obligation inherited from the past without intending any specific covenant (see Amos 1:9).

(b) Father in the Deuterocanonical Books

Turning to the deuterocanonical books (books found in the Greek but not the Hebrew canon of scriptures), we begin with the hymn of praise that comes at the end of the Tobit: "Exalt him [God] in the presence of every living being, because he is our Lord and he is our God; he is *our Father* and he is God forever" (Tb 13:4). Like the other passages we will examine, this prayer of praise discloses a very personal attitude toward God that recalls Isaiah 64:8 and anticipates the NT's prayerful relationship to God as "our Father." The Book of Tobit is a piece of edifying and fascinating fiction, whose main protagonists (Tobit, his son Tobiah, and Sarah, the bride-to-be) offer vivid examples of tenacious faith when tested by painful and even terrifying challenges. The hymn that praises God as our Father and our God forever may have been added later. At all events, the book and this concluding hymn represent God as free, just, and faithful in the lives of the protagonists. God shows the loving, paternal concern for Tobit, his family, and all those who suffer in exile (Tb 13:3–5).

Sirach elaborately addresses God as "Lord, *Father,* and Ruler of my life" (Sir 23:1) and, with slight variation, as "Lord, *Father,* and God of my life" (Sir 23:4). This address comes in a prayer for wisdom and self-control. True wisdom can be lived by those who confidently ask for the powerful help that God gives when saving individuals from falling into sin. In a psalm of thanksgiving that comes in the first of two appendices and that recalls the appeal to "my Father" of Psalms 89:26, the same book tells its readers: "I cried out. 'Lord, you are my *Father;* do not forsake me in the days of trouble'" (Sir 51:10). God's power ensures salvation for those in distress who appeal to him.

In denouncing those who trust idols to bring them and their ships safely across the sea, the Book of Wisdom turns to God and confesses: "It is your providence, O Father, that steers its [the ship's] course, because you have given it a path in the sea and a safe way through the waves" (Wis 14:3). God's fatherly providence powerfully controls ships, seas, and all creation. Earlier, Wisdom's account of the false way, entertained and followed by ungodly persons, includes their plans to torture and even kill the righteous person, who—among other things—"boasts that God is his father" (Wis 2:16).

(c) Similes and Corollaries

To complete this survey of Father language for God in the OT, we need to recall the use of similes, some corollaries, and then some data from the intertestamental literature. First of all, a number of passages compare God's activity toward the people with that of an ideal father. In the wilderness, God marvelously "carried" the people to their destination "as a father carries his son" (Dt 1:31); in the desert he also "disciplined" them "as a father disciplines his son" (Dt 8:5; see Wis 11:9–10). This language of discipline should not be taken to suggest a cold, authoritarian parent—still less a brutal, punishing father. It is inspired by a love that is concerned with training the beloved child. To encourage a wise and heartfelt trust in the God who also disciplines his children, the Book of Proverbs remarks: "The Lord reproves the son he loves, as a father the son in whom he delights" (Prv 3:12). Those who honor and serve God may meet with misfortune, but Proverbs encourages them to view such trials in a relationship of familial intimacy with God and even as proofs of the divine favor. One of the psalms introduces what is basically the same simile to celebrate the compassionate help God extends to individuals and to the chosen people as a whole: "As a father has compassion on his children, so the Lord has compassion on those who fear him" (Ps 103:13). Finally, in reference to the true worshipers who will be spared on the day of judgment, God is compared to a father: "They will be mine says the Lord of Hosts, my own possession…and I shall spare them as a man spares the son who serves him" (Mal 3:17).

We remarked above on the fact that the OT rarely applied to God the metaphor of Father; the last paragraph illustrates that paternal similes for God were also quite rare. In a somewhat unsymmetrical fashion, the OT used more generously the corollary of fatherhood when it spoke of God's sons (e.g., Dt 14:1) or children (e.g., Is 45:11). Israel had become God's "firstborn son" (e.g., Ex 4:22), "child," or "son" (e.g., Hos 11:1; Wis 18:13). Although a sense of collective sonship predominated in pre-Christian Judaism, royal and righteous persons were also at times singled out. The king, who stood between God and the people and was enthroned as the instrument of the will of the divine King, was named God's "son" (e.g., Ps 2:7). In the wisdom tradition, a righteous person could be called God's "child" or "son" (Wis 2:13,18; 5:5). The man who cared for widows and orphans "will be like a son of the Most High" (Sir 4:10), but it was above all the people as a whole who, through the divine choice and liberating activity, enjoyed the status of God's "sons" (e.g., Jer 3:22), "sons and daughters" (e.g., Dt 32:19; Is 30:1), or "children" (Is 1:2; see Jer 31:20). This language expressed the intimate closeness of Israel's relationship to God, and nowhere more clearly than in Hosea 11:1–4.

While the prophet elsewhere uses the metaphor of God as Husband to the people, here he introduces the tender and dramatic metaphor of loving parents bringing up their children. God does more than "call" repeatedly to the people whose idolatrous cult of foreign gods makes them insolent and ungrateful children that run away (Hos 11:1–2). The divine oracle portrays God's gentle, parental activity as follows: "It was I who taught Ephraim to walk, I who took them in my arms; but they did not know that I secured them with reins and led them with bonds of love, that I lifted them like a little child to my cheek, that I bent down to feed them" (Hos 11:3–4). No passage in the OT goes beyond this one in expressing God's tender, loving care for his rebellious children. Where the law allowed a rebellious son to be brought by his parents to the elders and then stoned to death (Dt 21:18–21), God's parental love will not surrender the people to their sinful choices. God is the most loving of parents, even when faced with children who are consistently unloving and unresponsive.

The intertestamental literature (or texts composed by Jews around the time of Jesus but not recognized as canonical scripture) includes a few examples of paternal and maternal language for God. Nothing surpasses the tenderness of a passage from the Thanksgiving Hymns of Qumran, which applies to God a metaphor ("Thou art a father") and two similes ("as a woman" and "as a foster-father"): "For Thou art a father to all [the sons] of Thy truth, and as a woman who tenderly loves her babe, so dost Thou rejoice in them; and as a foster-father bearing a child in his lap, so carest Thou for all Thy creatures."[6] One notices, however, that in the few places where the Dead Sea Scrolls introduce the theme of divine fatherhood and human beings' filial status (e.g., 4Q372.1.16), the relationship remains unrelated to God's "Spirit." As we will see in Chapter 3, Jesus *and his Spirit* enter the picture when Paul refers to our adoption as God's sons and daughters (e.g., Rom 8:14–17; Gal 4:4–6).

To sum up, naming God *Father* expressed his deep involvement in the story of Israel, its kingly leaders, and its righteous ones. The name has nothing to do with physical generation; Israel's king was not understood to be deified, as if he was in a gendered sense begotten from the deity. The use of the Father metaphor centered on God's free and creative choice of the people. This name conveyed the steadfast commitment and compassionate love of God in protecting, cherishing, and nourishing a people whose infidelity could also call for discipline. But despite all their sinful failures to live out their covenant with God, they could always call upon God as their Father. While occurring in a variety of historical, prophetic, and sapiential texts, this divine name cannot be called frequent in the OT, but it will become the favored name in the NT, as we will see later.

Wisdom, Word, and Spirit

Both in the history of Israel and beyond, the OT understood Wisdom, Word, and Spirit to serve as personified agents of divine activity. As personifications that were not yet formally recognized as persons, they operated with personal characteristics, and this was particularly so in the case of Wisdom. Let us look now at these divine personifications that provided the language that would be used later to express and elaborate the NT experience of the tripersonal God. The most striking case of such personification is that of Wisdom.

(a) Wisdom

Hokmah, or wisdom (as noun, adjective, or verb) occurs 318 times in the OT, and nearly 75 percent of these occurrences turn up in Job, Proverbs, Ecclesiastes (Qoheleth), Sirach, and Wisdom. Wise counsels are also found elsewhere: for example, Tobit 4:3–21; 12:6–13; and Baruch 3:9–4:4.[7] Personified Wisdom or Sophia becomes increasingly related to the divine work of creation, providence, and salvation and grows in dignity and power along with OT sapiential thinking. Within a monotheistic faith, Wisdom takes on functions and attributes of YHWH, and within a strongly patriarchal religion, Wisdom emerges in a feminine way. Let us track this development chronologically, as far as is possible, from Job to Wisdom.

Perhaps dating to the seventh century B.C. and probably containing some later additions, the Book of Job abruptly introduces Wisdom at the end of a long dialogue between Job and his three friends in a poem that scholars have variously called an interlude, a bridge, or a later insertion. The poem stresses the mysterious inaccessibility of divine Wisdom, which is quite beyond the reach of human beings (Jb 28:12–14, 20–21), utterly precious (Jb 28:15–19), and accessible only to God (Jb 28:23–27). At this early stage of reflection, Job 28 celebrates and does not formally personify Wisdom.[8] Here Wisdom appears as related to the works of creation, yet distinct from any particular work of creation. God, who controls the wind, the sea, the rain, and the thunderbolts, can alone see and know the way to Wisdom. Although many subsequent characteristics of Wisdom do not show up in this poem from Job, one persistent feature emerges: her mysterious inaccessibility. Wisdom will be seen constantly as divine gift rather than human achievement. The books of Proverbs, Sirach, and Wisdom may represent the availability of Wisdom, who invites all to her feast, dwells in Jerusalem, and graciously appears to those who love her. Nevertheless, the initiative remains hers. This mysterious inaccessibility will be reflected in Paul's teaching on the crucified Jesus. Only those divinely enabled to do so will recognize him as the Power and the Wisdom of God. What they confess appears as folly to all who follow the world's wisdom and have not yet accepted the grace to discern the divine Wisdom in person, whose life among them ended on a cross (1 Cor 1:18–2:8).

While it has reworked some or even much older material, the Book of Proverbs seems to date from the late sixth or early fifth century B.C.

Wisdom looms large in the first nine chapters (1:20–33; 3:13–24; 4:5–9; 8:1–9:6). Like a prophet Wisdom preaches her message, setting before her hearers a choice: either folly and disaster or fear of God and life. More precious than jewels, she proves a tree of life for those who grasp her (Prv 3:15, 18). Her claims are dramatic: Listening to her words will bring salvation, while disobedience entails destruction. Her role in creation is announced (Prv 3:19), to be developed in the famous description of her primordial relationship to God and creation (Prv 8:22–31). "Begotten" or "created" "long ago" as God's firstborn (Prv 8:22), Sophia not only existed with God before everything else but also cooperated in the divine work of creation (Prv 8:30–31). Delighting in God's company and then in the human community, Sophia is revealed here as profoundly related—to God, to all creation, and, in a particular way, to human creatures. Finally, Proverbs 9:1–6 depicts Wisdom as building her house and inviting the simple to join her feast of food and wine that symbolize the doctrine and the virtue that come from God.[9] Lady Wisdom's house and banquet will provide language for the NT and post-NT interpretation of Jesus, divine Wisdom in person.

Among the earliest deuterocanonical books and longest books of the Bible, Sirach contains the most extensive example of Jewish wisdom literature we have. It was originally written in Hebrew ca. 180 B.C. and two generations later translated into Greek.[10] Wisdom appears at the beginning of the book (Sir 1:1–30), at the halfway mark (Sir 24:1–34), and at the end (Sir 51:1–27). In the heavenly court, Sophia proclaims her divine origin:

> I came forth from the mouth of the Most High and covered the earth like a mist. I dwelt in the highest heavens, and my throne was a pillar of cloud. Alone, I compassed the vault of heaven and traversed the depths of the abyss. Over waves of the sea, over all the earth, and over every people and nation, I have held sway. Among all these, I sought a resting place. In whose territory should I abide? (Sir 24:3–7)

Sophia came forth "from the mouth of the Most High" as divine Word, dwells like God "in the highest heaven," and is enthroned like God "on a pillar of cloud." Like God, she is present everywhere (from "the vault of heaven" to "the depths of the abyss") and has universal dominion ("over all the earth" and over "every people and nation"). She covered "the earth like a mist," just as the divine Spirit or Breath covered the waters at creation (Gn 1:2).

Wisdom looked for a permanent home ("a resting place"). In a dialogue with her (that has no counterpart in the case of Word and Spirit), the Creator chose a place for her to dwell:

> The Creator of all things gave me a command, and my Creator chose the place for my tent. He said, "Make your dwelling in Jacob, and in Israel receive your inheritance." Before the ages, in the beginning he created me, and for all the ages I shall not cease to be. In the holy tent I ministered before him, and so I was established in Zion. Thus in the beloved city he gave me a resting place, and in Jerusalem was my domain. (Sir 24:8–11)

Existing with God from "the beginning" and enjoying eternal existence ("for all ages I shall not cease to be"), Sophia followed the divine choice of Israel and has made her home in Jerusalem. Settled in the holy city, she sends out an invitation for her great banquet: "Come to me, you who desire me, and eat your fill of my fruits. For the memory of me is sweeter than honey, and the possession of me sweeter than the honeycomb. Those who eat of me will hunger for more, and those who drink of me will thirst for more" (Sir 24:19–21). Here Sophia herself is the food and the drink, the source of nourishment and life. The NT will apply this language to Jesus (Mt 11:28), while John will go beyond Sirach by portraying Jesus as permanently satisfying: "Those who come to me will not hunger and those who believe in me will not thirst" (Jn 6:35).

At this point, Sirach innovates even further by identifying Sophia with that central symbol of YHWH's will and guidance for the people, Israel's Torah: "All this is the book of the covenant of the Most High God, the law that Moses commanded us" (Sir 24:23; see Bar 4:1–4). This identification seems a mixed blessing: On the one hand, it extends the influence of Sophia into the most sacred realm of Israel's relationship with God; on the other hand, this identification can be seen to curtail Sophia by confining her to "the manageable limits of a book."[11]

In his final poem (Sir 51:1–27), Ben Sirach speaks as an old man, at times almost identifying himself with the beloved Wisdom who has brought him such deep satisfaction and serenity:

> Draw near to me, you who are uneducated, and lodge in the house of instruction. Why do you say you are lacking in these things, and why do you endure such thirst? I opened my mouth and said, "Acquire wisdom for yourselves without money. Put your neck under her yoke, and let your souls receive instruction; it is to be found close by. See with your own eyes that I have labored but little and found for myself much serenity." (Sir 51:23–27)

This invitation to the "uneducated" and thirsty will be echoed in Jesus' offer to those who are poor and overburdened. If they take on his light yoke, they will find enduring peace (Mt 11:28–30). As divine Wisdom in person, Jesus invites his hearers to take up the yoke of his message rather than put, or rather leave, their neck under the yoke of the law.

Before leaving Sirach, we can observe how this book prefigures two aspects of the "economic" mission of the Son as divine Wisdom. On the one hand, while Wisdom is present to "every people and nation" (Sir 24:6), by the divine choice she dwells in Israel and finds her home in Jerusalem (Sir 24:8–11). A universal presence does not preclude God's choice of a special dwelling place for Wisdom. On the other hand, such a particular divine choice does not mean that Wisdom is absent elsewhere in the world and is unavailable for the whole human race.

Written probably shortly before Christ's birth and, in any case, the last of the OT books, the Book of Wisdom[12] yields much for our theme from its first half (Wis 1:1–11:1), which in turn is divided into two sections. The first (Wis 1:1–6:20) deals with retribution for good and evil and with the immortality that Sophia can bring.[13] The second section describes Sophia and her operations in the world and explains how she is to be found (Wis 6:21–11:1). Although closely and remarkably identified with God, she makes herself accessible: "One who rises early to seek her will have no difficulty, for she will be found sitting at the gate" (Wis 6:14). Indeed, she herself "goes about seeking those worthy of her, and she graciously appears to them in their paths, and meets them in every thought" (Wis 6:16).[14]

The second section merits close attention. It describes Wisdom and how Solomon is attached to her: Reputedly the wise man par excellence, he sought her and was blessed by her. As the divine artisan at work in all creation (Wis 8:6), she taught him (Wis 7:22). Her 21 attributes (i.e., the perfect number of 7 multiplied by 3) explain how Sophia can teach all things:

> There is in her a spirit that is intelligent, holy, unique, manifold, subtle, mobile, clear, unpolluted, distinct, invulnerable, loving the good, keen, irresistible, beneficent, humane, steadfast, sure, free from anxiety, all-powerful, overseeing all, and penetrating through all spirits that are intelligent, pure, and altogether subtle. For wisdom is more mobile than any motion; because of her pureness she pervades and penetrates all things. (Wis 7:22–24)

Here Sophia is identified with spirit, a spirit that "penetrates all things" and is thus immanent everywhere. This immanence is balanced by transcendence because Sophia is also portrayed as "holy, unique," "all-powerful," and all-seeing.

In a classic passage, the Book of Wisdom sets out Sophia's relationship to God:

> She is a breath of the power of God and a pure emanation of the glory of the Almighty; therefore nothing defiled gains entrance into her. For she is a reflection of eternal light, a spotless mirror of the working of God, and an image of his goodness. Although she is but one, she can do all things, and while remaining in herself, she renews all things; in every generation she passes into holy souls and makes them friends of God and prophets; for God loves nothing so much as the person who lives with Wisdom. She is more beautiful than the sun, and excels every constellation of the stars. Compared to the light she is found to be superior, for it is succeeded by the night, but against Wisdom evil does not pre-

> vail. She reaches mightily from one end of the earth to the other and she orders all things well. (Wis 7:25–8:1)

Right from the Book of Job, Sophia had been radically related to God. Now her connection is expressed in a manner that even goes beyond "begetting" (Prv 8:22) or "coming forth from God's mouth" (Sir 24:3). As R. E. Murphy says, in a sort of effusion, radiation, or emanation from the divinity, she emerges as a "reflection" or "mirror image" of God.[15] High language is also used of Wisdom's work in creating and conserving the world. After calling Sophia *the mother and fashioner* of all things (Wis 7:22), the author of Wisdom now celebrates her role in renewing and ordering all things (Wis 7:27; 8:1)—that is to say, in upholding and guiding creation. In short, Wisdom not only "lives with God" but is also associated constantly with all God's works (Wis 8:4).

The theme of the unity between Sophia and God reaches a significant climax in Chapter 10, which presents her in salvific terms. After Chapter 9 has already stated that human beings are "saved" by Sophia (Wis 9:18), the biblical author reinterprets Israel's history by assigning to Sophia the saving deeds normally attributed to YHWH. It was Sophia who was at work in protecting Adam, Noah, Abraham, Lot, Jacob, and Joseph. It was Sophia who through Moses delivered the Hebrew people in the Exodus:

> A holy people and blameless race, Wisdom delivered from a nation of oppressors. She entered the soul of a servant of the Lord and withstood dread kings with wonders and signs. She gave to a holy people the reward of their labors; she guided them along a marvelous way and became shelter to them by day and a starry flame through the night. She brought them over the Red Sea, and led them through deep waters. (Wis 10:15–18)

By attributing to Sophia the saving deeds of God in the OT story, the Book of Wisdom makes the identification between Sophia and YHWH closer than ever.

The NT will give Jesus the title of *Wisdom* (e.g., 1 Cor 1:24). It also has something to say about Jesus' being involved like Lady Wisdom in the creation and conservation of the world (e.g., 1 Cor 8:6; Col 1:16–17; Heb 1:1–2). The first Christians knew that Jesus had brought them the *new creation* of graced life through his death and resurrection, the culmination of salvation history or God's redemptive activity for the world. As agent of this *new* creation, Jesus must also be, so they recognized, the divine agent for the *original* creation of all things. Likewise being the central protagonist of salvation history, he was also seen to be active in the unfolding of that history prior to the incarnation (e.g., Jn 12:41; 1 Cor 10:4). Prompted at least in part by the Fourth Gospel's use of Logos in its prologue, Christian writers, as we will see, thematize Christ's activity before the incarnation, both in creation and in salvation history, in terms of the *Logos,* or Word of God, rather than in terms of Wisdom. Justin, Irenaeus, and others highlight the Logos's preincarnational presence and activity on behalf of the chosen people. In a later chapter, we will find them interpreting as "Logophanies" all the OT theophanies or appearances of God.

Before leaving the Book of Wisdom, we should note how it shares a strong sense of God's invisible transcendence with second-century Christian writers and a first-century Jewish author, Philo of Alexandria. The activity of Lady Wisdom (Book of Wisdom) or, equivalently, of the Logos (Philo, Justin, and Irenaeus) safeguards this transcendence. God is utterly beyond our world. The creation and conservation of everything as well as the divine activity within the history of salvation must take place through the agency of Wisdom or the Logos. We turn now to the Word as another major OT personification of the divine activity.[16]

(b) Word

Like Lady Wisdom, the Word is with God and is powerfully creative from the beginning (Gn 1:1–2:4). To cite the classical passage from Deutero-Isaiah:

> For as the rain and the snow come down from heaven, and do not return there until they have watered the earth, making it bring forth and sprout, giving seed to the sower and bread to the eater, so shall my word be that goes out from my mouth; it shall not

> return to me empty, but it shall accomplish that which I purpose, and succeed in the thing for which I sent it. (Is 55:10–11)

The psalms celebrate the creative and conserving Word of God: "Let all the earth fear the Lord; let all the inhabitants of the world stand in awe of him. For he spoke, and it came to be; he commanded, and it stood firm" (Ps 33:8–9; see Ps 148:5). Sirach also appreciates how the divine Word operates to conserve creation: by God's "Word all things hold together" (Sir 43:26), a sentiment that will be applied to Christ by Colossians 1:17.

At times, the OT scriptures set *word* in parallelism with *spirit* or *breath* as instruments of creation: "The Word of the Lord created the heavens; all the host of heaven was formed by the Breath of his mouth" (Ps 33:6); "Let all your creatures serve you, for you spoke, and they were made. You sent forth your Spirit, and it formed them" (Jdt 16:14). Solomon's famous prayer takes *word* and *wisdom* as synonymous agents of divine creation: "God of my fathers and Lord of mercy, you made all things by your Word, and by your Wisdom fashioned humankind" (Wis 9:1–2). *Word* also personified the divine activity in the story of the chosen people's deliverance from Egypt, at least when death came to the firstborn of the Egyptians. In a vivid personification of *Word* the Book of Wisdom declares: "Your all-powerful Word leaped from heaven, from the royal throne, into the midst of the land that was doomed; a stern warrior, carrying a sharp sword of your authentic command, he stood and filled all things with death" (Wis 18:15–16). *Word* also repeatedly expressed God's historical and saving revelation mediated in a special way through the OT prophets. The Word of the Lord comes to them; hence they can communicate divine oracles and declare, "Thus says the Lord." The prophets convey divine words of judgment over the people along with indications of God's will for them. In brief, *word* matches *wisdom* as a way of expressing God's creative, revelatory, and salvific activity.

(c) Spirit

Spirit shows up frequently (nearly 400 times) in the OT as a third way of articulating the creative, revelatory, and redemptive activity of

God.[17] When dealing with God's *spirit* (Hebrew *ruah;* Greek *pneuma*), the OT highlighted its power as *wind,* as the breath of life, or as the divine inspiration that comes upon prophets. At creation "the spirit" of God hovered over the surface of the water (Gn 1:2). Significantly, spirit takes possession of prophets to empower them to speak God's word.[18] I say significantly because this indicates further how in pre-Christian Judaism *word, wisdom,* and *spirit* were practically synonymous ways for speaking of God's manifest and powerful activity in the world. In celebrating God's creative power, the psalmist, as we saw above, uses *word* and *breath* (or *spirit*) as equivalent parallels: "By the Word of the Lord the heavens were made, and all their host by the Breath of his mouth" (Ps 33:6; see Ps 147:18). The work of creation can be expressed in terms of God's word or in terms of the divine spirit, as Judith's thanksgiving to God illustrates: "Let your whole creation serve you; for you spoke, and all things came to be; you sent out your Spirit and it gave them form" (Jdt 16:14; see Ps 104:29–30). Spirit and wisdom are likewise identified: When God gives wisdom, this is equivalent to sending "the holy Spirit" (Wis 9:17; see 1:4–5; 7:7,22,25). Other OT books link and even identify spirit and wisdom (Dt 34:9; Jb 32:8–9; Is 11:2). In short, like word and wisdom, the spirit was a way of articulating the divine activity and revelation in the world.

(d) Wisdom, Word, and Spirit

The NT and post-NT Christian language for the tripersonal God flowed from the Jewish scriptures. That language was deeply modified in the light of Jesus' life, death, and resurrection—together with the outpouring of the Holy Spirit. Nevertheless, naming God as *Father, Son* (Word or Wisdom), and *Spirit* found its roots in the OT. There Wisdom, Word, and Spirit functioned, frequently synonymously, to acknowledge the transcendent God's nearness to the world and to the chosen people—a nearness that did not, however, compromise the divine transcendence, or that otherness that sets God "beyond" all other beings. In their creative, revelatory, and redemptive involvement, Wisdom, Word, and Spirit took on divine roles, while staying clearly within God's control. At times almost identified with God (e.g., Wis

7:25–26), they remained distinct in function (Wis 9:4). These notions were available for the followers of Jesus, when they set out to express the "economic" missions in salvation history of the Son (as Wisdom and Word) and of the Spirit, as well as their inseparable role in the creation and conservation of the whole universe.

Thus these notions opened up the possibility of acknowledging the general work of the Son (named as Wisdom) *both* "over all the earth" and "for every people and nation" (Sir 24:6) *and* for those called in the special history of salvation (e.g., Sir 24:8–11; Wis 10:15–18). The divine Word had operated both in the general order of creation and in the specific order of redemption. It was the Word who created all things and peoples (e.g., Jdt 16:14; Wis 9:1–2), acted against the firstborn of the Egyptians (Wis 18:15–16), and spoke through the prophets to the chosen people of God. Likewise, the divine Spirit took possession not only of the OT prophets within the special story of salvation but could also impel a non-Israelite, Balaam, to utter important oracles (Nm 24:2; see Nm 22:1–24:25). In these ways the OT provided some lines for distinguishing between and holding together the role of Son/Wisdom/Word and Spirit within both the general and the special history of salvation. The OT fashioned in advance some insights into the creative, revelatory, and salvific functions of Word/Wisdom and Spirit for the history of God's people and beyond—in the history of all peoples and in the entire created order.

The last paragraphs have treated Word, Wisdom, and Spirit as roughly equivalent OT personifications for God's activity. At the same time, we do well to recall two of Wisdom's advantages. First, Wisdom enjoys more of a distinctive "face" than Word and Spirit; unlike them Wisdom also engages in dialogue with God (Sir 24:8). Second, although Spirit and Word influence the course of salvation history (e.g., through empowering and speaking through the prophets, respectively), the scriptures assign to Wisdom alone a whole set of salvific deeds normally attributed to YHWH in the deliverance from slavery in Egypt (Wis 10:15–18). Nevertheless, one should not overlook one advantage of Spirit, when compared with Wisdom and Word: They are not credited with being the divine gift in the final days. Through the prophet

Joel, God promises to pour out "my Spirit" rather than "my Wisdom" or "my Word" (Jl 2:28–29; see Acts 2:17–18; Ez 11:19; 39:29).

Conclusion

The most valuable feature of Wisdom, Word, and Spirit as expressive of the divine activity toward the human race (and the whole world) lay in their being not abstract principles but vivid personifications—something that was particularly true in the case of Wisdom. Wisdom called on men and women to listen to its message and to follow it, thus preparing the ground for the visible coming of Jesus and his Spirit. No one has appreciated this better than Gerhard von Rad, who wrote:

> Wisdom is the form in which YHWH's will and his accompanying of human beings (i.e., his salvation) approaches human beings. Wisdom is the essence of what men and women need for a proper life and of what God grants them. Still, the most important thing is that Wisdom does not turn toward human beings in the shape of an "It," teaching, guidance, salvation or the like, but of a person, a summoning "I." So Wisdom is truly the form in which YHWH makes himself present and in which he wishes to be sought by human beings. "Who finds me, finds life" (Prv 8:35). Only YHWH can speak in this way.[19]

One might well add: Only Jesus, prompted by his Spirit, can speak in this way.

The vivid personifications of Wisdom/Word and Spirit, inasmuch as they were *both* identified with God and the divine activity *and* distinguished from God, opened up the way toward recognizing God to be tripersonal. The leap from mere personifications to distinct persons is always, to be sure, a giant one. Nevertheless, without these OT personifications (and the Father/Son language applied to God), the acknowledgment of the Trinity would not have been so well and providentially prepared—by foreshadowings and by an already existing terminology.

2.
The History of Jesus and Its Trinitarian Face

"The testifier was the Father, the testified the Son, the Holy Spirit was the one who designates the testified one."

Theodore of Mopsuestia, *Fragment, 166*

The whole story of Jesus showed a trinitarian face. In other words, his history transposed to the human level the interpersonal life of the triune God. In particular, he lived in a human way his identity of being the Son in relationship to the Father. Jesus' life comes across that way—right from his virginal conception. Let us begin from there in discerning the trinitarian face of Jesus' history, looking for hints of God's tripersonal reality and certainly not yet for a fully deployed doctrine of the Trinity.

The Virginal Conception

Elsewhere, I have put the case for recognizing that Matthew and Luke presented the conception of Jesus as actually taking place not through normal sexual intercourse but through a special intervention of the Holy Spirit.[1] The most plausible alternative argues that these two evangelists created (or inherited) pieces of fiction that expressed a purely theological truth: Jesus was/is the Son of God. Their (differently articulated) theological statements were then quickly misunderstood to claim a historical virginal conception. Raymond Brown has drawn attention to the problems involved in crediting both Matthew and Luke, who wrote independently of each other and drew on different traditions, with having stated their theological faith in this way.[2]

I strongly suspect that it has been general convictions (e.g., that God never acts in such special ways as through a virginal conception) or difficulties at the level of meaning that have led many people to doubt or reject the virginal conception. In early Christianity, apocryphal gospels developed further biological aspects of Jesus' conception and birth so that their readers increasingly lost sight of the deep religious significance of those events. In modern times, I believe, many reject the virginal conception because they react against a particular caricature that has at times been offered as an explanation; for instance, that Jesus had to be virginally conceived because sexual intercourse is impure and he was/is uniquely holy. Such caricatures apart, we are still left with two questions: Was the manner of Jesus' conception virginal in the literal sense of being conceived through a special action of God without the sperm of a human father being involved? I answer yes, and that leaves me with the second question: What religious and saving significance does the miraculous manner of Jesus' conception convey—in particular, for the doctrine of the Trinity?

Traditionally the major value of his virginal conception has been to express Jesus' divine origin and identity, yet without denying his true humanity. Unique and all as his mother and his mode of conception were, he was conceived and "born of a woman" and "born under the [Jewish] law" (Gal 4:4), and that meant he was circumcised after eight days. All of this pointed to his humanity in its concrete particularity of being conceived and born a Jewish male. At the same time, the fact that he was conceived and born of a *virgin* pointed to his divinity. The Davidic Messiah was also God's own Son. This interpretation should be fitted into wider patterns provided by the NT, or at least into the chronological sequence of writers: from Paul, through Mark, Matthew, and Luke, to John.

Paul recognized the personal identity and saving function of Jesus Christ when "designated Son of God in power according to the Spirit of holiness by his resurrection from the dead" (Rom 1:4). Here, as elsewhere (e.g., probably in Phil 2:5–11), Paul's letters drew on very early traditions to confess Jesus' divinity, expressed in terms of his being Lord and Son of God and revealed above all by his resurrection from the dead and exaltation to the Father's right hand. Later on, in composing his gospel, Mark included a "baptism Christology": At the beginning of his ministry, Jesus is declared by God to be "my beloved Son" (Mk 1:11). Matthew and Luke, in their own differing ways, added a "conception Christology": The unique action of the divine Spirit at the conception of Jesus reveals that there never was a moment in his history when Jesus was not Son of God. Finally, other NT authors went "further back" to add a "preexistence Christology" (Jn 1:1–18; Heb 1:1–3). Without saying anything about the manner of Jesus' conception, John and Hebrews acknowledged in his coming on the human scene the incarnation of One who was "previously" "with God" and was now "made flesh." Thus the event of the virginal conception yielded a revelatory link for an exploration that characteristically started at the end with his risen (and divine) "postexistence" and finished at the beginning with his eternal "preexistence." The pattern is not, however, perfect. Preexistence texts (that express Jesus' divinity) surface early in the formation of the NT and are to be found already in Paul's letters (e.g., 1 Cor 8:6; 2 Cor 8:9; Phil 2:6), even if the apostle does not elaborate theologically on Jesus' preexistence.

We can spot other patterns of significance for trinitarian faith to which the event of the virginal conception contributed. Matthew names the newly conceived Jesus "Emmanuel, which means God with us" (Mt 1:23). Right from his conception and birth, Jesus fulfilled and expressed the presence of YHWH with his people. Then at the end, the same gospel—in a notable use of inclusion—shows the risen and exalted Christ meeting his disciples not only as one to whom "all authority in heaven and earth has been given" but also as one who promises: "I am with you always to the close of the age" (Mt 28:18,20). What Jesus became through the resurrection he had already been from the start: the fulfilled expression of YHWH's presence with his people.

In general, to name Christ's divinity is to speak of his relationship to the Father *in the Spirit.* The particular event of the virginal conception can be expected to yield meaning not only about Christ's divine filiation but also about his relationship with the Holy Spirit. Christians experienced the outpouring of the Spirit in the aftermath of Jesus' resurrection. They came to appreciate that the same Spirit sent to them by the Father and the risen Christ (e.g., Lk 24:49; Jn 14:26) had been actively present in the whole of Jesus' life—not only at the start of his ministry (Lk 3:22; 4:1,14,18) but even right back at his conception. In other words, the risen Jesus (with his Father) actively blessed the disciples with the Spirit, but in his entire earthly existence, he had himself been blessed by the Spirit—right from his very conception when he came into the world through the Spirit's creative power (Mt 1:20; Lk 1:35).

Thus the event of the virginal conception plays its part in revealing and clarifying a central truth: from the beginning to the end, there is a trinitarian face to the story of Jesus Christ. His total history discloses the God who is the Father, the Son, and the Holy Spirit.

We turn now to the synoptic Gospels' presentation of Jesus' ministry. In this chapter, we will ask questions about the earthly Jesus himself: that is to say, about stage one in the formation of the gospel traditions. But often an answer can be given only in terms of the way the evangelists themselves presented some scene or words—that is, at the third or final stage in the formation of these NT texts. That will be fully examined in Chapter 4.

Jesus' Baptism

Mark's Gospel (followed by those of Matthew and Luke) recalls a kind of appearance of the Trinity at Jesus' baptism in the voice of the Father, the obedience of the Son, and the descent of (and anointing by) the Spirit.[3] The Spirit descended on him "like a dove," and "a voice came from heaven, 'You are my Son, the Beloved; with you I am well pleased'" (Mk 1:10–11; see Ps 2:7; Is 42:1). Even if, according to Mark and—somewhat less emphatically—Luke (Lk 3:22), but not Matthew (Mt 3:17), the voice from heaven was directed to Jesus, these evangelists (and still less Matthew[4]) do not seem to be thinking of a call-vision like those of Moses (Ex 3:1–4:17), Isaiah (Is 6:1–13), Jeremiah (Jer 1:5–19), or Ezekiel (Ez 1:1–3:27),[5] as if the voice from heaven strengthened or even created Jesus' sense of communion with the Father, conveyed a divine commission, or confirmed a vocation already accepted. Mark admittedly represents the episode as Jesus' own visionary experience and personal hearing of a heavenly voice. Yet Mark, still less the other synoptic Gospels, does not want to report Jesus' inner experience, let alone any reply he made to the voice from heaven. They have no particular interest in Jesus' consciousness as such, even if Luke makes the baptism epiphany a prayer experience of Jesus (Lk 3:21–22) as he will do with the Transfiguration (Lk 9:29).

Rather the story of the baptism, in particular in the earliest version found in Mark, functioned to reveal Jesus' identity (as approved from heaven in his state of being God's beloved Son), to tell of his consecration, to introduce his activity, and to indicate the form that activity will take. The revelatory opening of the heavens, the sound of the Father's voice, and the descent of the (creative and prophetic) Spirit disclosed that with Jesus, *the* bearer of God's Spirit, the final time of salvation was being inaugurated. Mark 1:10 speaks of "the heavens being torn apart"; the evangelist will use the same verb (*schizo*) about the curtain of the temple being "torn in two"—symbolizing, among other things, the revelation of Jesus' identity to the centurion and through him to others (Mk 15:38). The baptism episode assures Mark's readers that Jesus was/is related to God in a special way and would initiate a heaven-blessed ministry. John's Gospel, while not directly recounting Jesus' baptism, implies it, twice adding the detail that the Spirit not only descended on Jesus but also "remained on him"; John further presents Jesus as the One "who baptizes with the Holy Spirit" (Jn 1:32–33), a theme we find at an earlier stage in the synoptic Gospels.

In Mark's narrative, John the Baptist says of the "mightier one" coming after him: "He will baptize you with the Holy Spirit" (Mk 1:8).

When following Mark at this point, Matthew and Luke add a significant phrase: "He will baptize you with the Holy Spirit *and with fire*" (Mt 3:11; Lk 3:16).[6] In the event, neither Mark nor Matthew report any coming of the Holy Spirit, as does Luke (Lk 24:49; Acts 1:8; 2:1–4), who also includes a reference to the "fiery" Spirit (Acts 2:3,19). Matthew will include the mandate to baptize "in the name of the Father, and of the Son, and *of the Holy Spirit*" (Mt 28:19). Where Luke clearly refers being "baptized with fire" to the fire of the Spirit at Pentecost, Matthew may intend this fire to be the judgment at the end (Mt 7:19; 13:40,42,50; 18:9) when the Son of man comes to judge all people (Mt 25:41). At all events, the three synoptic Gospels envision Jesus, after being baptized with the Holy Spirit at the outset of his ministry, to work as one empowered by God's Spirit. His baptism with the Holy Spirit signifies the coming of the final age and the fulfillment of God's promise to pour out the divine Spirit (Is 44:3; Ez 39:29; Jl 2:28–29).

According to Mark, the Spirit who had come down on Jesus "drove" him at once into the wilderness (Mk 1:12). Like Matthew (Mt 4:1), Luke puts this more gently: Jesus "was led by the Spirit" into the desert (Lk 4:1). For Luke, in particular, the earthly Jesus showed himself in his ministry of preaching and healing to be the paradigmatic Spirit-bearer (e.g., Lk 4:14,18–21; 6:19). Luke here approaches the Johannine conviction (Jn 1:32–33) that Jesus, like the Glory of the Lord on the Tent of Meeting (Nm 14:10), possessed the Spirit permanently and was the source of the Spirit. Unlike Matthew (Mt 11:25), Luke introduces Jesus' thanksgiving to the "Father, Lord of heaven and earth" by representing Jesus as "rejoicing in the Holy Spirit" (Lk 10:21–24); he depicts Jesus as delighting, under the influence of the Spirit, in his relationship to God acknowledged as Father.[7]

We have just been looking at the way in which three of the evangelists portray the story of Jesus in trinitarian terms. But what of Jesus himself and, in particular, his consciousness of sonship and awareness of the Holy Spirit? As we have seen, the gospel stories of Jesus' baptism, while coming from a historical episode (John did baptize Jesus), may not be used as sources of information about some deep experience

Jesus underwent on that occasion.[8] As John Meier convincingly argues, Jesus' consciousness of his sonship and of the Spirit could have "crystallized" before, during, or even after the baptism. Although we may properly imagine this consciousness to have been "developed intellectually and experienced existentially" by Jesus, we cannot be "more specific" about "exactly when and how this happened."[9]

The Spirit

Let us look first at Jesus' experience of the Spirit and then at his consciousness of sonship. Apparently he was aware of being empowered by the Spirit and deplored the attitude of some of his critics: so far from acknowledging God's Spirit at work in his ministry, they attributed Jesus' redeeming activity to Satan and so sinned against the Spirit (Mk 3:22–30). But he never unambiguously pointed to his deeds as signs of the Spirit's power. Matthew has Jesus say, "If by the Spirit of God I cast out demons, the kingdom of God has come upon you" (Mt 12:28; see 12:18). But here we may well be reading a redactional modification on the part of this evangelist. Luke seems to provide the original version of the saying: "If by the finger of God I cast out demons…" (Lk 11:20).[10] In any case, Jesus is never credited with an awareness of the Spirit that had anything like the same intensity as his consciousness of the God whom he called "Abba." He never, for instance, prayed *to* the Spirit: "Holy Spirit, all things are possible to you, but not my will but yours be done." Rather he prayed in the Spirit or with the Spirit in him. As far as the evidence goes, Jesus apparently described and thought of the divine Spirit in a fairly normal prophetic way: the dynamic power of God reaching out to have its impact on Jesus and through him on others. It took Jesus' resurrection and exaltation to initiate a new, characteristically Christian manner of thinking about the Spirit and the relationship of Jesus to the Spirit.

A much later "spiritual" interpretation of the Transfiguration (Mk 9:2–8 parr.) understood the bright cloud (Mk 9:7) to be not simply part of a general scenario of the divine presence and glory as in OT apocalyptic language, but to be a particular image of the Holy Spirit: "the whole Trinity appeared: the Father in the voice, the Son in the man, and the Spirit in the bright cloud."[11] This interpretation might have done better to associate the Spirit with Moses and Elijah, two heavenly figures in the Transfiguration who had been especially empowered by the Spirit during their earthly activity. In that way, one might recognize the Spirit at work by continuing to empower Moses and Elijah. In any case, a presence here of the Holy Spirit goes beyond what Matthew, Mark, and Luke intended when reporting this remarkable event. As at his baptism, Jesus said nothing, at least during the Transfiguration itself; Elijah and Moses did the talking (Mk 9:4 parr.). Unlike the baptism, the episode took place privately and on a high mountain, the symbolic border zone between heaven and earth, and not down at a major river and the scene of a religious revival for a general public.[12]

Jesus' Sonship

It was Jesus' sonship rather than any theme connected with the Spirit that Mark and Matthew exploit to structure a christological inclusion into their gospels. Mark begins with a double announcement of Jesus as the Son of God in the context of his baptism (Mk 1:1,11) and via the metaphorical sense of baptism as suffering (Mk 10:38) has the revelation of Jesus' divine sonship peak immediately after the crucifixion with the centurion's confession: "Indeed this man was Son of God" (Mk 15:39). The filial rather than a messianic secret forms the leitmotif. Matthew uses a double christological frame: the theme of "God with us" (Mt 1:23; 28:20) and that of the obedient Son of God who is tried and tested at the beginning (Mt 3:14–17; 4:1–11) and at the end (Mt 27:39,54).

The evidence from the ministry makes it clear that Jesus himself understood his relationship to God as sonship. Because it was/is a relationship with *God*, that automatically means that we are dealing with a *divine* sonship. But what kind of divine sonship did Jesus imply or even lay claim to? Merely a somewhat distinctive one, or a divine sonship intimate to the point of being qualitatively different and radically unique? To prevent things from becoming confused and confusing when examining the synoptics, we must distinguish what Jesus said (or seems to have said) about his divine sonship from anything others say about him in this connection. We come across Jesus speaking absolutely of "the Son" but never of "the Son of God." In an important passage, heavy with wisdom language (Mt 11:25–30; see Lk 10:21–22), Jesus refers to the Father, identified as "Lord of heaven and earth," and claims that a unique and exclusive (salvific) knowledge of "the Father" is possessed by "the Son" who is tacitly identified as "me": "All things have been delivered to me by my Father; and no one knows the Son except the Father, and no one knows the Father except the Son and anyone to whom the Son chooses to reveal him" (Mt 11:27). This is to affirm a unique mutual knowledge and relationship of Jesus precisely as *the Son* to the Father, a mutual relationship out of which Jesus reveals, not a previously unknown God, but the God whom he alone knows fully and really. A distinctively new feature in Father/Son talk has emerged here.[13]

Then Mark 13:32 (followed probably by Mt 24:36) also has Jesus referring absolutely to "the Son" and, with respect to the end of the age, (implicitly) acknowledging limits to his knowledge over against "the Father": "Of that day and of that hour no one knows, not even the angels in heaven, nor the Son, but only the Father."

Third, the parable of the vineyard and the wicked tenants reaches its climax with the owner sending to the tenants "my son" and their killing this "beloved/only son" (Mk 12:1–12 parr.). Mark or the pre-Markan tradition has apparently added "beloved/only" (see Mk 1:11) and almost certainly the reference to the resurrection (Mk 12:10–11), but the substance of the parable, with its allegorical reference to his own violent death (which says nothing about its expiatory value and its actual mode—by crucifixion), seems to derive from Jesus. A son could act as his father's legal representative in a way that slaves or servants could not; in the parable, this differentiates the son from the previous messengers. It seems that Jesus intended his audience to identify him with the son in the story. One should note also a sense of his mission being the eschatological climax of God's saving interventions (the "finally" of verse 6). Yet neither here nor elsewhere in the synoptic Gospels does Jesus ever come out into the open and say, "I am the Son of God." (See, however, Mt 27:43, where his taunters recall, "He said, 'I am the Son of God,'" even though Matthew's Gospel has never previously represented Jesus as saying just that.)

Three times the synoptic Gospels portray Jesus as referring to the divine sonship enjoyed by others here and hereafter (Mt 5:9; Lk 6:35; par. in Mt 5:44–45; Lk 20:36). All in all, even if every one of the references to his own divine sonship or that of others comes from the earthly Jesus himself, we are faced with much less use of this theme than we find in the OT. In a way that we have seen to be fairly widespread, the Jewish scriptures name the whole people, the Davidic king, and/or righteous individuals as children/sons/daughters of God. The situation comes across, however, as the opposite with God as Father. We saw in the previous chapter how the OT rarely calls YHWH *Father* and hardly ever does so in prayers addressed to God. Jesus seems to have changed that situation, spending his public ministry in dialogue with *Abba* and humanly aware of his oneness-in-distinction with the Father.

Mark's Gospel five or six times calls God *Father*—most strikingly in Jesus' prayer in Gethsemane: "Abba, Father, all things are possible to you; take this cup from me. Yet not my will but yours be done" (Mk 14:36). Even if *Abba* was not merely a child's address to its male parent,[14] Jesus evidently spoke of and with God as his Father in a direct, familial way that was unique, or at least highly unusual, in Palestinian Judaism. *Abba* was a characteristic and distinctive feature of Jesus' prayer life. In several passages in Matthew (e.g., 6:9; 11:25–26; 16:17), in one passage at least in Luke (11:2), and perhaps in other passages of those two evangelists, *Father* stands for the original *Abba*.[15] Jesus' example, at least in the early years of Christianity, encouraged his followers to pray to God in that familiar way (Gal 4:6; Rom 8:15). As J. D. G. Dunn points out, "the clear implication" of these passages is that Paul regarded the *Abba* prayer "as something distinctive to those who had received the eschatological Spirit"—in other words, "as a distinguishing mark of those who shared the Spirit of Jesus' sonship, of an inheritance shared with Christ."[16]

Altogether in the synoptic Gospels (excluding simply parallel cases), Jesus speaks of "Father," "my (heavenly) Father," "your (heavenly) Father," or "our Father" 51 times. Sometimes we deal with a Father-saying which has been drawn from Q, or a source (*Quelle* in German) containing sayings of Jesus used by Matthew and Luke (e.g., Mt 11:25–27; par. in Lk 10:21–22), or else we find a Father-saying which, while attested by Matthew alone (e.g., Mt 16:17) or by Luke alone (e.g., Lk 22:29), seems to go back to Jesus. Matthew shows a liking for *heavenly* and at various points may have added the adjective to sayings that originally spoke only of "your Father" or "my Father" (e.g., Mt 6:32). The same evangelist may at times have inserted *Father* into his sources (e.g., Mt 6:26; 10:29,32–33; 12:50; 20:23; 26:29). Even discounting a number of examples as nonauthentic, it is clear that Jesus spoke fairly frequently of God as Father.

Further, Jesus called those who did God's will *my brother, and sister, and mother,* but not *my father* (Mk 3:31–35 parr.). He invited his hearers to accept God as their loving, merciful Father. He worked toward mediating to them a new relationship with God, even to the point that they too could use *Abba* when addressing God in prayer. However, being his brothers and sisters did not put others on the same level with him as sons and daughters of God. Jesus apparently distinguished between "my" Father and "your" Father, a distinction upheld by Matthew. He was not inviting the disciples to share with him an *identical* relationship of sonship. No saying has been preserved in which Jesus linked the disciples with himself so that *together* they could say, "Our Father." When he encouraged the disciples to pray to God as Father, the wording *Our Father* (Mt 6:9, unlike Lk 11:2 where there is no "our") was for the disciples only.[17] If Jesus did actually say "*Our* Father," it was in a prayer he proposed for others ("Pray then like this"—Mt 6:9). He invited his hearers to accept a new relationship with God as Father; yet it was a relationship that depended on his (Lk 22:29–30) and differed from his. When Jesus spoke of "my Father," was he conscious of being "Son" in some kind of distinctive way, or was he aware even of a unique divine sonship vis-à-vis "Abba"?

At least we can say this: Jesus applied the language of divine sonship individually (to himself), filling it with a meaning that lifted "Son (of God)" beyond the level of his *merely* being either a man made like Adam in the divine image (Lk 3:38), or someone perfectly sensitive to the Holy Spirit (Lk 4:1,14,18), or someone bringing God's peace (Lk 2:14; 10:5–6) albeit in his own way (Mt 10:34; par. in Lk 12:51), or even a/the Davidic king (Lk 1:33) who would in some way restore the kingdom of Israel. We do not have to argue simply from the fact that Jesus referred to himself (obliquely) as *the Son* and to God as *my Father*. He not only spoke like *the Son* but also acted like *the Son* in knowing and revealing the truth about God, in changing the divine law, in forgiving sins (outside the normal channels of temple sacrifices and the ministry of the levitical priesthood), in being the one through whom others could become children of God, and in acting with total obedience as *the* agent for God's final kingdom. All this clarifies the charge of blasphemy brought against him at the end (Mk 14:64 par.); he had given the impression of claiming to stand on a par with God. Jesus came across as expressing a unique filial consciousness and as laying claim to a unique filial relationship with the God whom in a startling way he addressed as *Abba*.

Even if historically he never called himself *the only* Son of God (see Jn 1:14,18; 3:16,18), Jesus presented himself as *Son* (uppercase) and not just as one who was the divinely appointed Messiah and in that sense *son* (lowercase) of God.[18] He made himself out to be more than just someone chosen and anointed as divine representative to fulfill an eschatological role in and for the kingdom. Implicitly, Jesus claimed an essential, "ontological" relationship of sonship toward God that provided the grounds for his functions as revealer, lawgiver, forgiver of sins, and agent of the final kingdom. Those functions (his "doing") depended on his ontological relationship as Son of God (his "being").

Inasmuch as Jesus experienced and expressed himself as the Son, that means that the YHWH of the OT was now known to be Father. The revelation of *the* Son necessarily implied the revelation of the Father.

Coming and Being Sent

To complete the trinitarian accounting of the history of Jesus, we need to recall some further data that might indicate how Jesus conceived his *mission*. At times he expressed his mission as one who had been sent by God. Taking a child into his arms, he remarked: "Whoever receives one such child in my name receives me; and whoever receives me receives not me but him who sent me" (Mk 9:36–37 parr.). As we saw from the parable of the wicked tenants, Jesus obliquely referred to himself as the "Son" who had finally been "sent" (Mk 12:6 parr.). He expressed the limits set to his mission as being "sent" to the lost sheep of the house of Israel (Mt 15:24). But on other occasions Jesus went beyond the normal prophetic "I was sent" to say, "I came." He said about his ministry, for instance, "I came not to call the righteous but sinners" (Mk 2:17 parr.); "I came to cast fire upon the earth; and would that it were already kindled!" (Lk 12:49; see also Lk 12:51; par. in Mt 10:34–35).

A startling example of "coming" language turns up when Jesus explains why he must proclaim the message in other towns: "That is what I came out to do" (Mk 1:38). This statement, which may be due to the evangelist, leaves us with the question: Whether or not the saying goes back to Jesus, can we account for this "coming out" simply in terms of Jesus' coming from Nazareth (Mk 1:9; see 6:1–6), given that Mark, unlike Luke (see Lk 4:16–30), does not make much of Jesus' coming from Nazareth? From where does Mark think that Jesus "came out" to do his work? The "coming" language is also connected with a major self-designation used by Jesus: "The Son of man came not to be served but to serve" (Mk 10:45 par.). Occasionally the language of "coming" and of "sending" is combined, as in a passage from Q:

> Jerusalem, Jerusalem, the city that kills the prophets and stones those who are *sent* to it! How often have I desired to gather your children together as a hen gathers her brood under her wings, and you were not willing! See, your house is left to you. And I tell you, you will not see me until the time comes when you say,

> "Blessed is the one who comes in the name of the Lord." (Lk 13:34–35; par. in Mt 23:37–39)

Without insisting on the authenticity of every "sending" and "coming" logion, we can say that they are numerous and various enough to encourage the conclusion that the earthly Jesus conceived of his mission both as one who came and as one who had been sent by the Father. Here it is well to recall that the OT prophets shared a radical sense of being *sent* by God, but never purported to *come* in their own name. Furthermore, they never presented themselves as "sons of God," nor were they ever called that.

Apropos of "being sent" and "coming," it is interesting to note how Paul and John maintain this double terminology when articulating Jesus' mission. Paul writes not only of God's "sending his own Son" (Rom 8:3; see Gal 4:4) but also of Jesus' taking the initiative by "becoming poor" (2 Cor 8:9), "emptying himself, taking the form of a slave," and "being born in human likeness" (Phil 2:7). John likewise affirms not only the sending of God's Son (Jn 3:17,34; 20:21), but also represents the Son of man as "descending from heaven" (Jn 3:13). The double terminology can be embodied in the same statement in the Fourth Gospel, as when Jesus declares: "I have *come* down from heaven, not to do my own will, but the will of him who *sent* me" (John 6:38).

Conclusion

We move on now to the trinitarian testimony from the first Christian writer, Paul, underlining again the difficulty of extracting much from the synoptic Gospels about the inner experience and awareness of the earthly Jesus himself. Two of them (Matthew and Luke) convey the trinitarian implications of the virginal conception, at least in the sense that their narratives involve God (the Father), the Son, and the Holy Spirit. When we move to the public story of Jesus, we must cautiously refrain not only from finding doctrine in an anachronistic fashion but also from being too confident about our reconstructions of the original flow of events. The opening scene of the baptism illustrates the difficulty. Jesus was baptized, the evangelists appreciate some kind of trinitarian dimension in that event, but it remains almost impossible to reach firm conclusions about how Jesus himself experienced that occasion. His ministry exhibits him as living out a filial relationship and mission as One sent/coming from the Father; yet the synoptic record of the ministry yields little about his sense of the Holy Spirit. We detect more at the level of the evangelists' appreciation of Jesus' story: in what, for instance, Mark and Matthew develop about the Father/Son relationship and what Luke appreciates about the role of the Holy Spirit in the ministry.

3.
The Trinity According to St. Paul

"May I breathe my last breath in the protection of your close embrace, with your all-powerful kiss! May my soul find herself without delay there where you are whom no place circumscribes, indivisible, living and exulting in the full flowering of eternity, with the Father and the Holy Spirit, true God, everlasting, world without end!"

St. Gertrude of Helfta, *The Herald of Divine Love*

"Let all rise from their seats to show honor and reverence to the Blessed Trinity."

The Rule of St. Benedict

In Western iconography, the "throne of grace (*Gnadenstuhl*)" is undoubtedly the most important representation of the Trinity. Turning up for centuries in a painted or carved form, it shows the Father holding the cross with the Son dead on it (or the Father simply holding the body of the Son) with the Holy Spirit as a dove hovering between them. One cross links the three figures; their unity is also expressed by their being turned toward each other. Frequently, as in the version by El Greco exhibited in the Prado, the dead body of the Son already hints at the luminosity of the coming resurrection. The classical Eastern icon of the Trinity, created by St. Andrew Roublev and to be found at the Tretiakov Gallery in Moscow, presents the three "angels" who visited Abraham and Sarah (Gn 18:1–15). A divine unity and harmony pervades the composition, in which the three figures sit around the one table and are entirely referred to each other in mutual self-gift. The Roublev icon (and the sacred tradition behind it) is one of the few representations of the Trinity in which the Holy Spirit has a human face, albeit in angelic style. The presence of a chalice on the table hints at the cup of the passion (see Mk 10:38–39), and the table itself brings to mind the Last Supper, celebrated just before Christ's death and resurrection. Despite the obvious differences between the Roublev icon and the "throne of grace," they converge in representing the Trinity in the light of Good Friday and Easter Sunday—something that also characterizes the witness of St. Paul and the pre-Pauline tradition cited by the apostle.

The doctrine of the Trinity is grounded in God's self-disclosure in the whole Easter mystery. The crucifixion revealed the utter sinfulness and lostness of the world. Through our archetypal representatives (Judas, Caiaphas, and Pilate), the will to run our own affairs and distance ourselves from God seemed to have its own way and even enjoy its triumph. The apparently definitive collapse of Jesus' mission could lead one to despair and even cynicism about God, or at least about human creatures who are supposedly made in the divine image and likeness. It was precisely in the crucifixion and the resurrection that the tripersonal God was powerfully engaged against sin and for our deliverance. Jesus' message about the powerful coming of the divine reign and the infinite mercy of Abba was vindicated when Jesus received radically new, indestructible life from God and with God (e.g., Rom 6:9–10; Acts 13:34). The resurrection revealed that the tripersonal God was/is present in suffering and on/around the cross—a dramatic truth valued by artists who painted or sculptured "the throne of grace." The cross was named by Paul as an "offense" and "folly" to others (1 Cor 1:23) and was accepted by Christians as *the* mysterious way of divine self-communication and salvation. The "foolishness" and apparent powerlessness of the nonviolent Trinity is the foolishness of the cross and vice versa.

Let us look first at the Father/Son (or Father/Lord) relationship and then at what Paul indicates about the Holy Spirit. At the end of the chapter, we will examine the triadic formulas and language we find in Paul's letters.

The Father/Son Relationship

The new experience of God (the Father) conveyed by the resurrection of the crucified Jesus produces an attribute that turns up right from Paul's earliest letter. The apostle begins that letter by reminding the Thessalonians not of some abstract doctrine but of their experience in that they have "turned to God from idols, to serve a living and true God, and wait for his Son from heaven, *whom he raised from the dead*" (1 Thes 1:9–10). This adjectival clause, "God (the Father) who raised Jesus (from the dead)," may well be a pre-Pauline formula that the apostle has taken over.[1] At all events, it turns up regularly in his writings. He begins his letter to the Galatians with an appeal to "God the Father who raised him [Jesus] from the dead" (Gal 1:1). He warns the Corinthians against fornication by recalling their bodily destiny: "God raised the Lord and will also raise us up by his power" (1 Cor 6:14). In Pauline terms, God may be said simply to have raised Jesus from the dead (Rom 4:24; 8:11; 10:9) or to have raised him by his glory (Rom 6:4) or to have raised him by his power (1 Cor 6:14). Paul calls Christ's risen existence life "out of the power of God" (2 Cor 13:4). At times (e.g., Rom 4:25; 6:9; 1 Cor 15:4,13), the letters use a divine passive: "Christ was raised" or "has been raised (from the dead)"; the reader is meant to understand "by God (the Father)." The formula-like clause "God (the Father) who raised Jesus (from the dead)," which also turns up in post-Pauline literature (e.g., Acts 3:15; 4:10), draws attention to the new, Christian, and Pauline understanding of YHWH as the Father who has raised his dead Son.

The identification of God (the Father) as the agent of Jesus' resurrection leads Paul to acknowledge that his specifically Christian doctrine of God stands or falls over this point. If Christ has not been raised from the dead, "we are even found to be misrepresenting God because we testified of God that he raised Christ" (1 Cor 15:15). It would be bad enough for us to entertain a false faith and to indulge futile hopes about ourselves (1 Cor 15:14,17–19); it is obviously even worse to be misrepresenting God in a fundamental way. Put positively, this means that Paul describes and almost defines God as the Father who has resurrected his Son (and who offers us in turn the hope of resurrection to new and eternal life). This Pauline language raises questions for those who are sensitive to the axiom about trinitarian actions *ad extra* being common to all three divine persons. Should one interpret the apostle's repeated attribution of Jesus' resurrection to the Father as "merely" appropriation, or are we confronted here with something that is "proper" to the Father? A later chapter will face this question.

What interests us in this chapter is the new, specific attribute: "God (the Father) who raised Jesus from the dead." This is not a *general* truth about God, expressed, for instance, by such adjectival attributes as *eternal, merciful, all-powerful,* and *faithful,* or by nouns as when the psalmist confesses, "God is King" and "the Lord is my Shepherd." YHWH is now revealed as One who has not only sent his Son (e.g., Rom 8:3; Gal 4:4) but also as One who has brought the Son back from the dead to a new, transformed life and sent "the Spirit of his Son into our hearts" (Gal 4:6). These new verbal attributes resemble the specific OT confessions of YHWH as the One who "saw" his people's misery, "led" them out of captivity, and "brought" them to a land flowing with milk and honey (e.g., Dt 26:5–9). To name YHWH as *the Father* who raised Jesus coheres with what we will shortly examine in Pauline usage: the name *Father* that Jesus had used moves from the margins of Jewish faith and piety to the center and will enjoy a continued and even enhanced centrality in Christian language about God. The new, specific attribute for God as *both* the Father and Resurrector of Jesus *and* the Sender first of Jesus and then of the Holy Spirit inevitably raises questions about distinctions within the divine unity, that is to say, about

YHWH "sharing" divinity with two other distinct subjects or persons (to employ the language of a later age).

As regards the crucified and risen Jesus, his life, activity, and death left no reasonable doubt that he was a distinct individual or person, to use anachronistic terms. (These terms come from later ages, which developed the notion of distinct rational individuals or persons with powers to know, love, and act freely.) The crucial question took rather this form: Was/Is he a *divine* individual, on a par with YHWH whom he had called and addressed as *Abba*? In the case of the Holy Spirit, the key issue—at least for many people—was the opposite.[2] The Spirit, being the Spirit of God, was obviously divine. But were/are we dealing with a distinct, divine individual or person?

We begin with Jesus. Resurrected, exalted to God's "right hand," and installed as the final mediator of salvation (e.g., Rom 8:34), is Jesus understood by Paul to be divine (in the proper, high sense of that word)? How does the apostle think of the relationship between God (the Father) and the exalted Jesus?

(a) Divine Lord

One of the oldest (and briefest) Christian prayers occurs as a closing benediction from Paul: "Maranatha" (1 Cor 16:22). Transliterated into Greek from two Aramaic words, in this context *Maranatha* probably means "Our Lord, come!" rather than "Our Lord has come." The NT ends with the same prayer (but in Greek): "Come, Lord Jesus" (Rv 22:20). In this way, Christians prayed that the risen and exalted Jesus would come for them in his post-Easter glory. The synoptic Gospels show how Jesus was remembered as speaking of himself as the Son of man who would come in glory to judge and save at the end.[3] Yet the early Christians did not pray "Come, Son of man" but "Come, Lord Jesus." In what seems to be its meaning here, the title *Lord* directs attention to the divinity of Jesus, who uniquely shares now in God's sovereign rule and will mediate eternal salvation in the life to come (e.g., 1 Thes 1:10).

Applying *Lord* (*Kyrios*) as a high or divine title to the crucified and risen Jesus began very early in Christianity. Our oldest Christian document, 1 Thessalonians, calls him by that title 24 times. In a passage that parallels the synoptic Gospels' language about the apocalyptic Son of man's future descent from heaven at the parousia (or final coming at the end of history), Paul does not use that designation but six times writes of the coming Christ as "Lord" (1 Thes 4:13–5:3). Elsewhere in the same letter he also gives Jesus the title of *Kyrios* in an eschatological context, that is, a context connected with the end of history (e.g., 2:19; 3:13). Altogether Paul uses that title for Jesus around 230 times and does so sometimes in passages that seemingly derive from an earlier tradition (e.g., Rom 10:9; Phil 2:11). The mark of a Christian was the confession of Jesus as their resurrected, sovereign Lord (Rom 10:9). To name the crucified and exalted Jesus as receiving the adoration of the universe and the name *Lord* to "the glory of God the Father" (Phil 2:10–11) obviously raises the questions: Who is Jesus with his cosmic authority and what is his relationship to God the Father?

In the postresurrection situation, Paul maintained the earthly Jesus' own realistic practice by speaking of God (*ho Theos*) as *Abba* (Rom 8:15; Gal 4:6), *the Father* (e.g., Gal 1:1; Phil 2:11), or the *Father of our Lord Jesus Christ* (e.g., Rom 15:6; see 2 Cor 11:31). Adopted as sons and daughters of God, empowered by the Spirit, and imitating their elder brother, Jesus, Christians could pray familiarly to God as *Abba*. The apostle kept up this distinctive name for God (as *Abba* or *Father dear*) in contexts that are closely linked with the glorious resurrection of the crucified Jesus (e.g., Rom 8:11; Gal 1:1). Then there was Paul's typical greeting to his correspondents, which ran as follows: "Grace to you and peace from God our Father and the Lord Jesus Christ" (e.g., Rom 1:7). Here the apostle set Christ as the source of integral salvation ("grace and peace") on the same level as YHWH—without, however, identifying him with YHWH because he was not Abba. In relation to the one Lord Jesus Christ, God was called *Father*, with Father naming God here (as in other settings [e.g., Gal 1:1]), and implying that the Lord Jesus Christ was/is God's Son.

That Paul's resurrection faith entailed trinitarian, or at least binitarian, belief also emerged clearly when he split the confession of monotheism expressed in that central Jewish prayer, the Shema, or "Hear, O Israel" (Dt 6:4–5). The apostle glossed *God* with *Father* and

Lord with *Jesus Christ* to put Jesus as risen and exalted Lord alongside God the Father: "For us there is *one God, the Father,* from whom are all things and for whom we exist, and *one Lord, Jesus Christ,* through whom are all things and through whom we exist" (1 Cor 8:6). Here the title *one Lord* expanded the Shema to contain Jesus. Using the classic monotheistic text of Judaism, Paul recast his perception of God by introducing Jesus as *Lord* and redefining Jewish monotheism to acknowledge a personal distinction within the godhead and produce a christological monotheism.[4] Interestingly, the apostle did not need to argue for this redefinition of monotheism. He assumed that his Corinthian readers and hearers would agree with him. By and large, Paul reserved *God* for *the Father,* whereas he used *Lord* (or *Son of God*) for Jesus. In its highest religious sense "Lord" referred to Jesus more often than to the Father in the Pauline letters.

Paul's redefining of Jewish monotheism also involved acknowledging Christ as agent of creation ("through whom are all things and through whom we exist"). To speak of Christ in such terms was to attribute to him a divine prerogative, that of creating human beings and their universe. To be the agent of eschatological salvation (that is, of God's final kingdom) was equivalent to being the agent of the *new* creation (2 Cor 5:17; Gal 6:15). Now, what held true at the end must be true also at the beginning; eschatological claims about Christ led quickly to protological claims or claims about "first things," namely, that he was involved in the divine act of creation. Back in Chapter 1, we examined three OT personifications of God's activity in creating, sustaining, and relating to the world: Wisdom, Word (or Logos), and Spirit. Our earliest Christian writer (Paul), in applying to Christ the title of *Sophia* or *Wisdom,* was in fact expressing his divine identity, just as one of the last NT writers (John) did when he gave the title of *Logos* to Jesus of Nazareth. John quite explicitly associated the Logos with the divine work of creation (Jn 1:3,10). Paul, although he both attributed to Christ the divine prerogative of creation (1 Cor 8:6) and called him the Wisdom of God (1 Cor 1:17–2:13), did not quite clinch matters by writing of "the one Wisdom of God, Jesus Christ, through whom all things exist." It is significant, however, that after calling Jesus "the

Power of God and the Wisdom of God" (1 Cor 1:24), Paul went on in the same letter to attribute to Jesus the functions of Lady Wisdom—in creation (1 Cor 8:6) and in preexistent, saving activity for the chosen people (1 Cor 10:4).

Before pursuing further these reflections on the way Paul gave Jesus the high title of *Lord* and *Wisdom,* it may be well to recall some lexical facts. In biblical Greek *kyrios* (somewhat like the Italian *signore,* the Spanish *señor,* and the German *Herr*) spans a wide range of meaning: from a polite form of address (*Sir*) right through to God as the One who has absolutely sovereign rights over human beings and their world. In the Septuagint, the (Hebrew) divine name *YHWH* (not pronounced out of reverence but replaced by *Adonai,* "Lord") was rendered *Kyrios* or "Lord," and, especially in the prophetic books, God could be called the Lord of hosts. In applying *Lord,* the NT at times applies to Jesus this central name for the one true God.

To situate this claim, let us review the range of usage for this term in the entire NT. (1) *Kyrios* could be simply a respectful way of addressing a man (e.g., Mt 21:30; 25:11; 27:63; Jn 4:11; 12:21; Acts 16:30). (2) It was also a way of addressing a teacher or a rabbi (e.g., Mt 8:25; see Mt 17:15; Mk 4:38; 9:17). (3) The designation could suggest authority, in the sense of one with the power to perform mighty works (e.g., Mt 8:25). (4) *Kyrios* may denote the owner of property (Mk 12:9; Lk 19:33) or the master of slaves (Lk 12:42–47; Eph 6:5; Col 4:1). In some parables, the "master" or *kyrios* is a metaphor for Jesus (e.g., Mt 25:18–24, 26). (5) Because of their power, political rulers (Mt 27:63) could lay claim to a certain "divinity" and as "lords" could even demand worship (see Acts 25:26). (6) *Lords* might also refer to so-called gods who were supposed to have rights over human beings (1 Cor 8:5). (7) Finally, the NT speaks not only of God (e.g., Mt 5:33; 11:25; Mk 12:29–30; Acts 2:39; 4:26; Rom 4:6–8; 11:2–4) but also of Jesus as *Kyrios,* and often does so in a way that clearly raises Jesus above the merely human level (e.g., Mk 12:36–37; Lk 19:31; Jn 13:13–14; Phil 2:11; Rv 22:20–21).

The word of the Lord, to which OT prophets and prophetical books often appeal, becomes for Paul the word of the Lord Jesus, that is to say, the message about and from the Lord Jesus, or perhaps the message that is the Lord Jesus (1 Thes 1:8; see 2 Thes 3:1). Where deliverance has been promised to those who "call upon the name of the Lord" (Jl 2:32; it is 3:5 in the Hebrew text), Christians "call upon the name of our Lord Jesus Christ" (1 Cor 1:2). Passages in the OT that call God *Kyrios* are referred by Paul to Christ: Romans 10:13 cites Joel 2:32; Philippians 2:10–11 echoes Isaiah 45:23–24 and acknowledges the exalted Jesus as "Lord" to "the glory of God the Father." These Pauline passages read as applying to Jesus or being fulfilled in Jesus OT verses that speak of God as *Lord*.[5] The risen Christ is understood by the apostle to share God's lordship over all created beings "in heaven and on earth or under the earth" (Phil 2:10). In particular, Christ's lordship makes him sovereign over all angelic beings in heaven (Col 1:16–17; 2:8–10). Not surprisingly, in Paul's letters and elsewhere in the NT it is not always clear whether the writers mean God or Christ when they speak of the *Kyrios* (e.g., Acts 9:31; 1 Cor 4:19; 7:17; 2 Cor 8:21).

To fill out Paul's account of Christ's lordship, it is helpful to note how he and other early Christians also appropriated to Jesus the rubric of "the day of YHWH (the Lord)." They acknowledged Christ as Lord not only of all space (being worshiped by the angels and all creatures in heaven, on earth, and under the earth) but also of all time and history. The day of YHWH was the day when God was to intervene decisively against the wickedness of Israel (Jer 17:16–18; Am 5:18–20; Ez 7:1–27; Zep 1:14–18; Jl 2:1–2), of Babylon (Is 13:6,9), or of Egypt (Ez 30:3). On this doomsday, God would judge sinners and manifest the divine glory (Is 2:11–12). Jeremiah (Jer 30:5–9) and later prophets came to fill the phrase with a somewhat more positive sense, which had not been totally lacking in earlier usage. "The day of the Lord" would bring Israel's restoration at a time of final conflict and victory (Zec 14:1–21). This doomsday of judgment was to destroy evildoers and to spare the good (Mal 3:13–4:3). In essence, to talk of that day was to see God as the awesome future of history, not only for the chosen people but also for all nations.

Paul and other NT writers took the doomsday term and reapplied it to Christ's parousia or final coming (1 Thes 5:2), "the day of our Lord

Jesus Christ" (1 Cor 1:8; 5:5; 2 Cor 1:14; Phil 1:6,10; 2:16). The day of God's final and decisive intervention in judgment was now understood to be and identified with the day of Christ's final and decisive intervention in judgment. The Lord Jesus Christ was to carry out the future function of God. The expectation of doomsday associated God and Christ to the point of their being interchangeable.

(b) The Son of God

We have been concentrating on Paul's attribution of the divine title *Lord* to the crucified and risen Jesus. Before taking up the apostle's testimony to the Holy Spirit, a word on his use of another title that is highly relevant from a trinitarian point of view: the Son of God. Paul's first letter calls Jesus God's Son (1 Thes 1:10), and subsequently the apostle continues to introduce that title—often at key places in his letters (1 Cor 15:28; 2 Cor 1:19; Gal 1:16; 2:20; 4:4; Rom 1:3–4; 8:3, 32). In his seven certainly authentic letters (Rom, 1 and 2 Cor, Gal, Phil, Phlm and 1 Thes), he speaks 15 times of Jesus as God's Son. It is significant that Paul himself never tries to prove that Jesus is the Son of God; he takes it for granted that this belief is simply shared by the early Christians to whom he writes. Further, in some cases when Paul calls Jesus by that title, he seems to draw on earlier formulations that take us back to the opening years of Christianity (e.g., 1 Thes 1:10; Rom 1:3–4). He writes of the Son being "sent" (Rom 8:3; Gal 4:4), "revealed" (Gal 1:16), and "raised" (1 Thes 1:10) by the Father. A Deutero-Pauline letter (or one probably not written by Paul himself but later by one of his associates) speaks of "the beloved Son" of the Father (Col 1:13) and then proceeds to acknowledge in him the divine prerogative of creating and conserving the world (Col 1:16–17).

The title *Son* has its particular place in Paul's theology of the cross: "God did not spare his own Son but gave him up for us all" (Rom 8:32). Unlike Abraham's son, Isaac (Gn 22:1–18), Jesus was not spared. In the OT story, the collective "son of God," the people, repeatedly suffer, and so too do the righteous individuals who call God their Father (Wis 2:10–20). The OT language and narrative had done at least something to prepare Paul's language about the Son of God not being spared and "giving himself up" for us (Gal 2:20). The OT had done nothing like that to prepare the way for speaking of the "Lord" being put to death (Rom 4:24–25; 1 Cor 2:8) or for identifying the crucified Jesus as the "Wisdom" of God (1 Cor 1:18–2:5). Like the other two important personifications of the divine activity (Word and Spirit), the OT never describes Wisdom as suffering, let alone being put to death.

In the last chapter, we saw how Jesus, when calling others to open themselves to God's kingdom, was apparently conscious of a qualitative distinction between *his* sonship and *their* sonship, which was derived from and dependent upon him. His way of being Son was different from theirs. In his own way, Paul (and later on John) maintained this distinction. The apostle expressed our new relationship with God as taking place through an "adoption" (Rom 8:15; Gal 4:5), which makes us "children (*tekna*) of God" (Rom 8:16–17) or, alternatively, "sons of God" (Rom 8:14; Gal 4:6–7). John would distinguish between the only Son of God (Jn 1:14,18; 3:16,18) and all those who through faith can become "children (*tekna*) of God" (Jn 1:12; 11:52; 1 Jn 3:1–2,10; 5:2). Paul (and subsequently John) likewise maintained and developed the correlative of all this, Jesus' stress on the fatherhood of God. More than 100 times, John's Gospel was to name God as *Father*. Paul's typical greeting to his correspondent, as we noted above, was "Grace to you and peace from God *our Father* and the/our Lord Jesus Christ."

If he distinguishes between our graced situation as God's adopted children and that of Jesus as the Son of God, what does Paul understand the latter's "natural" divine sonship to entail? Beyond question, the crucified Christ's resurrection from the dead is the major focus in Paul's presentation of the divine sonship (e.g., Rom 5:10). The apostle thinks primarily of the risen Son's redemptive and revelatory impact on Christian believers, on Paul's own life and ministry, and on the future of the entire universe (e.g., 1 Cor 15:20–28). Nevertheless, the apostle does not want to say that Jesus *became* God's Son for the first time through his resurrection from the dead. Here several passages in Romans and Galatians prove relevant.

Paul writes of God "sending his own Son in the likeness of sinful nature and to deal with sin" (Rom 8:3). In a similar (but not identical) passage, the apostle says that "when the fullness of time had come, God sent his Son, born of a woman, born under the law (Gal 4:4)." This language of sending obviously raises central questions about the relationship between the Sender (the Father) and the Sent (the Son). Does Paul think here of an eternally *preexistent* Son coming into the world from his Father to set us free from sin and death (Rom 8:3,32) and make us God's adopted children (Gal 4:4–7)? Our answer will, in the first place, partly depend upon the way we interpret other Pauline passages that do not use the title *Son of God* (2 Cor 8:9; Phil 2:6–11). These latter passages present a preexistent Jesus taking the initiative, through his "generosity" in "becoming poor" for us and "assuming the form of a slave."

Second, our answer will also depend on whether we judge 1 Corinthians 8:6 and Colossians 1:16 to imply that as a preexistent being the Son was active in creation. It should be noted that 1 Corinthians 8:6, without referring as such to "the Son," runs as follows: "There is one God, the Father, from whom all things and for whom we exist, and one Lord, Jesus Christ, through whom are all things and through whom we exist." Naming God as *the Father* moves us toward talk of the Son. In the case of Colossians 1:16, the hymn (Col 1:15–20) does not give Jesus any title. However, he has just been referred to (Col 1:13) as God's "beloved Son."

Third, it should be observed that the language of "sending" (or even, for that matter, "coming" with its suggestion of personal purpose and initiative) simply by itself does not necessarily imply personal preexistence. Otherwise we would have to ascribe such preexistence to John the Baptist, "a man sent from God," *the* great prophet who "came to bear witness to the light" (Jn 1:6–8; see Mt 11:10,18; par. in Lk 7:27,33). In the OT, angelic and human messengers, especially prophets, were "sent" by God, but one should recall at once what we observed in the last chapter: No prophets sent by God (and we can add here, not even John the Baptist) were ever called God's sons. It makes a difference that in our Pauline passages it is God's Son who was sent. Here, being "sent" by God means more than merely receiving a divine commission and seems to include coming from a heavenly preexistence and enjoying a divine origin.

Fourth, in their contexts, the three Son-of-God passages we are looking at (Rom 8:3,32; Gal 4:4) certainly do not focus on the Son's preexistence but on his being sent or given up to free us from sin and death, to make us God's adopted children, and to let us live (and pray) with the power of the indwelling Spirit. Nevertheless, the apostle's soteriology (or doctrine of salvation) presupposes here a Christology that includes divine preexistence. It is precisely because Christ is the preexistent Son who comes from the Father that he can make us God's adopted sons and daughters.

The Sending of the Spirit

Let us turn now to the Holy Spirit. The NT writers, in particular Luke and John, understand the relationship between Jesus and the Spirit to be transformed by the resurrection, or at least to be disclosed as strikingly different from what seemed to be the case during Jesus' earthly ministry. The exalted Jesus is now seen to share in God's prerogative as Sender or Giver of the divine Spirit. Paul, however, differs here from Luke and John. Although he speaks of the risen Christ as having become "a life-giving Spirit" (1 Cor 15:45), he never quite says that Christ has sent or will send the Spirit. The closest he gets comes in 1 Corinthians 15:45, which presents Jesus as the source of "spiritual" life as well as of the "spiritual" body. Luke and John talk of Christ as co-sending the Spirit. Exalted "at the right hand of God and having received from the Father the promise of the Holy Spirit," Christ along with the Father pours out the Spirit with the perceptible effects that follow (Acts 2:33; see Lk 24:49; Jn 16:7; 20:22).

When referring to the bestowal of the Spirit, Paul says that "God has sent the Spirit of his Son into our hearts" (Gal 4:6). Or Paul uses the divine passive, which does not explicitly name the divine Giver or Sender: "The Holy Spirit has been given to us" (Rom 5:5); to each Christian "is given" some manifestation of the Spirit (1 Cor 12:7,8). Or else Paul writes of Christians "receiving" the Spirit without stating from whom the Gift comes (1 Cor 2:12; Gal 3:2); the apostle speaks simply of "receiving the Spirit" (Rom. 8:15) even in a chapter that is perhaps his classic statement on Christian existence in the Spirit and that talks repeatedly and realistically of the Spirit (Rom 8:1–27).

At the same time, Paul speaks not only of "the Spirit of God" (Rom 8:9; 1 Cor 2:11,12,14) but also, occasionally, of "the Spirit of (Jesus) Christ" or "the Spirit of God's Son" (Rom 8:9; Gal 4:6; Phil 1:19). The genitive (the *of* form in English) is exquisitely ambiguous; it can be read as an objective genitive (the Spirit that brings us to God/Christ), as a genitive of origin (the Spirit that comes from or is drawn from God/Christ),[6] or even perhaps as a genitive of identity (the Spirit that is God/Christ). The third (grammatical) possibility leads us to a further, major reflection on the postresurrection function and understanding of the Holy Spirit.

In Paul's letters, the Spirit is not only characterized by a relationship to the risen and exalted Christ but also, in the experience of believers, is almost identified with Christ (i.e., the Spirit who is Christ or who is the presence of Christ). The Spirit "in us" (Rom 5:5; 8:9,11,16; Gal 4:6) is nearly synonymous with talk about our being "in Christ" (Rom 6:3,11,23; 16:11; 1 Cor 1:30; 3:1; 4:15; Phil 3:1; 4:1–2). Paul appreciates that coming to Christ involves the Spirit (Gal 3:1–5), who makes preaching effective and empowers conversion (1 Thes 1:4–6). Hence, Christians' experience of the Spirit merges with their experience of the risen Christ (1 Cor 6:11). The divine Spirit dwelling "in you" (Rom 8:9,11) is, for all intents and purposes, equivalent to "having the Spirit of Christ" or to Christ being "in you" (Rom 8:9,10). This near-functional identity allows J. D. G. Dunn to say not only that for Paul "the Spirit is the medium for Christ in his relation" to human beings but even that "*no distinction can be detected in the believer's experience*" between the exalted Christ and the Spirit of God.[7]

Nevertheless—and this is vitally important about Paul's thinking regarding the relationship Christ/Spirit—it is patent that neither the apostle nor other NT authors finally identify Christ with the Spirit. Jesus was conceived through the power of the Holy Spirit (Mt 1:20; Lk 1:35)—a statement that cannot be reversed. It was the Word and not the

Spirit that became flesh (Jn 1:14). It was the Son and not the Spirit who was sent "in the likeness of sinful flesh" to deal with sin (Rom 8:3) and who was not "spared" but "given up for us all" (Rom 8:32). The Spirit was not "handed over to death for our sins and raised for our justification" (Rom 4:25). The Father raised Jesus and not the Spirit from the dead (e.g., Gal 1:1). Through his resurrection, Christ and not the Spirit became "the firstborn" of a new eschatological family (Rom 8:29) and "the first fruits of those who have fallen asleep" (1 Cor 15:20).

It is the indwelling Spirit that helps us pray *Abba* and witnesses to Christ (Rom 8:15–16; Gal 4:6; 1 Cor 12:3), and not an indwelling Christ who makes us pray like that and witnesses to the Spirit. (Here, however, we should recall that the earthly Jesus himself first taught his disciples to pray *Abba* and that he witnessed to the Spirit—at least according to Luke [e.g., Lk 10:21–24] and John [e.g., Jn 16:7].) Finally, unlike the Spirit, it is the crucified and resurrected Jesus who at the end will subject all things to his Father (1 Cor 15:24–28). Paul's and, more broadly, the NT's story of Christ's mission, conception, ministry, death, and resurrection with its aftermath distinguish him from the Holy Spirit. A whole series of events and actions are attributed either to Jesus or to the Holy Spirit but are not interchangeable. Much of what is attributed to Jesus cannot be attributed to the Holy Spirit, and vice versa.

Finally, what of the individual or personal identity of the Spirit—to ask an anachronistic question? Like the OT, which can name the divine Spirit in an impersonal way (as breath or wind), Paul at times speaks of the Spirit impersonally, for example, as being "poured" (Rom 5:5), as "seal" (2 Cor 1:22; see Eph 1:13; 4:30), as "first fruits" (Rom 8:23), or as a "down payment" (2 Cor 1:22; 5:5; see Eph 1:14). Nevertheless, he also writes of the Spirit in clearly personal language as "leading" (Rom 8:14), "witnessing" (Rom 8:16), "interceding" (Rom 8:26–27), having aims or aspirations (Rom 8:27), "searching" and "knowing" (1 Cor 2:10–11), "distributing" gifts (1 Cor 12:11), and "crying out" in the human heart (Gal 4:6). Talk of "choosing" (1 Cor 12:11) and "freedom" (2 Cor 3:17) also seems incompatible with the Spirit being impersonal. In summary, the language of Paul's letters implies that the Spirit is a personal subject who engages in personal activities.

Triadic Formulas

Last of all, the Pauline letters yield a number of triadic formulas and other triadic passages about God, which range from the fairly simple (e.g., at the start of Romans) to the more formal (e.g., at the end of 2 Corinthians). Romans opens with what may be a kerygmatic/credal tradition in which the order is God (the Father), the Son, and the Spirit: "the gospel concerning his [God's] Son, who was descended from David according to the flesh and was declared to be Son of God with power according to the Spirit of holiness by resurrection from the dead" (Rom 1:3–4). On the basis of and from the time of his resurrection, Jesus is proclaimed the Son of God with power (see 1 Cor 6:14); the Spirit is characterized by holiness and imparts holiness (see Rom 15:16).

The final form of 2 Corinthians concludes with an elaborate, trinitarian benediction that could be drawn from the tradition and that certainly differs from the briefer benedictions with which Paul normally concludes his letters; for instance, "the grace of the Lord Jesus Christ be with you" (1 Cor 16:23). At the end of 2 Corinthians, as happens also in Romans 5:1–11, Paul emphasizes the soteriological functions of the Trinity or the Trinity "for us": "The grace of the Lord Jesus Christ, the love of God, and the fellowship of the Holy Spirit be with all of you" (2 Cor 13:13). In comparison with the order that goes back to Matthew 28:19 (Father/Son/Holy Spirit), this closing benediction from Paul maintains the Holy Spirit in the third place but changes the order of the first two figures, names them differently (*Lord Jesus Christ* instead of *the Son* and *God* instead of *the Father*), and speaks not of their "name" but of *grace, love,* and *fellowship*—associated, respectively, with the first, the second, and the third figures. Placing *the Lord Jesus Christ* ahead of *God* highlights the historical mediation of revelation and salvation through Christ, and ending with *fellowship* underlines the communion created by the Holy Spirit and toward which the gracious activity of the Lord Jesus Christ and loving concern of God (the Father) aim. This closing benediction is a summary of salvation history that associates Christ with *God* and *the Holy Spirit* in bestowing spiritual blessings. *Grace* and *love* have already characterized the divine dealings with human beings, who can now through faith and baptism share in the new fellowship produced by the Holy Spirit. At the same time, Paul's triadic formulas and other trinitarian passages are not rigidly the same.

In an earlier letter, the apostle speaks in a different order and more succinctly of *Spirit, Lord,* and *God* (an order that reverses the first and the third figures in Matthew's baptismal formula) and insists that spiritual gifts come from the one ("the same") divine source and should contribute to "the common good" (1 Cor 12:7): "There are varieties of gifts, but the same Spirit; and there are varieties of service, but the same Lord [Jesus]; and there are varieties of working, but it is the same God [the Father] who inspires them all in every one" (1 Cor 12:4–6).

The triadic synopsis of salvation history found in Galatians 4 follows the order of Matthew's baptismal formula:

> When the fullness of time had come, God *sent* (*exapesteilen*) his Son, born of a woman, born under the law, in order to redeem those who were under the law, so that we might receive adoption as sons [and daughters]. And because you are sons [and daughters], God *sent* (*exapesteilen*) the Spirit of his Son into our hearts, crying, "Abba! Father!" (Gal 4:4–6)

This trinitarian summary of salvation history comes across as fairly concrete and specific: It opens with a reference to "the time" having fully come, the time when the system of law observance, the "curse" from which all of God's people were to be redeemed (Gal 3:13–14) came to an end through the work of Christ and the Spirit. This happened with Jesus' human birth into the Jewish people. Thus redemption from the law reached the Jews, adoption was offered to both Jews and Gentiles, and the Holy Spirit came. In this soteriological view of the Trinity, salvation is initiated by God (see the divine "love" of 2 Cor 13:13), effected by Christ through his incarnation, life, death, and resurrection (see Rom 4:25), and appropriated by participating in the Holy Spirit (see Rom 5:1–5). The "evidence" for the christological statement about our adoption as sons and daughters is provided by the indwelling Spirit and the Spirit's use of the Son's language, "Abba! Father!" The indwelling of the Spirit is the way that both the Father and the Son are present in the believer's life. The Son, who effected the redemption and secured "sonship" for us, now indwells through the Spirit. The same verb is used for the Son *and* the Spirit being sent by the Father; this parallel language suggests that both the Son *and* the Spirit preexisted with the Father, from whom they were sent on two related missions.

To complete the picture, let us note four triadic formulas in Ephesians: the first has the order Christ/Spirit/Father ("through him [Christ] we have access in the one Spirit to the Father" [Eph 2:18]); this recalls 1 Cor 6:11 ("You were justified in the name of the Lord Jesus Christ and in the Spirit of our God"). The second uses the order Father/Spirit/Christ: "I bow my knees before the Father, from whom all fatherhood takes its name in heaven and on earth that he may grant you to be strengthened with might through his Spirit…and that Christ may dwell in your hearts through faith" (Eph 3:14–17). God's fatherhood, which is all-encompassing ("from whom all fatherhood takes its name in heaven and on earth"), entails the power through the Spirit to confess in faith Jesus as Son. The third formula follows the sequence of 1 Corinthians 12:4–6 (Spirit/Lord Jesus/God the Father): "There is one body and one Spirit…one Lord [Jesus], one faith, one baptism, one God and Father of all, who is over all and through all and in all" (Eph 4:4–6). Through the Spirit, believers can believe in Jesus as Lord and call on the Father of all, the one God whose fatherhood is on a cosmic scale, "over all and through all and in all" (Eph 4:6; see 1 Cor 15:24–28). Fourth, the same order (of Spirit/Jesus/Father but modified at the end by a return to "our Lord Jesus Christ") appears in the next chapter: "Be filled with the Spirit, as you sing psalms and hymns and spiritual songs among yourselves, singing and making melody to the Lord [Jesus] in your hearts, giving thanks to God the Father at all times and for everything in the name of our Lord Jesus Christ" (Eph 5:18–20). This order, from the Spirit through the Son to the Father, helps to bring out how the Father is the ultimate source and goal of all things.

All in all, Paul (along with the Deutero-Pauline Letter to the Ephesians) witnesses to a soteriological view of the tripersonal God, from whom comes our initial adoption, ongoing guidance, and future inheritance:

> For all who are led by *the Spirit* of *God* are sons (and daughters) of *God*. For you did not receive a spirit of slavery to fall back into fear, but you have received a *Spirit* of adoption. When we cry "*Abba! Father!*" it is that very *Spirit* bearing witness with our spirit that we are sons (and daughters) of God, and if sons (and daughters), then heirs, heirs of *God* and joint heirs with *Christ*. (Rom 8: 14–17)

Salvation takes place because we are loved by the Lord Jesus, elected by God the Father, and sanctified by the Spirit (2 Thes 2:13; see 1 Thes 1:4–6). In what may be an allusion to baptism, Paul reminds the Corinthians how they have been enabled to inherit "the kingdom of God" the Father: "You were washed, you were sanctified, you were justified in the name of the Lord *Jesus* Christ and in the *Spirit* of our *God*" (1 Cor 6:10–11).

The OT scriptures had told of the divine glory filling the temple (e.g., 1 Kgs 8:11; Ez 43:1–5); by calling the Israelites God's sons and daughters and very occasionally naming God as Father, these same scriptures had prepared the way for the image of the people as God's family. To these two OT possibilities, Paul added the theme of the body; the Holy Spirit made these three images a living reality. The Spirit realizes the divine presence by indwelling the *temple* of the community and individual believers (1 Cor 3:16–17). Together through the Spirit, they make the one *body* of Christ (1 Cor 6:19; 12:12–27; Eph 4:4), the one *family* of God (2 Cor 6:18; Gal 4:5–7). The change to human hearts promised through the prophets (Jer 31:31–34; Ez 11:19–20) has been fulfilled, with the indwelling Spirit mediating and guaranteeing our future glory (1 Cor 1:22). As always, Paul's Pneumatology (or doctrine of the Spirit) and trinitarian teaching remain firmly situated within the full "economic" context of salvation history.[8]

Conclusion

To sum up: Paul continues to be monotheistic and does not abandon the Jewish faith in one God professed by the Shema (Dt 6:4). "God is one," the same God for Jews and gentiles alike (Rom 3:29–30). As the apostle insists with the Galatians, "God is one" (Gal 3:20). In the face of pagan idols, the "so-called (many) gods" and many "lords," the apostle's christological monotheism does not tamper with the confession that "there is one God" (1 Cor 8:4–6). At the same time, Paul's monotheism is christological and pneumatological, and this is a new development. Basing himself on the existing Christian tradition and on his own experience, he sets Jesus (as the divine Lord or the Son) and the (Holy) Spirit alongside the Father or God (*ho Theos*). Although we certainly do not find here (or even later in the NT) anything like the eventual, full-blown doctrine of God as three in one and one in three (Father, Son, and Holy Spirit), nevertheless, the Pauline teaching about the Trinity (based above all on the resurrection of the crucified Jesus and the coming of the Holy Spirit) and subsequent NT witness provide a foundation and a starting point for that doctrinal development. But there are still obvious limits: for instance, while Paul (1 Cor 8:6) and some others (e.g., Jn 1:3; Heb 1:2) attribute to the Son the divine work of creation, no NT author says anything about the activity of the Spirit in the creation of the world. Where the OT, as we saw in Chapter 1, presents the divine Spirit as operative in the original creation, this thought is not as such picked up by the NT.

Within the NT itself, post-Pauline authors, notably Luke and John, were to take further the doctrine of the Spirit. Even statistics reflect the course that the development was to take. In his seven (certainly) authentic letters, Paul uses *S/spirit* 113 times; he uses *Holy Spirit* only 13 times, and he does this especially when he is concerned to stress the Spirit as the source of holiness who reproduces God's holiness in people. Luke in particular was to prove decisive not only in establishing the name *Holy Spirit* but also in helping to clarify the personal identity of the Spirit who is co-sent by the Son.

4.
The Trinity in the Witness of Luke, Matthew, Hebrews, and John

"I will see and consider the Three Divine Persons seated on the royal dais or throne of the Divine Majesty."

St. Ignatius Loyola, *The Spiritual Exercises*

This chapter aims to unfold further testimony from the NT that has relevance for the development of trinitarian doctrine. My purpose is not to survey and appraise all that the NT has to teach on the Father, the Son, and the Holy Spirit. I want rather to highlight some major themes from the NT authors that will flow into the story of trinitarian faith and practice.

Luke/Acts

Let us look at some trinitarian patterns that emerge from Luke's Gospel and from the Acts of the Apostles. First of all, along with Matthew, Luke reports the Q-saying about the intimate, mutual knowledge between Father and Son and does so in a way that introduces the Holy Spirit:

> At that same hour, Jesus rejoiced in the Holy Spirit and said, "I thank you, Father, Lord of heaven and earth, because you have hidden these things from the wise and intelligent and have revealed them to infants; yes, Father, for such was your gracious will. All things have been handed over to me by my Father; and no one knows who the Son is except the Father, or who the Father is except the Son and anyone to whom the Son chooses to reveal him." (Lk 10:21–22; par. in Mt 11:25–27)

Luke also reports Jesus' testimony to himself and his decisive role for the final salvation of human beings, a role expressed in terms of the *Son of man:* "I tell you, everyone who acknowledges me before others, the Son of man also will acknowledge before the angels of God; but whoever denies me before others will be denied before the angels of God" (Lk 12:8–9; par. in Mt 10:32–33[1]). The future and final salvation of human beings with God is understood to depend upon their present relationship with Jesus. Here, high claims about Jesus' function and identity are hardly less than explicit. When defending himself against the charge of unjustified friendship with public sinners, Jesus tells a parable about a uniquely merciful father (Lk 15:11–32). Obviously, Luke attributes to Jesus and his divine Father the same loving, forgiving attitude toward sinful men and women. By including these two Q-sayings and the parable of the merciful father (introduced by two other parables about divine mercy toward the lost and sinful [Lk 15:3–10]), the evangelist prompts the questions: Who did Luke think Jesus was/is?[2] What relationship did Luke think Jesus had vis-à-vis the Father and the Holy Spirit? These sayings and the three parables, inasmuch as we can establish that they go back to the earthly Jesus, raise similar questions about Jesus' consciousness of his own identity and relationship to the Father (and the Holy Spirit).

We noted in Chapter 2 how, in Luke's view, the earthly Jesus has a pneumatic existence as the paradigmatic Spirit bearer. But Jesus also enjoys a divine prerogative in being the Co-Sender of the Spirit and performs that function in the aftermath of his resurrection from the dead. In a surprisingly discreet instruction, the risen Jesus tells his disciples: "You must wait in the city until the power from above comes down upon you" (Lk 24:49). A repetition of this command occurs in the opening chapter of Acts and is somewhat more explicit: "Do not leave Jerusalem, but wait for the promise of my Father, that I told you about. For John baptized with water, but in a few days you will be baptized with the Holy Spirit" (Acts 1:4–5). In the former case, only the "from above" hints at the source from whom/which the power will come; in the latter case, the Holy Spirit is called "the promise of my Father." In the event, as we shall shortly see, the risen Jesus is also involved in the divine action of pouring out the Spirit. Both passages name the Spirit in a less than fully personal way: as "the power" and "the promise." This will be so also when the next chapter speaks of "the gift of the Holy Spirit" (Acts 2:38, i.e., "the gift that is the Spirit"). One must add that this language of *power, promise,* and *gift* does not necessarily exclude personal connotations; after all, Jesus himself is "the power of God" (1 Cor 1:24). Mark has Jesus speak of "the Son of man sitting at the right hand of the Power" (i.e., God; Mk 14:62; see Mt 26:64; Lk 22:69). A Deutero-Pauline letter (Eph 4:7) writes of "the gift of Christ" (i.e., "the gift that comes from and is Christ"; see Rom 5:15). What may be puzzling in Acts 1:5 is the promise about being "baptized with the Holy Spirit." After all, Luke 3:16 has spoken of baptism "with the Holy Spirit *and with fire*." But Acts 1:5 does not repeat the latter phrase. In the event, tongues of fire will visibly symbolize the coming of the Holy Spirit (Acts 2:3).[3]

The Acts of the Apostles offers a trinitarian view of the resurrection and a resurrectional view of the Trinity. In his Pentecost discourse, Peter explains the phenomena the people have just perceived: "This Jesus God raised up, and of that all of us are witnesses. Being therefore exalted at the right hand of God, and having received from the Father the promise of the Holy Spirit, he has poured out this that you both see and hear" (Acts 2:32–33). The sending of the Spirit is not merely Jesus' own gift; he receives "from the Father" the promised Spirit before pouring out the Spirit. Faced with this and similar passages in Acts, we may well ask: What does Luke make of the relationship between the Spirit, the Father, and the exalted Jesus who is enthroned at the Father's "right hand" and is Co-Sender of the divine Spirit?

The missionary discourses of Peter continue to expound the death and resurrection of Jesus in a trinitarian key:

> The God of our fathers raised up Jesus, whom you had killed by hanging him on a tree. God exalted him at his right hand as Leader and Savior that he might give repentance to Israel and forgiveness of sins. And we are witnesses to these things, and so is the Holy Spirit whom God has given to those who obey him. (Acts 5:30–32)

Two items in this passage invite comment. The *God* and *Father* of Acts 2:33 is here identified with YHWH, *the God of our fathers* (see also Acts 3:13). The witnessing role lets the Holy Spirit emerge in a more personal way. It is not that the mighty wind and fire of Acts 2:1–4 ignore or even exclude personal connotations; after all, fire symbolizes the presence and glory of the Lord (Gn 15:17; Ex 3:2; 19:18; Ps 104:4; Ez 1:4,13,14,27; Heb 12:29). Associating God with wind (Ps 104:3–4; Ez 1:4) and fire offers a more dynamic divine scenario than naming God as *my Rock* or *my shield.* Nevertheless, witnessing is a blatantly personal activity.

In the Lucan scheme, the risen Jesus needs to be withdrawn from the visible scene before the coming of the Holy Spirit. The ascension does not, however, mean that Jesus has gone away, as if he were on a very long sabbatical leave in another universe. He remains dynamically, if invisibly, present in and to the church. Here distinctions may seem to become a little blurred. Luke can move from cases of faithful guidance by the ascended Lord (Acts 9:10–16; 18:9–10; 22:17–21) to cases of guidance by the Holy Spirit (Acts 8:29; 10:19; 16:6) without distinguishing very clearly between them. He reports at least once guidance by "the Spirit of Jesus" (Acts 16:7). Does Luke mean here the Spirit that comes from Jesus, the Spirit who is somehow Jesus, or the Spirit who brings us to Jesus? Are the risen Jesus and the Holy Spirit interchangeable? As regards the initial coming of the Spirit, Luke distinguishes Jesus as divine Co-Sender from the divine Spirit who is sent or poured out (Lk 24:49; Acts 2:33). But in the spread and life of the Christian community, Luke often refers to the powerful guidance of

Jesus and that of the Spirit in a seemingly undifferentiated manner. Such faithful and sure guidance suggests, incidentally, a personal property. Only persons can guide other persons. Hence, the Spirit seems here to be personal, like Jesus himself.

In the last chapter, we recalled how Paul names God's Spirit as *the Holy Spirit* rather infrequently: only 13 times in the seven letters generally regarded as authentic or written directly by the apostle himself. John's Gospel speaks of *the Spirit* 20 times but of *the Holy Spirit* only 4 times. Luke, however, in his Gospel and Acts refers 54 times to *the Holy Spirit*. Right from the start Luke shows his liking for *the Holy Spirit* not only in his opening chapter (1:15,35,42) but also in the account of Jesus' baptism. There, he changes Mark's *the Spirit* (Mk 1:10) to *the Holy Spirit* (Lk 3:22). Luke's preferences helped to settle the traditional name for the third divine person as *the Holy Spirit* rather than as *the Spirit*. Does the Lucan usage intend to stress the distinct, individual, or "personal" (to speak anachronistically) identity of the Spirit, or does the evangelist want to insist that the Spirit's outpouring and interiorly empowering people will not take away from the transcendent otherness and holiness of the Spirit as the Spirit of/from God? Perhaps this usage aims principally at expressing the central purpose of the Spirit's mission—to be *the* source of holiness by reproducing the characteristics of divine holiness and so creating truly holy men and women. Does Luke wish instead to distinguish *the* Holy Spirit from various spirits (and demons) believed to be around in the gentile world (see, e.g., 1 Thes 4:1; Gal 4:3; Eph 2:1; Col 2:8)? Whatever Luke's reason or blend of reasons, his terminology of *the Holy Spirit,* through the early creeds and liturgy, came to establish itself as standard.[4]

What we do not yet find in the Lucan writings is a trinitarian formula for baptism. Acts depicts the first Christians as baptizing in the name of Jesus and the gift of the Holy Spirit being connected with baptism. On the day of Pentecost, Peter calls on his hearers: "Repent, and be baptized every one of you in the name of Jesus Christ so that your sins may be forgiven; and you will receive the gift of the Holy Spirit" (Acts 2:38). Luke writes of the gift of the Holy Spirit both as following on baptism in the name of Jesus (Acts 8:14–17; 19:1–7) and as preceding baptism in Jesus' name (Acts 10:44–48). Although these passages link Jesus and the Spirit in the context of baptism, nevertheless, the Father is not introduced, still less a trinitarian formula for baptism.[5]

Paul's letters likewise echo the practice of being baptized "into" or "in the name of" Jesus (e.g., 1 Cor 1:15), presenting baptism as a sacramental reenactment of the first Good Friday and Easter Sunday: "Do you not know that all of us who have been baptized into Christ Jesus were baptized into his death? Therefore, we have been buried with him by baptism into death, so that, just as Christ was raised from the dead by the glory of the Father, so we too might walk in newness of life" (Rom 6:3–4). Here, "the glory of the Father" (i.e., the glorious power of the Father) connects baptism with the first person of the Trinity. Occasionally, the apostle associates the Holy Spirit with baptism (e.g., 1 Cor 6:11; 12:13). In the first of these passages, by invoking, for example, "the Spirit of *our God*" (1 Cor 6:11), Paul brings in God the Father, but he nowhere connects a trinitarian confession as such with baptism. This is done by Matthew, who puts into the mouth of the risen Jesus the tripartite formula: "Make disciples of all nations, baptizing them in the name of the Father and of the Son and of the Holy Spirit" (Mt 28:19).[6]

Matthew

The order and the names (the Father, the Son, and the Holy Spirit) found in Matthew's baptismal formula have become standard for Christian faith. Beyond implying some distinctness and equality, however, the formula clarifies little about the relationship among the Father, the Son, and the Holy Spirit. To speak of the Father, the Son, and the Holy Spirit offers only (to adopt the language of a later age) a minimal identification of the three persons in their relationship to each other, apart from the unity of three being implied by the singleness of "the name." Unlike Paul, who (1) introduces no such trinitarian confession but (2) understands baptism as sacramentally reenacting the dying and rising of Jesus, Matthew (1) draws on the liturgical practice of his community to make the trinitarian confession central to the administration of baptism but (2) as such does not refer to any reenactment of Christ's death and resurrection. Nevertheless, the setting in which Matthew introduces the baptismal formula suggests two things: the powerful, salvific revelation of the Trinity is particularly connected with Jesus' dying and rising; the fundamental, new determination of life for the baptized brings decisively important blessings from the Father, the Son, and the Holy Spirit. This soteriological motif remains to the fore, as we shall see, in the story of trinitarian reflection and debate. Matthew's point of arrival (the confession of the Trinity in association with baptism) became the point of departure for the development of creeds as they emerged in a baptismal context.[7]

Hebrews

Although containing no explicit reference to baptism, the Letter to the Hebrews yields a rich testimony to trinitarian faith in a way that goes beyond what we gleaned from Paul. As with the apostle's letters, Hebrews is centered on Christ, blends wonderfully christological and soteriological motifs (or Jesus in himself and Jesus for us), develops a theology of the cross, and includes some elements for a Christology of preexistence. Hebrews differs from the Pauline letters by criticizing not the Mosaic law but the levitical priesthood of the OT cultic system. Jesus is qualified by his divine sonship to be not only kingly Messiah (Heb 1:8–9) but also High Priest, being "the great High Priest" as Son of God (Heb 4:14–10:31).

Hebrews differs also in that it treats the scriptures not as the written word of God but as the spoken word of the tripersonal God. Paul introduces quotations from the scriptures with such rubrics as *it is written* (e.g., Rom 9:13,33; 11:8,26; 14:11; Gal 4:27), *the Scripture says* (Gal 4:30), *Moses says* (Rom 10:19), *Isaiah says* (Rom 10:20), or *David says* (Rom 11:9). Hebrews, however, puts biblical quotations into the mouth of either God (the Father) or the Son or the Holy Spirit; positions are supported scripturally through the *spoken* word of the tripersonal God.

It is rare that anyone else is allowed to speak the words of scripture as Moses does in Heb 9:19–20. By putting biblical texts into the mouths of the Father, the Son, and the Holy Spirit, Hebrews vividly appropriates the OT scriptures to articulate faith in the tripersonal God.

In texts drawn from the scriptures, God (the Father) speaks to the Son as Son (Heb 1:5) and as Lord (Heb 1:10–12). In these words addressed to the Son, there is a Christology of divine and eternal lordship. Here, the divine being of the Son is so closely associated with the divine being of the Father that OT language apropos of YHWH (and the Father) can be applied to the Son. Son of God in his being, Jesus functions as high priest on our behalf. As the Father says to him, "You are a priest forever" (Heb 7:17,21). Then the Son speaks to God the Father: "I will proclaim your name to my brethren, in the midst of the congregation I will praise you" (Heb 2:12). Even more important, on the occasion of his coming into the world, the Son says to the Father: "Sacrifices and offerings you have not desired, but a body you have prepared for me; in burnt offerings and sin offerings you have taken no pleasure. Then I said, 'See, God, I have come to do your will'" (Heb 10:5–7). Finally, Hebrews puts the words of scripture into the mouth of the Holy Spirit (Heb 3:7–11; see 10:15–17).

In short, Hebrews draws on the biblical texts for a trinitarian doctrine, one might say drama, in which the Father speaks to the Son and to us in the Son (Heb 1:2), the Son addresses the Father, and the Holy Spirit bears witness to us. The salvific revelation in history, solemnly enunciated in the opening verses (Heb 1:1–4), does nothing else than continue *ad extra* (to the outside) the communion that exists *ad intra* (on the inside) between Father, Son, and Holy Spirit, a communion that Hebrews boldly lets its reader overhear in the words of the scriptures.[8] The Letter to the Hebrews resembles Luke and Matthew in that it presents the saving revelation of the tripersonal God in the context of Jesus' death and its glorious aftermath. It differs in that the language of entrance into the heavenly sanctuary (Heb 4:14; 6:20; 9:12,24) and of heavenly enthronement (Heb 1:3; 8:1; 10:12; 12:2) takes precedence over that of his resurrection from the dead (Heb 13:20).

Johannine Writings

When we turn to trinitarian themes in the Johannine writings, we find an abundant use of the Father/Son language. For instance, the Gospel of John calls Jesus *Son* 17 times and *Son of God* 9 times. In his identity and "work" as Son, Jesus is the divine Revealer of God the Father. We also run up against the christological title of *Logos,* or *the Word,* which became a central, high title for some centuries to come. The portrayal of the Word in the prologue to John's Gospel shows a marked resemblance to what is said about Lady Wisdom in Proverbs 8:22–31 and Sirach 24:1–12. Yet that prologue speaks of the Word, not the Wisdom, becoming flesh and does not follow Baruch in saying that "Wisdom appeared on earth and lived among human beings" (Bar 3:37). The evangelist develops the theme of the Son of God as the Revealer who brings the divine self-revelation (Jn 1:18); he is the *Logos,* as being spoken word or rational utterance rather than as being mere thought or meaning that remains within the mind. When focusing in a classic passage on what "God has revealed to us through the Spirit" (1 Cor 2:10), Paul writes of the hidden and revealed *Wisdom* of God (1 Cor 1:17–2:13). Despite the availability of such wisdom language and conceptuality, John speaks of "the Word" (Jn 1:1,14; see 1 Jn 1:1; Rv 19:13). The prologue of the Fourth Gospel does not open by saying, "in the beginning was Wisdom, and Wisdom was with God, and Wisdom was God" (see Jn 1:1).

Why did John choose Word and not Wisdom? Several considerations may have told against the latter and for the former. First, given that *Sophia* was personified as Lady Wisdom (see Chapter 1 above), it could have seemed awkward to speak of this female figure "being made flesh" when Jesus was male. Second, along with other themes, Wisdom was described as the radiantly beautiful woman whom Solomon sought as his wife (Wis 8:2,9,16). The NT imagery developed before the final composition of John's Gospel portrayed Jesus in the role of Solomon rather than of Wisdom: He was the husband seeking and caring for his wife, the church (e.g., Eph 5:25–27).

Third, in Hellenistic Judaism the law of Moses had been identified with Wisdom (Sir 24:23; Bar 4:1–4) and credited with her characteristics. To announce then that "Wisdom was God and was made flesh" could have been felt to suggest that "the Torah was God and was made flesh." Within a few years, Christians were to identify the Son of God and the *Logos* with law or the law.[9] But neither John nor any other NT authors identified Christ with the Torah. Fourth, Paul, Luke (especially in Acts), and other NT witnesses had prepared the way for John's prologue by their use of *logos* for God's revelation through Christ. As J. D. G. Dunn rightly argues, the background for John's choice of *Word* is *also* to be found in the earlier books of the NT and not just in the OT, Philo, and other such sources.[10]

Both in NT times and later, the Johannine *Word* offered rich trinitarian possibilities. First, it offered the possibility of identification and distinction. On the one hand, words proceed from a speaker; being a kind of extension of the speaker, they are, in a certain sense, identical with the speaker ("the Word was God"). On the other hand, a word is distinct from the one who utters it ("the Word was with/in the presence of God"). Thus, Christ was/is identified with, yet distinct from, YHWH. Second, God has been uttering the divine word always ("in/from the beginning"); the Word "was" (and not "came to be") God. In this context, *Word* opens up reflection on the personal, *eternal* preexistence of the Logos-Son. God has never been without the Word.

Third, we do not need John Osborne and other modern playwrights to be reminded of the fact that words reveal their speakers. Shamefully or happily, words express what is on our mind and in our heart. In the OT, *the word of God* repeatedly denotes the revelation of God and of the divine will. John's Gospel can move smoothly from the language of the Word to focus on "God the only Son who has made the Father known" (Jn 1:18). This Word offers light to everyone coming into the world (Jn 1:9), a theme soon developed, with the help of Philo, Middle Platonic, and/or Stoic thought, by Justin Martyr, Origen, and others.[11] As the Son of God sent from the Father or the Son of man who has come down from heaven, in a unique and exclusive way Jesus communicates heavenly knowledge and does so in a way that frees and nourishes human beings. The Word of revelation is liberating truth (Jn 8:32) and the bread of life (Jn 6:25–59).

Early believers raised the question of the saving self-revelation of the tripersonal God to non-Christians. Here *Logos* language quickly proved to be helpful. In his first *Apology*, Justin wrote: "We have been taught that Christ is the first begotten of God and that he is the Word (*Logos*) of whom the whole human race partakes. Those who have lived according to the Word are Christians, even though they have been considered atheists: such as, among the Greeks, Socrates, Heraclitus, and others like them" (46.1–4). Wherever there was the *Logos*, there was some true light and genuine knowledge of God. Like Justin, Origen acknowledged how this happened beyond and before Christianity: "It is not true that [God's] rays were enclosed in that man [Jesus] alone....or that the Light, which is the divine *Logos*, which causes these rays, existed nowhere else.... We are careful not to raise objections to any good teaching, even if their authors are outside the faith" (*Contra Celsum,* 7.17).

Fourth, John's *Logos* teaching opened the way for Christians not only to recognize the influence of the *Logos* beyond Christianity but also to dialogue with non-Christian thinkers. Those who endorsed Jewish, Platonic, and Stoic strands of thought about the *Logos* could find a measure of common ground with Christians, who, nevertheless, remained distinctive with their faith that "the Word was made flesh." In the ancient world, the notion of the *Logos* probably offered a more effective bridge to contemporary culture than that of "wisdom" or "Wisdom."

Finally, when John and other NT Christians called the crucified and risen Jesus the Word (and Wisdom) of God, they were not only expressing his divine identity but also drawing attention to the fact that their faith did not look back simply to the incarnation or even merely back to Jesus' prehistory in the call and story of the Jewish people. By maintaining that the whole world was created through the divine Wisdom and Word (Jn 1:3,10; 1 Cor 8:6; Col 1:16; Heb 1:2) they interpreted Jesus as the divine agent of all creation, which right from the beginning carried a trinitarian face or at least a binitarian one. No NT witness seems to attribute the creation of the world to the agency of the Spirit. Yet more than once the NT draws attention to the *creative* work of the Holy Spirit (e.g., 1 Cor 12:1–11) for believers' new life in Christ, which Paul calls "a new creation" (Gal 6:15), a divine work that is analogous to that of first creating the world.[12]

What of the Holy Spirit in the Johannine testimony? According to John, the Spirit comes from Jesus, is sent by Jesus, or is bestowed by Jesus (Jn 7:39; 15:26; 19:30,34; 20:22). At the same time, the sending or giving of the Spirit does not involve merely Jesus; the sending of the Spirit depends on the Father as does the primordial inner-trinitarian proceeding: "When the Paraclete comes whom I will send you from (*para*) the Father, the Spirit of truth who proceeds (*ekporeutai*) from (*para*) the Father, that One will bear witness about me" (Jn 15:26). John also talks about the Father giving the Spirit (Jn 14:16–17) or sending the Spirit (Jn 14:26), albeit in response to Jesus' prayer and in Jesus' name. Further, the evangelist associates the Spirit not only with witnessing to Jesus (Jn 15:26; see also 1 Jn 5:7–8) but also with new birth and life (Jn 3:5–8; 4:10,14; 7:37–39), with truth and teaching (Jn 14:16–17,26; 16:13–15), and with mission and the forgiveness of sins (Jn 20:22–23).

Even if the coming of the Spirit (Jn 14:16–17,25) seems to merge with the return of Jesus himself (Jn 14:3,18,23,28), in John's Gospel the Spirit is not equated with Jesus but enjoys some individual identity. Although both Jesus (1 Jn 2:1) and the Spirit (Jn 14:26; 15:26; 16:7) are called *Paraclete,* the Spirit is styled *another Paraclete* (Jn 14:16). Jesus is called *the Truth* (Jn 14:6) but not *the Spirit of truth* (Jn 14:17). The personal language applied to the Spirit (e.g., *sent, coming, witnessing,* and *teaching*) allows some sense of a distinct person to emerge. So too does the name *Paraclete.* Whether we translate this name as "Helper," "Consoler," "Advocate," or "Counselor," we use personal terms.[13]

Before leaving John's Gospel, we should note that its witness to the revelation of the tripersonal God (as also holds true with Paul, Luke, Matthew, and the Letter to the Hebrews) is located firmly in the context of Jesus' death and resurrection (Jn 13:1–21:25). Beyond question, the Fourth Gospel also witnesses to that revelation being communicated through the incarnation (Jn 1:1–18) and the public ministry (Jn 1:19–12:50). As the Revealer right from the start (Jn 1:14), Jesus has manifested the glory of God the Father (Jn 17:4). But the account of the Last Supper, the passion, and the resurrection articulates the trinitarian revelation even more clearly, above all as regards the Holy Spirit.

Conclusion

Like the earlier chapters, this fourth chapter has examined in the context of their historical development and authorial intention various biblical texts that bear on trinitarian faith. The post-NT reception of the scriptures was to pass over some items in this witness. It would not make much of the brilliant way Hebrews used the inherited Jewish scriptures to let the divine persons express themselves. The history of trinitarian reception was to attend massively, however, to Jesus' virginal conception and baptism, the triadic baptismal formula supplied by Matthew 28, the gift of the Spirit in John 19 and 20 (along with numerous verses in the last discourse from John's Gospel), John's prologue, various christological hymns such as Philippians 2:6–11, and the Pentecost scene in Acts 2, reading as well many verses of the OT in a christological and trinitarian fashion. Something of that history of reception will emerge in the chapters that follow. Here, I simply want to acknowledge the need for full-length studies on the reception of the trinitarian witness from the Bible—the reception not only of the passages to which these chapters have attended but also of others as well.

The Historical Developments

5.
THE TRINITY BEFORE NICAEA

"Who then is God? He is Father, Son, and Holy Spirit, one God. Seek no further concerning God; for those who wish to know the great deep must first review the natural world. For knowledge of the Trinity is properly likened to the depth of the sea."

St. Columban, *Instruction on the Faith*

"Monarchians pushed the argument for unity to extremes and rejected any plurality within the Godhead."

Eric Osborn, *The Emergence of Christian Theology*

At the heart of his appeal to the Galatians, Paul recalls their *experience* of what God's Spirit has done and continues to do for them. How can they then imagine that justification comes through the works of the law (Gal 3:1–5)? It is a similar challenge that primarily holds together post-NT reflection on the tripersonal God. What must God be like to account for the salvation experienced through Christ's life and resurrection from the dead along with the gift of the Spirit? Other factors also fuel the development of trinitarian theology: in particular, the illuminating authority of the scriptures and the insights of cultivated reason as it strove to understand and interpret the created world and human life. In the light of religious experience, the inspired scriptures, and philosophical reason, what must or could be said about God and the distinguishable divine relationships? Is the life of Jesus the human life of God's Son? Does Jesus' story belong to God, so that we can say that (the Son of) God suffered and died on the cross, or are suffering and death utterly incompatible with being God?

Their inherited monotheistic faith (see Mk 12:28–34; Rom 3:29–30) posed difficult questions for early Christians after they encountered the divine in Jesus, who addressed YHWH as *Abba* and with the Father gifted them with the divine Spirit. Is there dialogue within God, or—to use the language of a later age—are there personal distinctions "built into" the one God and the one divine life? If there are such distinctions within God, what are the relations between these personal distinctions (lowercase) or Distinctions (uppercase)? Having experienced through Jesus a certain threefoldedness within the deity, how should the early Christians relate to God and think of God—in particular, on the occasion of their entrance into the church through baptism and participation in the Eucharist? Were they to think of the Father, the Son, and the Holy Spirit as so distinct and even separate as to amount to three gods who had decided to live and work together for human salvation?

A letter from Pope Dionysius (d. 268), which we will come to, shows how this heterodox option of tritheism was real and feared. Where tritheism sacrificed the vital identity of Father, Son, and Holy Spirit to their multiplicity, the opposite heresy of modalism took monotheism so rigidly that it sacrificed the multiplicity of the divine persons to their unity. The modalist option entailed holding that the divine persons were united to the point that all three were incarnated in Christ. This logically meant that Jesus was praying to himself when he prayed to "Abba" and—in a conclusion drawn by the Patripassians ("the Father sufferers")—that the Father died on the cross. From the outset, Christian thinkers had to walk a fine line between lapsing into tritheism or retreating to rigid monotheism when they sought to explicate their new experience of God made possible by Jesus and his Spirit. In this chapter, we leave behind the biblical roots of trinitarian belief. We move to the development of trinitarian doctrine and begin by examining the second- and third-century attempts to understand and interpret the Trinity. St. Justin Martyr (d. ca. 165), St. Irenaeus (d. ca. 200),

Tertullian (d. ca. 220), and Origen (d. ca. 254) will prove the main protagonists. As regards their biblical sources, it should be recalled that they lived, taught, and wrote at a time when the Christian canon, or normative list of authoritative scriptures, was still being formed.[1]

St. Justin Martyr

In dialoguing with Jewish, Middle-Platonic, and Stoic thinkers and defending his Christian faith before a wider Roman public, Justin drew on the OT scriptures, some Christian scriptures, and, in particular, on what he called "the memorials of the apostles" (above all, what came to be known as the Gospels of Matthew and Luke), his experience of baptism (e.g., *First Apology,* 61) and Eucharist (e.g., ibid., 65–66), and the philosophies he had studied. He dedicated his attention to reflecting on the Father and the Son (or *Logos*), paying relatively little attention to the Holy Spirit. Here he differed from Athenagoras, a slightly later second-century apologist who initiated a trinitarian (philosophical) reflection that included the Holy Spirit.

(a) Christ's Divinity

Justin's robust faith encouraged him in the view that one could establish Christ's divinity from OT prophecies (*First Apology,* 30–53) but could Justin then accept Christ as divine without sacrificing faith in the one God? That this issue concerned Justin deeply came through his long argument that worshiping Christ did not contradict monotheism (*Dialogue,* 48–108). In dealing with the divine names and appellations, Justin added an attribute not found explicitly as such in the emerging NT by insisting on the unbegotten or unoriginated character of the Father. The Father is "prior" to all, and his eternal Son is begotten before the created universe and is the agent of all creation (see e.g., Jn 1:3; 1 Cor 8:6; Col 1:16–17):

> The Father of all has no name given him, since he is unbegotten. For a being who has a name imposed on him has an elder to give him that name. "Father," "God," "Creator," "Lord," and "Master"

> are not names, but appellations derived from his benefits and works. His Son (who alone is properly called Son, the Word [*Logos*] who is with God and is begotten before all creation, when in the beginning God created and ordered all things through him) is called Christ because he was anointed. (*Second Apology,* 5)

The language of "the Word who is with God" echoed John 1:1, just as the creation of "all things through him" echoed John 1:3; the claim that only the divine Son "is properly called Son" related to the Johannine scheme in which Jesus is the only begotten Son and those who believe in him become "children" of God (e.g., Jn 1:12–13). We see here how Justin called God (*ho Theos* as in normal Pauline and Johannine usage) the Father of all or Creator.

In this passage from the *Second Apology*, Justin introduced two "high" christological titles (*Son* and *Word*) and one "low" one (*Christ*). In another passage, he added to *Son* and *Word* some further, high titles: "God has begotten of himself a certain rational Power as the beginning before all other creatures. The Holy Spirit indicates this Power by various titles: sometimes the Glory of the Lord, at other times Son, or Wisdom, or Angel, or God, or Lord, or Word" (*Dialogue*, 61; see *First Apology,* 12). "A certain rational Power" and "Wisdom" recall Paul's language of Jesus' being "the Power of God and the Wisdom of God" (1 Cor 1:24). The scriptures also name God (the Father) as "the Power" (e.g., Mk 14:62). "The Glory of the Lord" evokes the divine Shekinah with its many OT associations (e.g., Ex 40:34–38) and the Johannine (e.g., Jn 1:14; 2:11) and Pauline (e.g., 2 Cor 4:6; see also Heb 1:3) language of "glory" connected with Christ. Justin was the first postapostolic Christian writer to identify Jesus with the divine Wisdom of Proverbs 8:22 (e.g., *First Apology,* 23; *Dialogue,* 129). The list also attributed to Jesus a title never given him by the NT, *Angel*. In the face of the current angelology, some NT writers (e.g., Heb 1:5–14) had to insist that Christ was superior to the angels. In the second century, however, Justin drew on the OT tradition in which *the Angel of the Lord* could interchange with *YHWH* or *the Lord* (e.g., Gn 31:11,13; Ex 3:2,4–5). In Justin's list, *Angel* as a divine title is preceded by four other divine titles (*Power, Glory of the Lord, Son,* and *Wisdom*) and followed by another three high titles (*God, Lord,* and *Word*). We will see shortly how Justin valued this title *Angel* for safeguarding the Father's invisible transcendence and expressing the Son's mediatorial role. Unlike other high titles he applied to Jesus (e.g., *Son, Lord, Word, Wisdom,* and *God*), Justin's talk of *Angel* did not enjoy a solid follow-up (much as the naming of Jesus in Heb 3:1 as *Apostle* lapsed).

Justin's recognition of the Son's or Word's divinity called for reflection on the Father/Son relationship. To interpret the generation of the Word, Justin appealed to the sun sending forth its rays or a fire kindling "another" fire. Just as in these analogies, the begetting of the Son did not mean an "amputation, as if the essence (*ousia*) of the Father were divided" (*Dialogue*, 128).[2] Here Justin anticipated a question that was to be long debated in the fourth century, the consubstantiality (or being of "one substance") of the Father and the Son (or Word) in that they share the same essence or *ousia*. By that time, thanks to Tertullian, Justin's image of *Light from Light* had entered the Nicene Creed (DH 125; ND 7). Was Justin, in using this material language of the sun emitting its rays and fire kindling another fire, influenced by the Stoic idea (as Tertullian later was) that nothing can be real unless it is in some sense bodily? These sunny and fiery metaphors also raised the question: Is the product on the same level as or less than the source? At all events, St. Athanasius (d. 373) found in the sun and its radiance a favorite image for the eternal begetting of the Son, while the Bible itself had earlier applied to God the metaphors of the sun and fire (e.g., Ex 24:17; Heb 12:29).

Besides initiating the postapostolic identification of the Son with the divine Wisdom of Proverbs 8:22, the metaphor of *Light from Light,* and the eternal begetting from the divine essence (*ousia*), Justin was also the first Christian writer to discover a trinitarian (or, in his case, a binitarian) meaning in Genesis 1:26: "Then God (*Elohim*) said, 'Let us make humankind in our image, after our likeness.'" Jewish thinkers, prior to Justin, had been drawn into debate over such plurals used by or about God in the scriptures. To Justin, the "let us make" suggested at least two divine persons (to use the language of a later age): before the creation the divine Offspring talked with the Father (*Dialogue,* 62;

see 129). What we meet, however, in Genesis 1:26 is a plural of intensity in *Elohim* and of deliberation in the "let us make"—the kind of plural of deliberation used when someone ponders something or engages in a soliloquy (as in the modern expression "let us think about that"). The plural here may also or may alternatively refer to heavenly but nondivine beings who compose God's court: "the host of heaven" of 1 Kings 22:19 or "the sons of God" of Job 1:6.

Justin wrote further of "*another* God besides the Creator" (*Dialogue,* 50), who is "distinct in number but not in mind" (ibid., 56).[3] Yet talking of the Son as "another/second God," as Origen was also going to do (*Dialogue with Heracleides,* 2.3), could end up destroying monotheism (by alleging in polytheistic style a second or third god) or else lapsing into an unacceptable subordinationism in which the Son lacks the true divinity of the Father and is a secondary God. Nevertheless, sharing the one mind, inasmuch as mind belongs to the essential characteristics of God, necessarily entails sharing the same divinity. Being nondistinct in mind seems an early intimation of later reflections on the one divine nature, or *physis* (with its divine mind and will), that will develop through Origen, the Cappadocians, St. Augustine, St. Thomas Aquinas, and others. To adopt a language that emerged much later than Justin, the oneness of the divine mind shared by the three divine persons will leave us with the challenge: Can we in any way distinguish the three persons on the basis of consciousness? Does their sharing in the one divine mind mean that there is no room left for differentiating their consciousnesses?

(b) The Trinity

In his *First Apology,* Justin introduced the notion of the Son of God being "second," adding a reference to the Holy Spirit as being "in the third place."

> We worship the Creator of the universe...with the word of prayer and thanksgiving...expressing our thanks to him in words, with solemn ceremonies and hymns.... The Master, who taught us this worship and who was born to this end, was crucified under Pontius Pilate.... We are sure that he is the Son of the true God,

> and hold him the second in order, with the Spirit of prophecy in the third place. I shall show that the honor we pay is rational. (13)

The sense of subordination ("the second in order" and "in the third place") might put orthodox nerves on red alert about the equality in communion between the three divine persons. It would be a pity, however, to miss the liturgical context for Justin's summary of the new, trinitarian faith of Christians. The Creator, or Father, is worshiped in liturgy that was "taught" by the divine Son (i.e., presumably what was taught by Jesus at the Last Supper). Naming the Holy Spirit as *the Spirit of prophecy* points to the inspired scriptures from which Justin drew in expounding his trinitarian theology and in doing so in a "rational" or philosophical way. Few passages suggest as much about the methodology followed by Justin and bequeathed to his successors: the context of thanksgiving and salvation experienced in worship, the confession of the tripersonal God expressed in developing creeds ("the Creator of the Universe," "the Son of the true God," who is "the Master born [and then] crucified under Pontius Pilate," and "the Spirit of prophecy"), the authoritative biblical testimony, and the requirements of rational thought.

Before leaving behind this passage from the *First Apology,* let us note that Justin (and to some extent Irenaeus and Tertullian after him) did not always clearly distinguish the Spirit from the incarnate Logos (e.g., *First Apology,* 33). This has been well indicated by J. N. D. Kelly.[4] To Kelly's discussion, one might add the fact (noted in Chapter 1) that the OT at times took God's Logos and Spirit as parallel and interchangeable personifications of the divine activity; this parallelism would have encouraged Justin and other deeply biblical theologians to entertain at times this identification. To be sure, the clear and definitive statement of the Holy Spirit's divinity and distinct identity (vis-à-vis the Father and the Son) would come only in the late fourth century at Constantinople I (381). Yet already in Justin's brief references (see above and below) the distinct divine status of the Spirit was starting to come through, not least in Justin's clear statement that Christians venerated the Spirit (*First Apology,* 6).

(c) The Missions

With the references in the *First Apology* (see above Justin's words about the Son born and then crucified under Pontius Pilate) and "the Spirit of prophecy," we have reached the *missions* of the Son and the Holy Spirit in the history of salvation. Applying to God the Father late Middle Platonism's (1) emphasis on the utter transcendence, invisibility, and unknowableness of God and (2) doctrine of the *logos spermatikos,* or "logos in seed" (shared with Stoicism and also related to Philo's thought about the principle of intrinsic intelligibility and mediation at work in the cosmos and history), Justin develops the Johannine theme of the preexistent Logos as universal mediator of creation and revelation.

"The seeds of the Word" have been dropped everywhere (*Second Apology,* 8) and, at least to some extent, in every person (ibid., 10). In one way or another, the whole human race shares in the Logos (*First Apology,* 46). Many people live only "according to a fragment of the Logos" (*Second Apology,* 8); Christians live "according to the knowledge and contemplation of the whole Logos, who is Christ" (ibid.). Justin applies the universal mediation of the Logos to Greek history, interpreting it to be a prelude and preliminary to Christ and Christianity:

> Plato's teachings are not contrary to Christ's but they are not in all respects identical with them: as is the case with the doctrines of others, the Stoics, the poets, and the prose authors. For each, through his share in the divine generative Logos, spoke well, seeing what was suited to his capacity...whatever has been spoken aright by anyone belongs to us Christians; for we worship and love, next to God, the Logos who is from the unbegotten and ineffable God.... All those writers were able, through the seed of the Logos implanted in them, to see reality darkly. For it is one thing to have the seed of a thing and to imitate it up to one's capacity; far different is the thing itself, shared and imitated in virtue of its own grace. (Ibid., 13)

While claiming to know "in virtue of its own grace" the incarnate Logos "who is from the unbegotten and ineffable God," Justin and other Christians do not deny some presence and impact ("the seeds") of the Logos in the life and thought of Plato, the Stoics, poets, and prose authors—an impact that makes their teachings in certain respects identical with those of Christ.

Several decades later, Origen was to say something similar but in terms of the divine rays being mediated by the Light and not being confined to where they are fully found—in the history of Jesus: "It is not true that [God's] rays were enclosed in that man [Jesus] alone…or that the Light which is the divine Logos, which causes these rays, existed nowhere else…. We are careful not to raise objections to any good teaching, even if the authors are outside the faith" (*Contra Celsum,* 7.17). In the fourth century Athanasius of Alexandria would argue that, because human beings are "rational (*logikoi*)," they all share somehow in the Logos/Word; they have in themselves at least "some shadows of the Word" (*De Incarnatione Verbi,* 3.3; see 5.1; 6.4).[5] More than ever the revealing and redeeming role of the Logos/Son and of the Holy Spirit in the lives of non-Christians remains a vital theme for reflection.[6]

Here I simply wish to register the inclusive view of Justin (and others): all human beings share (at least partly) in the Word, understood more along the lines of reason or the interior word than that of the expressed, spoken word. As Justin puts matters, "Christ is the First-born of God, and…he is the Word of whom all human beings have a share. Those who lived according to reason are Christians, even though they were classed as atheists: for example, among Greeks, Socrates and Heraclitus" (*First Apology,* 46). Probably the most important pre-Socratic philosopher, Heraclitus (d. 475 B.C.) held that everything is in a state of eternal flux. Justin may have listed him here as a foil to Socrates, associated with Plato in arguing for a world of changeless ideas. Both philosophical extremes, Heraclitus and Socrates, had some share in the same divine Word.

Belief in Christ as "the First-born of God" is Justin's basic hermeneutical principle for expounding not only the history of humanity in general but also that of the OT in particular. As preexistent Logos, the Son was prior to creation and mediated creation and sowed his seeds everywhere. As Angel, he was the one who encountered

Abraham, Jacob, Moses, and others in OT theophanies (*Dialogue,* 75). Out of the burning bush, for instance, he spoke to Moses (*First Apology,* 62). Because "the Creator of all things" is so utterly transcendent and ineffable, this "Author and Father of all things" has "never appeared to anyone and never spoken in person." It was a God and Lord different from "the Creator of all things" who addressed the OT patriarchs and others and who is therefore "called Angel" because "he announces and brings about the will of God" (*Dialogue,* 56). In the light of the Father's words at Jesus' baptism and transfiguration, in the tradition of the synoptic Gospels, one wonders how Justin could affirm that the "Father of all things" has "never spoken in person."

In his concern to protect the absolute transcendence of "the Author and Father of all things," who is beyond all names and descriptions, Justin developed the theme of the intermediary roles of the Son, who is "another" or "second" God. As Logos, he mediates and is present in all creation; as Angel, he reveals the divine will in the OT theophanies, which in effect become Logophanies. When the Neoplatonic notion of intermediaries became popular a century or more later, the stage was set for Arius's full-blown subordination of the Logos.[7] Justin's subordinationism, however, did not lead him to anticipate Arius and deny the genuine divinity of the Logos.

Convictions about suffering encouraged some second-century and subsequent authors to deny the Son's genuine divinity. Here Justin disagreed with Greek philosophy's insistence that God's eternal immutability was not to be compromised by talk of a divine person's true incarnation and death. Trypho spoke not only for Jews when he challenged Justin's faith in the incarnation: "You are attempting to prove what is incredible and impossible in practice: namely, that God deigned to be born and to become man" (*Dialogue,* 68). The question has persisted to our own day: How could the Son of God enter human history, while remaining truly divine? Cultured pagans found even more offensive Justin's faith in the crucified Christ as "second God." Justin admitted that "they accuse us of madness, saying that we attribute to a crucified man a place second to the unchanging and eternal God, the Creator of all things" (*First Apology,* 13). How could God, who is impassible, immutable, and eternal, be "changed" not only by becoming related to events in time and space but even by becoming subject to appalling suffering and death through crucifixion?[8]

(d) Trinitarian Confession

In Justin's writings, the trinitarian confession comes through most firmly when he echoes credal statements and confesses "the true God" (also named the *Father and Maker of all things*), the Son, and the Holy (or prophetic) Spirit. In his *First Apology* Justin writes: "We revere and worship him [the true God], and the Son, who came from him and taught us these things...and the prophetic Spirit" (6). Later in the same work he speaks of "the Father of the universe," "his Son," and "the Holy Spirit" (65, 67). Some of this language may be taken from prayers for the eucharistic service. At all events, the rite of baptism provides a trinitarian pattern for other passages in the *First Apology.* Justin explains to his pagan readers what happens when Christians are baptized: "They receive washing in water in the name of God the Father and Master of the universe, and of our Savior Jesus Christ, and of the Holy Spirit" (61). A few lines further on, Justin describes baptism even more fully: "Over him who has chosen to be reborn and has repented of his sins *the name of God the Father* and Master of the universe is named.... And he who is enlightened is washed in *the name of Jesus Christ,* who was crucified under Pontius Pilate, and in *the name of the Holy Spirit,* who through the prophets announced beforehand the things relating to Jesus." It is clear that prior to Justin a trinitarian confession, which followed Matthew's order (Father, Son, and Holy Spirit), already accompanied the rite of baptism.[9]

Justin made an invaluable, initial contribution to trinitarian teaching. He reflected on God in the light of his shared Christian experience (especially that of the liturgy), of the inspired scriptures (in a situation when the canon was still somewhat fluid), and of the requirements of philosophical thought. His sense of the ineffable transcendence of the Father and Creator of all things led to a certain subordination of the Son—and of the Holy Spirit, to the extent that the Spirit was thought of. At the same time, Justin held that the Son, sharing in the essence (*ousia*) and mind of God, was/is truly divine. His presentation of the Son as the Logos, who creates, organizes, and affects the whole cosmos, allowed for a positive view of the religious situation of non-Christians. Without developing the language of "the crucified (Son of) God," Justin upheld God's real involvement in human history and suffering. His faith in the tripersonal God revealed in Jesus Christ led not only to debate with Jews and cultured pagans but also to a stand before the Roman public that brought martyrdom. Justin's trinitarian faith was literally a matter of life and death.

St. Irenaeus

Thirty or so years younger, Irenaeus may have met Justin in Rome before going to Gaul and a ministry as bishop of Lyons. The first and still perhaps the greatest biblical theologian, Irenaeus drew from St. John's Gospel a faith in the Logos eternally coexisting with the Father "before" truly becoming flesh, and from St. Paul a sense of Jesus as the last or second Adam who draws together in one great trinitarian project the whole story of creation and salvation. He expanded Paul's dyadic confession of 1 Corinthians 8:6 to include the Holy Spirit and speak of the orthodox faith "in one God almighty, from whom are all things,…and in the Son of God, Jesus Christ our Lord, through whom are all things, and in the saving dispensations by which the Son of God became man; and in the Spirit of God, who in each generation publicly discloses among human beings the saving dispensations of the Father and the Son, as the Father wills" (*Adversus Haereses,* 4.33.7).

(a) Marcion and the Gnostics

When expounding the common body of Christian doctrine or "rule of faith,"[10] Irenaeus also had to contend with the reductionist, anti-Jewish heresy of Marcion and the variegated theories of the Gnostics. Marcion, who was expelled from the Roman Christian community in 144, asserted that the OT Creator or Demiurge differed, by being just to the point of cruelty, from the merciful Father proclaimed by Jesus; in so doing,

Marcion rejected all the Jewish scriptures and reduced the Christian scriptures to a truncated version of Luke and 10 (emended) letters by Paul. Against Marcion, Irenaeus (for whom the figures of Adam and Eve and Genesis 1–3, among other items, were essential components in the doctrine of redemption) maintained the authority of the Jewish scriptures, accepted the four gospels, and defended the identity of YHWH as "the Father" of Jesus Christ. Marcion, he commented, "divides God into two and calls one God good and the other just. In so doing he destroys the divinity of both" (ibid., 3.25.3). There cannot be more than one case of deity. Eventually the fourth-century Nicene-Constantinopolitan Creed was to target Marcionite error with its confession of "*one* God, *Father* almighty, maker of heaven and earth." The Jewish Creator God is identical with the *Father* of our Lord Jesus Christ.

The Gnostics, headed by Valentinus (who lived in Rome for almost 30 years until ca. 165), claimed fresh revelations and added to the scriptures. In their antimaterial scheme of things, spiritual knowledge, or *gnosis,* meant that the pneumatics (or people of the higher spirit) were already saved, the psychics (or people of the *psyche* or living soul) could be redeemed, whereas the hylics (or people of matter) were incapable of deliverance from matter and so remained beyond (or rather below) redemption. In opposition to Valentinus and other Gnostics, Irenaeus set forth the "true *gnosis*," which was "the teaching of the apostles and the ancient doctrinal structure of the church that is meant for the entire world" (ibid., 4.33.8). On the basis of the rule of faith and liturgical practice, Irenaeus insisted on salvation being mediated through the flesh; this cohered with the missions of the Holy Spirit and the Son. "Human beings," he wrote, are made "spiritual" not by the abolition of the flesh "but by the outpouring of the Spirit" (ibid., 5.6.1). Renewal in the image of God comes about "not by getting rid of the material body but by sharing in the Spirit" (ibid., 5.8.1). Irenaeus drew a strong connection between the reception of Christ in the Eucharist and our bodily salvation: "Flesh is nourished by the body and blood of the Lord" (ibid., 4.18.5; see 5.2.2–3). Hence, "our bodies, after partaking of the Eucharist, are no longer corruptible but have the hope of eternal salvation" (ibid. 4.18.5). Before adding something more about the saving missions of the Son and the Holy Spirit, let us recall several points in Irenaeus's trinitarian doctrine where he anticipated developments to come.

In a confession of the Son's eternal existence that rejected in advance Arian heresy, Irenaeus declared that the Son "did not begin to be; he existed always with the Father" (ibid., 3.18.1). By thus confessing the Son's eternity, Irenaeus assigned to him a central attribute of God. In sarcastic debate with various Gnostics and with Marcion, he wrote of the eternal generation of the Son:

> If anyone asks us how the Son was "produced" from the Father, we reply that no one understands that "production" or "generation"...or whatever term anyone applies to his begetting, which in truth is indescribable. Valentinus does not understand it, nor Marcion, nor Saturninus, nor Basilides, nor angels, nor archangels, nor principalities, nor powers. Only the Father who begat him knows, and the Son who was begotten. Thus, since his generation cannot be described, sensible persons do not exert themselves to talk of "begettings" and "productions," or undertake to explain what is indefinable. All certainly know that a word is "emitted" from the mind; and so those who have thought out the term "emissions" have not hit on anything important, nor have they discovered some hidden mystery in applying to the only-begotten Word of God a meaning which is a matter of common knowledge. They call him indescribable and unnamable and then, as if they had assisted at his birth, they talk grandly about "the production and generation of his first beginning," and liken him to a word "emitted" by human speech. But we shall not go astray if we say about him, as about matter, that God "produced" him. For we have learned from Scripture that God is the first source of all. But whence or how he "emitted" material substance the Scriptures have not revealed. And it is not our duty to indulge in conjectures and make guesses about infinite matters which concern God. The knowledge of such things is to be left to God. (ibid., 2.28.6)

Although he leaned toward a negative or apophatic theology (writing of the mysterious generation of the Son as "indescribable," "indefinable," and better "left to God"), Irenaeus did indulge some "conjectures" about the Son or Word of God being generated like the immanent word "emitted" from the mind (*logos endiathetos*) or the exterior word in human speech (*logos prophorikos*). Applying to the generation of the Logos the analogy of thought emerging from our mind or a word from our lips was to become a theological commonplace (see e.g., Athanasius, *Contra Gentes*, 41)—aided, of course, by the Logos language in John's prologue. In particular, the "psychological" model of the Word being generated by the Father like thought coming from the mind as a kind of divine "Brainchild" was to be widely used.

Irenaeus's analogy with the production or emission of "matter" and "material substance" was less fortunate. Such production did and does mean a beginning, whereas Irenaeus acknowledged that "the Son always co-exists with the Father" (*Adversus Haereses,* 2.30.9). Nicaea's confession of the Son being "begotten and not made" would push aside Irenaeus's analogy with the creation of material substances.

Where Irenaeus proved more successful was in the parallel he drew between "that pre-eminent birth which is from the Most High Father" and "that pre-eminent generation which is from the Virgin" (ibid., 3.19.2). After the parallel had been developed by various writers, in 451 the Council of Chalcedon was to canonize this scheme of double generation: the Son's eternal, divine generation from the Father and his human generation in time from the Virgin Mary.

(b) The Two Hands of God

Irenaeus, like Justin, wished to safeguard the transcendence and invisibility of the Father—right from the initial moment of creation. Here Irenaeus followed Justin's interpretation of Genesis 1:26, made it clearly trinitarian, and added the image of God's two hands:

> In carrying out his intended work of creation, God did not need any help from angels, as if he did not have his own hands. For he has always at his side his Word and Wisdom, the Son and the Spirit. Through them and in them he created all things of his own free will. And to them he says, "Let us make human beings in our image and likeness." (ibid., 4.20.1)[11]

In the work of revelation, the mediatorial role of the Word likewise protects the Father's transcendence: "The Word of God, present with his handiwork from the beginning, reveals the Father to all to whom he wills, when the Father wills and how he wills" (ibid., 4.6.7). A little later, Irenaeus added: "Through his Word all his creatures learn that there is one God, the Father, who controls all things, and gives existence to all.... the Son makes the Father known from the beginning. For he has been with the Father from the beginning" (ibid. 4.20.6).

No one has ever been "outside" or excluded from this omnipresent, mediatorial role. In revealing to them the one God and Father, the Word "is always present to the human race" (ibid., 3.18.1) and not just to some groups of men and women. At the same time, only the Word could play this role: "No other being had the power of revealing to us the things of the Father, except his own proper Word" (ibid. 5.1.1). This universal presentation of the Son (and of the Spirit) retains enduring significance for reflection on revelation and salvation for all.

Without furthering Justin's particular "angel" Christology, Irenaeus followed him in "protecting" the Father's transcendence by assigning to the Son or Logos the divine theophanies in the OT. "It is he himself [the Logos] who says to Moses, 'I have surely seen the affliction of my people in Egypt, and I have come down to rescue them.' From the beginning he was accustomed, as the Word of God, to descend and ascend for the salvation of those who were in distress" (ibid., 4.12.4; see 3.6.2). This identifying as Logophanies the divine theophanies enjoys a long liturgical impact, for instance, in the week of preparation for Christmas in the Latin rite. The antiphon for Vespers on December 18 addresses the Son, whose coming is prayed for, as *Adonai* who appeared to Moses at the burning bush.

When expounding the Son's incarnation, Irenaeus had to confront the Valentinian Gnostics, who appealed to John's Gospel and sharply differentiated between Christ the Only-begotten (*Monogenes*), supernatural aeon, or *Nous* (Mind), on the one hand, and the historical figure of Jesus the man, on the other. Irenaeus insisted: "John knows one and the same Word of God; it is he that is Only-begotten, and it is he that was incarnate for our salvation" (ibid., 3.16.2). The "Only-begotten" of

John's prologue is identical with the Word who became flesh as our Lord Jesus Christ, suffered, and then rose from the dead (ibid., 1.10.3; 3.16.1,6). The language of person and personal identity was not yet available, but it is clear that for Irenaeus the Son or Word who lived eternally with the Father was the one and same subject who became "incarnate for our salvation" to suffer, die, and rise to new life (ibid., 3.12.2; 3.16.9). Almost two centuries later, St. Gregory of Nazianzus (d. 389) protested that anyone "who introduces two sons, the one being that of God and of the Father, and the second being that of the mother, instead of *one and the same* Son," has departed from true faith (*Epistola,* 101.18). These words almost form a gloss on what Irenaeus repeatedly affirmed against the Gnostics (e.g., *Adversus Haereses,* 3.82; 3.9.3; 3.17.4). Eventually the Council of Chalcedon in its christological definition (DH, 301–02; ND 614–15) was to adopt three times Irenaeus's language about the eternal Son of God being "one and the same" subject as Jesus Christ.

To complete this quick account of Irenaeus's trinitarian doctrine, let us observe how he identified preexistent, divine Wisdom with the Holy Spirit and not (as Justin and many other church writers did) with the Son:

> We have shown at length that the Word, that is the Son, was always with the Father. And God tells us, through the mouth of Solomon, that Wisdom, that is the Spirit, was with him before the whole creation: "the Lord created me for his works as the beginning of his ways; he established me before the ages [Prv 8:22–23]." (*Adversus Haereses,* 4.20.3)[12]

Any discussion about the Spirit being the Wisdom of God is obviously less important than the question of the Spirit's relationship to the Son.

We quoted above Irenaeus's language about God's two hands. This terminology could imply parallel missions and even no (direct) relationship between the Son and the Spirit. In another vein, however, Irenaeus interprets human salvation through a kind of vertical, trinitarian line (starting from the Spirit to the Son, and continuing upward from the Son to the Father): "Through the Spirit we rise to the Son;

through the Son we rise to the Father" (ibid., 5.36.2). Another passage, which distinguishes the Trinity and seemingly assigns them different spheres of activity by varying the verbs ("prepares, leads, and gives"; "works, fulfills, and approves"), spells out similarly the story of salvation and revelation (from the Spirit, to the Son, and on to the Father): "The Spirit prepares human beings for the Son of God; the Son leads them to the Father; the Father gives them immortality.... Thus God was revealed: for in all these ways God the Father is displayed. The Spirit works, the Son fulfills his ministry, the Father approves" (ibid. 4.20.4,6). Here, incidentally, it is clear how the human predicament for which salvation provides the solution is not thought of so much as sin but as death (and, to some extent, as the need for knowledge that divine revelation satisfies). Through the Spirit and the Son, human beings receive immortality and incorruptibility from the Father.

Lastly, the Holy Spirit, in preparing "human beings for the Son of God," also emerges as the life-creating "Gift of God" who is intimately linked with the church: "Where the Church is, there is the Spirit of God; and where the Spirit of God is, there is the Church and every kind of grace" (ibid., 3.24.1).Through the bestowal of the Spirit in baptism, men and women are released from the burden of sins. Their possession of the Spirit, Irenaeus holds with hope, will be crowned at the resurrection of the flesh: "It is by virtue of the Spirit that believers will rise again when the body is united anew to the soul" (*Epideixis,* 42). Here and elsewhere Irenaeus overcomes a certain "binitarianism" to be observed in the writings of Justin and other apologists.

(c) The Rule of Faith

The vital relevance of trinitarian faith came strongly through Irenaeus's writings. The real incarnation of the Son and the gift of the Spirit provided the means for that incorruptibility and immortality that constitute the heart of salvation. Irenaeus insisted robustly on the trinitarian "rule of faith" shared by orthodox Christians:

> For the Church, although scattered throughout the whole world as far as the limits of the earth, has received as handed down from the apostles and their disciples its *faith* in *one God the Father*

> almighty, who made the heaven and the earth and the seas and all the things in them; and in *one Christ Jesus the Son of God,* who was made flesh for our salvation; and in *the Holy Spirit,* who through the prophets proclaimed the saving dispensations. (*Adversus Haereses,* 1.10.1)

In this passage, as well as expounding mainline trinitarian belief that was expressed above all in the baptismal liturgy,[13] Irenaeus also rejected both the Marcionite separation of the NT God the Father from the OT Creator who made all things, and the Gnostic denial of the Son of God being truly made flesh for our salvation. A true incarnation brought together creation and redemption in the one drama of salvation. He firmly held together the work of creation and our "fleshly" redemption.

Apropos of the Son and the Spirit, we have seen above the strong link acknowledged between the Spirit and the visible communities of the church gathered around their bishop and sharing the same rule of faith. We have observed also the universal mediatorial role of the Word in revealing God. For Irenaeus, however, the Word does not "float free" of the incarnated, crucified and risen Jesus whom Christians follow. Through sharing in the Eucharist, their "flesh is nourished by the body and blood of the Lord...their bodies, after partaking of the Eucharist, are no longer corruptible, having the hope of eternal resurrection" (ibid., 4.18.5). It is one and the same Son who is present to men and women everywhere and whom Christians receive in the Eucharist. All in all, Irenaeus has much more to say about the Son than about the Holy Spirit. He does not reflect on the "origin" of the Spirit, whereas, albeit reluctantly, he does help to initiate the psychological model of the Word being generated like thought coming from the mind or like speech coming onto our lips.

Tertullian

A somewhat younger contemporary of Irenaeus, Tertullian fashioned a trinitarian vocabulary for the Latin world. He did so in a fairly polemical context as, on the one hand, he opposed polytheism and rejected Gnostic divisions of divinity, refusing to let anyone tamper with God's oneness and uniqueness. His monotheistic faith made him attack Marcion for attempting to divide God: "If God is not one, then there is no God" (*Adversus Marcionem,* 1.3). On the other hand, Tertullian had to contend with the modalist "monarchianism" of Noetus, Praxeas, and other heterodox Christians. Their rigid view of the "one principle (*mone arche*)" sacrificed personal distinctions within God; creation and redemption were seen merely as different modes in the way that for a time God acts externally and offer no information about God's eternal being. The distinctions between Father, Son, and Holy Spirit are no more than transient manifestations and not permanent presentations of the divine being. These heterodox Christians denied any distinctions within the divinity and aimed to defend at all costs the unique "mon-archy" of God (the Father). Their rigorous or undifferentiated monotheism led Noetus and Praxeas to teach a patripassian doctrine, according to which it was God the Father, and not a distinct Son, who was born into human history, suffered, and died on the cross (Tertullian, *Adversus Praxean,* 2). Slightly later in the third century, Sabellius, who was condemned by Pope Callixtus (see DH 112; ND 301), and the Sabellians brought the Holy Spirit into their version of modal monarchianism. The Father in the OT, the Son in the incarnation, and the Holy Spirit at Pentecost were interpreted to be merely three self-manifestations of the one God, three different relationships that the one God assumed successively in creating, redeeming, and sanctifying.

Faced with Christian modalists (and pagan polytheists), Tertullian wrestled with the question: Is the divinity of the Son (and of the Holy Spirit) compatible with genuine monotheism? In particular, Tertullian directed his criticisms against Praxeas, who had "driven away the Paraclete and crucified the Father" (*Adversus Praxean,* 1), and so made enduring contributions to trinitarian thought. He wrote of God's one "substance" and three distinct but undivided "persons" (ibid., 2,12). The distinction (not separation) of the persons does not compromise the unity of substance and the true divine monarchy.

In writing of one divine substance (*substantia*) in three persons, Tertullian was the first Christian writer to exploit the term *person* in theology, the first to apply *Trinity* (*Trinitas*) to God (*De pudicitia,* 21.16; *Adversus Praxean,* 8), and the first to develop the formula of *one substance in three persons*. The Latin *essence* (*essentia*) had for the time dropped out of use in favor of *substance*. Hence where the Greeks wrote of *ousia*, Tertullian used *substantia,* a term already applied to God by Seneca (d. A.D. 65). Where *substance* stood for the common fundamental reality shared by Father, Son, and Holy Spirit, Tertullian understood *person* as the principle of operative individuality. One could be led astray by the historical background of the Latin *persona* (and the Greek *prosopon*), as if the term meant only a mere mask or a mere manifestation. But Tertullian was no modalist monarchian when he wrote of the persons in God. At the same time, one must obviously beware of interpreting Tertullian in the light of later, especially modern, theories of personhood, which expound persons as conscious selves and autonomous subjects. Yet in the late second and early third century, he made a good start in applying the language of *persons* and *substance* to the one God revealed as Father, Son, and Holy Spirit. The standard trinitarian formula has remained *three persons,* whereas *one nature* and *one essence* have often replaced Tertullian's *one substance*.

When following the trinitarian interpretation of Genesis 1:26 already adopted by Justin and Irenaeus, Tertullian explains why God speaks in the plural: "There was already attached to him his Son, a second person, his own Word; and a third, the Spirit in the Word (Spiritus in Sermone)" (*Adversus Praxean,* 12). It is the other key term in Tertullian's trinitarian vocabulary, *substance,* that is more problematic. Inasmuch as he is influenced by the Stoic view that nothing can be real unless it is in some sense bodily, he could write: "Who will deny that God is a body, although God is spirit? For a spirit is a body, of its own kind, in its own form" (ibid., 7). "Materializing" language comes easily to him.

This tendency emerges when Tertullian attempts to show how God is a differentiated, triune unity; the divine substance is extended, with the Son and the Spirit sharing in it and being distinct persons, yet without being separated. He introduces three material analogies: a root producing a shoot and fruit; a spring issuing in a river and a canal; the sun producing a ray and the point of focus of a ray:

> The Son was "produced" from the Father, but not separated from him. For God produced the Word...as a root produces the shoot, a spring the river, the sun a ray.... The Spirit makes the third from God [the Father] and the Son, as the fruit from the shoot is the third from the tree, the canal from the river the third from the source, the point of focus of a ray third from the sun. But none of these is divorced from the origin from which it derives its own properties. Thus the Trinity derives from the Father by continuous and connected steps. (Ibid., 8)

The related images of the sun, light, and radiance enjoy some biblical background and do so in reference to all three divine persons (e.g., Ps 27:1; Lk 2:78–79; Jn 9:5; Acts 2:3; Heb 1:3). The OT calls God "the fountain of living waters" (Jer 2:13). The NT applies the theme of the fountain and the stream to the Holy Spirit (Jn 7:38–39; Rv 22:1) but not yet to the generation of the Son.[14] Tertullian himself seems to have introduced the image of the root with its shoot and fruit, albeit that NT language of fruits, first fruits, and harvest (e.g., 1 Cor 15:20; Gal 5:22; 6:8) offered some encouragement for this image.[15]

The point of the three analogies is to maintain that the Son and the Spirit are distinct from the Father as individual persons but not as substance. This way of looking at the dynamic "derivation" of the Son and the Spirit, Tertullian argues, does not subvert the unity of the one divine substance or "monarchy." The Son and the Holy Spirit remain derived from the Father without a real separation taking place. The analogies drawn from dynamic operations serve well enough to link the three persons through relationships of origin that do not separate them.

As regards the relationship between Father and Son, Tertullian emphasizes how the Son has been brought forth but not separated or divided from the Father:

> The Son is not other than the Father by separation from him but by difference of function, nor by division but by distinction.... The Father is the whole substance [of deity], while the Son is derivative and a portion of the whole.... The Father is other than the Son, as being greater, as he who begets is other than the begotten, the sender than the sent, the creator than the agent of creation. (Ibid., 9)

Here, the language about " being greater" evidently refers to John 14:28 ("The Father is greater than I"). The "sender than the sent" echoes John 14:26 about the sending of the Spirit, along with Pauline passages about the sending of the Son and the Spirit (Rom 8:3; Gal 4:4–6). The reference to "the agent of creation" also has its NT background (e.g., Jn 1:3; 1 Cor 8:6) and even more so the language of "he who begets" and "the begotten" (e.g., Jn 1:14,18). The statement about the Father being the whole substance of deity while the Son is a portion of the whole could, however, readily imply that the Son does not enjoy the fullness of divinity.

A little earlier in the same work, Tertullian added something to what Irenaeus had done toward initiating the psychological model of the Trinity—at least as regards the generation of the Word/Son. Encouraged by John's statements about the Logos, Tertullian presented the Son as *Ratio* or the Word in God's mind and as *Sermo,* the Word as spoken.

> God is rational and Reason (*Ratio*) existed first *with* him, and from him extended to all things. That Reason is his own consciousness of himself. The Greeks call it Logos, which is the term we use for discourse (speech) (*sermo*).... Speech is in you something *distinct* from yourself; by speech you talk in thinking, and think in talking. (Ibid., 5)

The being "with" and being "distinct" allowed Tertullian to distinguish the Son and the Father, without separating them.

Reflecting further on "the divine consciousness," Tertullian joins Justin and others in identifying divine Wisdom with the second person of the Trinity: "This mode of operation of the divine consciousness is revealed in the Scripture also under the title of Wisdom…with [God] creating (*condens*) and begetting (*generans*) his own consciousness.… When God first willed to bring forth (*voluit edere*)…he first produced (*protulit*) his Word (*Sermonem*)" (ibid., 6). Tertullian's identification of the Word/Son as divine Wisdom fitted into a broad consensus among the patristic authors, but any literal version of God truly "*creating* his Word" had no future in mainline trinitarian teaching, which would be built around Nicaea's eternally "begotten" but not at some point willingly "made/created." Tertullian appears to have held that the divine Word, after existing within the Father's mind, then became a distinct person in a "complete birth (*nativitas perfecta*)" (ibid., 7) only when creation began. Before creation, the Word was not yet perfect (expressed) Word, and before the incarnation not yet perfect Son. The Word/Son was brought into existence before and in view of creation and incarnation.

When reflecting on the economy of creation and salvation, Tertullian had an inclusive view of Reason/Logos "extending to all things" and being active in the OT dispensation right from the time of Adam. Tertullian followed Justin and Irenaeus in maintaining that "It was the Son who descended from time to time to have converse with human beings, from Adam to the patriarchs and prophets" (ibid., 16). It was the same Son who became incarnate and suffered. Against Gnostics and others who tampered with this true incarnation "for our salvation," Tertullian emphasized its fleshly reality (*Adversus Marcionem,* 2.27; *De Resurrectione Carnis,* 8). Against the Patripassianists, he insisted: "The Father did not suffer with the Son.… It is as impossible for the Father to 'suffer with' as it is for the Son to suffer in respect of his divinity" (*Adversus Praxean,* 29). When he wrote of the Crucified God, Tertullian meant only the Son, adding that Christ died as man, not as "Word and Son of God" (ibid.). Against those who alleged that the Father died on the cross or at least suffered with the Son, he pressed into service his spring/river image:

> If a river is defiled by some muddying, although the one substance comes down from the spring and there is no interruption at the

> spring, yet the malady of the river will not attach to the spring. Although the water which suffers [injury] belongs to the spring, so long as it suffers not in the spring but in the river, it is not the spring that suffers, but the river which [has come] from the spring. (Ibid.)

Despite some faulty steps that we have noted, Tertullian's input into Western trinitarian theology was permanently assured by a pioneering vocabulary that served the West (*Trinity,* three *persons,* and one *substance*), by at least one of his analogies (*light from light*), and by his furthering the psychological model of the Trinity (at least on the side of thought and knowing rather than loving—that is to say, for the generation of the Son and not the procession of the Spirit). He underlined the role of the Son's real incarnation for an integral salvation that includes our bodily resurrection. Along with Justin and Irenaeus, Tertullian witnessed to the emergence of formalized creeds (in particular, the Old Roman Creed) used for the trinitarian confession that accompanies baptism.[16]

Origen

The last writer we will look at before moving to Arius and the Council of Nicaea is the Alexandrian Origen. As with his theology in general, he developed his reflections on the Trinity through exegesis and spirituality and often in response to heterodox views of the time.

Against the adoptionists, who excluded Christ's divinity and held that he was a mere creature adopted by God (at his baptism or resurrection), Origen insisted on the eternal generation of the Son (who is identified with Wisdom or the Word) and repudiated the notion that "there was a time when he was not" (*De Principiis,* 1.2.9; 4.1.2; 4.4.1):

> How could anyone believe that God the Father could have existed at any time without begetting Wisdom?… We must believe that Wisdom is without any beginning…. He is called the Word because he is as it were the interpreter of the secrets of the mind of God…. It is an eternal and ceaseless generation as radiance is

> generated from light.... Nothing is ungenerate, that is with underived existence, except only God the Father. (Ibid., 1.1.2–6)

Here, along with the theme that went back to Justin and Tertullian, Origen explicated the eternal generation of the Word as "light from light."[17] Justin, as we noted above, had underlined the "unbegotten" character of the Father who "has no name given him." Origen, followed by the Cappadocians and others, stressed even more the "ungenerate, underived" existence of the Father. As regards the eternal generation of the Son, he maintained against the Valentinian Gnostics that this generation did not entail a division of the divine substance or essence (*ousia*).

In an exegetical work, Origen saw the Holy Spirit as derived from the Word, called the three divine persons *hypostaseis* (in the sense of (a) three individual subjects and not in the sense of (b) three "substances"), and underscored the "unbegotten" character of the Father: "The Holy Spirit came into being through the Word, the Word being anterior to the Spirit.... There are really three persons (*hypostaseis*), the Father, the Son, and the Holy Spirit, and we believe that only the Father is unbegotten" (*Comm. in Ioannem,* 2.10). When writing of the Holy Spirit's coming into being through the Word, Origen did not want to undercut the Spirit's eternal existence: "The Spirit...is ever with the Father and the Son; like the Father and the Son he always is, and was, and will be" (*Comm. in Ep. ad Romanos*, 6.7). Origen recognized how language had to be used in an extended way when claiming of the Son and of the Holy Spirit (as well as of the Father) that "there was never a time when he was not." He wrote: "We have to apologize for using such phrases as 'there was never a time when he was not.' For these words have temporal significance; but when they are used of the Father and the Son and the Holy Spirit, they are to be understood as denoting something 'supra-temporal'"(*De Principiis,* 4.4.28).

Although he would not call the Son and the Holy Spirit inferior in power, Origen favored a certain "subordinationism" that highlighted the place of the Father as the ultimate principle: "The Son and the Holy Spirit excel all created things to a degree that admits of no comparison, and are themselves excelled by the Father to the same or even greater degree" (*Comm. in Ioannem*, 13.25). Origen's conception of the Father as the ungenerated source of the Son's mission encouraged him to develop a picture of the "subordinate" Mediator, somewhat along the lines of Middle Platonism. As Logos, the Son brings about creation, and as Word and Wisdom reveals the divine mysteries ("interpreting the secrets of the mind of God"). Origen's stress on the transcendence of the Father leveled down the real divinity of the Son and the Spirit.

From the second century (the period of Justin and Irenaeus) and into the first half of the third century (the period of Tertullian and Origen), the baptismal command from Matthew 28:19 provided the creative ground plan for constructing the questions concerning the tripersonal God ("Do you believe in the Father?" and so forth) and answers that encouraged the formation of an embryonic creed. Such questions evoked the threefold baptismal profession of faith in the Trinity found in the *Apostolic Tradition* of Hippolytus that dates from ca. 216 (DH 10; ND 2). Baptismal creeds, (with the Old Roman Creed crystallizing around the middle of the third century and giving rise to other creeds), arose in the West and the East and were then followed by conciliar creeds, the first being that from the Council of Nicaea (325). The evidence from the second and third century, collected by J. N. D. Kelly and others, records the faith of the catechumens and the communities that welcomed them, when in a dramatic experience of deep personal relevance they confessed and were united with the tripersonal God.

Arius

Born shortly after Origen died, Arius (d. ca. 336) like others in Alexandria inherited Origen's trinitarian teaching: the Father, the Son, and the Holy Spirit as three *hypostaseis* or distinct subsistent realities who share in the one divine nature but manifest a certain subordination (of the Son and the Spirit to the Father).[18] Arius apparently wanted to push this subordination much further. The Father is absolutely beyond the Son and, being unoriginated and unbegotten, is the only true God.

A generation "from the essence/substance (*ousia*)" would misinterpret the divinity in physical categories and wrongly suggest that the one and immutable divine substance could be changed and divided into two or three parts. Like the modalist monarchians (e.g., Sabellius), Arius and his followers wanted to preserve an absolute "mon-archy" of God, but unlike the Sabellians and other modalist monarchians, they held onto the real difference of identity between the Father and the Son. (Arius had practically nothing to say about the Holy Spirit.) Where Sabellianism asserted a strict unity of the divine essence without any real distinction of subjects, Arianism distinguished the subjects while denying their unity of essence. As Athanasius reported the Arian position, they considered the Son strictly inferior to and, in fact, infinitely different from the Father (*Contra Arianos,* 1.6).

In an incoherent statement ridiculed by Athanasius, Arius described the Son/Logos as being created before the beginning of the world, out of nothing, and by the will of the Father, but not created "like one of the creatures." Using a phrase repudiated, as we have seen, by Origen in the previous century, Arius denied that the Son was coeternal with the Father: "There was a time when he was not." Because Arius apparently understood *unbegotten* and *eternal* as synonymous, he had to deny the Son's eternity. The Son must be "later" than the Father; otherwise he would be "unbegotten" like the Father. Arius summed up his doctrine of God as follows: "The Son…has nothing proper to God in his essential property, for he is neither equal nor yet consubstantial with him" (*Thalia,* 8–9). In particular, Arius and his followers noted how the Logos experienced, at the time of the passion, emotions of terror and dismay and so was held by them to fall infinitely short of the serene impassibility of the Father.

After initially speaking of the Son as created out of nothing, Arius subsequently allowed for the Son being "generated" by the Father but persisted in considering this act of generation to be in effect a creation. The only creature directly created by the Father, the Son carried out the will of the Father by creating everything else and so acting as a kind of demiurge, a Logos to be located very high in the hierarchy of being and exercising divine power between God and the universe, but less than

God. Hence, the One who became incarnate was not truly divine but below the level of God. Christ was also not truly and fully human. According to Arius, the Logos took the place of the human soul in Christ. The Council of Nicaea, however, concerned itself only with rebutting Arius's challenge to Christ's divinity.

6.
From Nicaea I to Constantinople I

"As the Arians in denying the Son deny also the Father, so also these men [the Pneumatomachians] in speaking evil of the Holy Spirit speak evil also of the Son."
St. Athanasius, *Letter to Serapion*

"The kiss of God is the gift of the Spirit."
St. Bernard of Clairvaux, *Devotion to Christ*

The crisis of doctrine initiated by Arius and his followers provoked the Emperor Constantine into calling the First Council of Nicaea (A.D. 325) in search of religious peace. In the event, the crisis over the divine status of Jesus and the tripersonal identity of God lasted for most of the century—at least down to Constantinople I (A.D. 381). Others have reported and interpreted well the ins and outs of a dramatic century of christological and trinitarian debate.[1] This chapter aims rather to present the results of the debates: the credal statements of 325 and 381. For the sake of clarity and convenience, I will set out here the creed that resulted from Nicaea I, the first ecumenical council in the history of Christianity, and will do so in the fuller form that resulted from Constantinople I. Phrases that do not occur in the Creed of Nicaea are italicized; words from the Creed of Nicaea that do not turn up in the Creed of Constantinople appear in square brackets. It is hard to overestimate the importance of the Nicene-Constantinopolitan Creed; it became the sole baptismal confession of the East and the eucharistic creed of all Christians. In both the East and the West, this was and remains the most significant confession of faith in the tripersonal God.

> We believe in one God, Father almighty, maker *of heaven and earth,* of all things visible and invisible;
>
> And in one Lord Jesus Christ, the only begotten Son of God,
> begotten from the Father *before all ages,*
> [that is from the essence/substance of the Father, God from God],
> Light from Light, true God from true God, begotten not made,
> of the same essence/substance as the Father,
> through whom all things came into existence, [things in heaven and things on earth],
> who because of us human beings and because of our salvation
> came down *from the heavens,*
> and was incarnate *from the Holy Spirit and the Virgin Mary*
> and became man, and *was crucified for us under Pontius Pilate,*
> and suffered and *was buried*,
> and rose again on the third day *according to the Scriptures* and ascended into heaven,
> and *sits on the right hand of the Father,*
> and will come *again with glory* to judge living and dead,
> *of whose kingdom there will be no end.*
>
> And in the Holy Spirit,
> *the Lord and Life-giver, who proceeds from the Father,*
> *who with the Father and the Son is together worshiped and together glorified,*
> *who spoke through the prophets;*
> *in one, holy, Catholic and apostolic Church.*
> *We confess one baptism to the remission of sins;*
> *we look forward to the resurrection of the dead and the life of the world to come.*
> *Amen.* (Translation mine, see DH 125,150; ND 7,12)

Nicaea I and Constantinople I

Nicaea I, speaking four times of "the Father," once of the (correlative) "Son," and never of "the Word" or "Logos," confessed that the Son is "from the essence/substance (*ousia*) of the Father, God from God, Light from Light, true God from true God, begotten not made, of one essence/substance (*homoousios*) with the Father." In his state before the incarnation, Jesus is given three titles: *Lord, Christ*, and *Son of God*, to which we could add the quasi-title that might well be put in uppercase, *the Only Begotten*. With the exception of *Christ,* these are all high, divine titles. Nicaea I also refers to Jesus in divine terms protologically ("through whom all things came into existence, things in heaven and things on earth"), incarnationally ("came down"), and eschatologically ("will come to judge living and dead"). In appended condemnations, the council anathematized those who said of the Son that "there was a time when he was not" or that "he was created from nothing and is of different *hypostasis* or *ousia* from the Father" (DH 126; ND 8).

This was to hold that the Son is truly the Son of God and not less than God. In the generation (not creation) of the Son, the substance of the Father has been fully communicated. The Son comes *from* the Father, but, not being created *by* the Father, is coeternal with the Father. Arius found these propositions quite unacceptable. He could elaborate his own reductive explanations for other expressions like "the Son of God"; he could take that to mean that the Son came into existence *after* the Father and hence was/is not on a par with him. But Arius could not confess that the Son was "naturally" (and not by some creative act of the divine will) generated from the very "substance of the Father" and was/is always there with the Father.

Nicaea spoke out clearly for Christ's divinity, but three of its terms continued to run into difficulties well after the Council: *ousia, homoousios,* and *hypostasis*. *Ousia* (used here as "being," "reality," "essence," or "substance") had a checkered background in Gnostic and Christian circles before it came to be adopted in Nicaea's teaching about the Son being "of the same essence/substance (*homoousios*)" as the Father. In the second century, Valentinian Gnostics had taught a triple consubstantiality: The human spirit is consubstantial (*homoousios*) with God, the soul with the demiurge, and matter with the devil. In the third century, the term came up when Paul of Samosata was deposed in 268 as bishop of Antioch. In speaking of the Logos as *homoousios* with the Father, he was apparently suspected of using the term in a modalist or Sabellian sense and so holding that the unity of the *ousia* was such that there was no personal distinction between the Father and the Son/Logos. When Nicaea pressed *homoousios* into service, the council almost inevitably recalled a bogey-figure (Paul of Samosata) and caused some to fear a lapse back into Sabellianism. As we shall see in a moment, when its appended anathema used *hypostasis* as synonymous with *ousia,* Nicaea compounded this fear.

The other question for *homoousios* was the meaning of *homo-*, or "the same," (as opposed to *homoi-* in *homoiousios,* or "of a similar essence"). In what sense does the former term apply to the Father *and* to the Son? Is it a question of the total identity of the same individual essence—the *one* being which they share as two particular subjects—or is the adjective to be understood in an "abstract" way as denoting the being or essence common to different individuals (e.g., siblings in a human family) who are of the same being merely in that sense? The latter interpretation would lead to bitheism (the Father and the Son as two gods) or tritheism (the Father, the Son, and the Holy Spirit as three gods). It is clear from the whole tenor of the Nicene Creed that the former meaning was intended. The Son also possesses the unique and indivisible divine being that is proper to the Father. Nevertheless, *homoousios* needed clarification because it could be wrongly understood to support a Sabellian doctrine about the Father, the Son, and the Holy Spirit constituting an identical and undifferentiated unity, with the persons as being no more than mere names or modes.

When used both in the NT and in (Platonic and Stoic) philosophy, many meanings for *hypostasis* cluster under two headings: the *hypostasis* as (1) the primordial essence or (2) as the individuating principle, subject, or subsistence. This basic ambiguity in the term had already surfaced in 262 when Pope Dionysius, understanding *hypostasis* in sense (1), condemned those who divided the one, divine "mon-archy" into three *hypostaseis* (DH 112–15; ND 301–03). To do that would obviously split the one divine essence into three divine essences and come up with three gods. Shortly before Dionysius's condemnation, however, Origen had confronted Sabellian modalism by speaking of the triune God as three individual *hypostaseis* and obviously used meaning (2) of the term. This terminological problem was further bedeviled by the fact that Western (Latin) Christians, at least since the time of Tertullian, took the Greek *hypo-stasis* to correspond to their Latin term *substantia*: that is to say, they naturally understood *hypostasis* in sense (1) above. Hence, when Eastern (Greek) Christians acknowledged the three *hypostaseis* of God, Westerners were easily shocked as they interpreted such a statement to mean three separate divine substances—in a word, tritheism. However, from their point of view the Greeks could readily misunderstand Latin talk about the one divine *substantia* as lapsing into the modalist position of one *hypostasis* in sense (2) of the word and hence as a denial of any personal distinctions in God.

The upshot for Nicaea of this inherited ambiguity about *hypostasis* was that taking *ousia* and *hypostasis* as equivalents ran the risk of *homoousios* being understood in a Sabellian way. (The Sabellians treated the terms *ousia* and *hypostasis* more or less as synonyms for an individual substance.) Father and Son would then not only be of the same *ousia* but also of the same *hypostasis*—in sense (2) of *hypostasis*. Then there would be no real distinction between Father and Son; they could not be distinct, individual subsistences or subjects.

After Nicaea, some bishops, while opposed to Arius, continued to prefer a term that had been discussed and rejected by the Council: *homoiousios*, in the sense of the Son "being of like being/substance" with the Father. The supporters of Arius rejected both *homoousios* and *homoiousios*. Eventually, from around 355 Aetius and Eunomius even developed the "Anomean (dissimilar)" doctrine, according to which the Son is not only the first creature but also in essence simply "unlike" the Father and thus radically inferior.

Then there were many bishops and others who simply remained uneasy about or antagonistic to the term *homoousios*. At least four reasons fueled their unease.

(1) The word was not found as such in the scriptures, even if it was not antibiblical.

(2) It had been condemned in the controversy over Paul of Samosata back in 268, but as Athanasius insisted, the term had turned up then in a different setting and in connection with an error that was alien to Arius (*De Synodis*, 41,43–45).

(3) We have already seen how, on the one hand, *homoousios* could be rigidly interpreted in a modalist, Sabellian sense, as if the Father and the Son were identical not only in substance but also as personal subjects. On the other hand, however, the term could be taken in a broader sense. Individual beings of the same species separately exemplify the same nature and can be said to share in the same substance (e.g., a brother and sister who are "of the same substance" as their parents).

(4) Finally, *homoousios* might be applied to material substances such as masses of bronze that can be cut up into parts and turned into such particular, separate objects as coins. Some at least of the older "material" analogies for the relationship between the Father and the Son were open to this misunderstanding.

Everything depended upon what was meant by *homo* in *homoousios*. It was easier to deal with some misinterpretations. Thus St. Basil of Caesarea (d. 379) could sweep aside (4): Orthodox faith was not talking materialistically of one divine substance (*ousia*), as if it were some "stuff" out of which Father, Son, and Spirit were made. It was the two opposite possibilities under (3) that troubled Basil more when analyzing various misunderstandings of *homoousios*. Those who failed to acknowledge in God the identity of essence were lapsing into polytheism and in effect believing in three gods. Those, however, who forced *homoousios* to the extreme of disallowing any personal distinctions within the godhead, were returning to Jewish monotheism or a similar, if Christian, undifferentiated view of God, Sabellianism. In a letter written in 375 to the leading Christians of Neocaesarea (in Pontus), Basil stated:

> It is indispensable to clearly understand that, as he who fails to confess the identity of essence (*ousia*) falls into polytheism, so he

> who refuses to grant the distinction of the *hypostaseis* is carried away into Judaism.... Sabellius...said that the same God...was metamorphosed as the need of the moment required, and spoken of now as Father, now as Son, and now as Holy Spirit. (*Epistola*, 210.5)[2]

By that time the battle, led by Basil, St. Hilary of Poitiers (d. 367), and Athanasius in support of *homoousios* and its correct interpretation, had almost been won. The term pointed to the identity of essence or being between the three divine persons. As regards the divine essence/substance, the Father, the Son, and the Holy Spirit are one. Athanasius drew on John and Paul to teach that the Father was/is never without his Word (i.e., the Son shares the divine eternity); that the Word/Son enjoys the exclusively divine prerogative of creation (e.g., Jn 1:3; 1 Cor 8:6); and that the "natural" Son of God makes our filial adoption and deification possible. Although insisting from around 350 on Nicaea's term, Athanasius accepted, nevertheless, those who without using *homoousios* confessed that the Son is "from the substance" of the Father and, as the "natural" Son, eternally with the Father.

The letter from Basil quoted above signals both the triumph of Nicaea's teaching on the common essence or *ousia* shared by Father and Son (and Holy Spirit) but also a partial switch away from the council's terminology (at least as found in the appended anathema). No longer are *ousia* and *hypostasis* being used as equivalents. Like Gregory of Nazianzus, Basil writes of one *ousia* or divinity (the one, identical essence of God) and three *hypostaseis* or *prosopa* (individual, personal subsistences with their particular properties) in God. Seven years later, this trinitarian terminology was officially adopted after Constantinople I. In its letter to Pope Damasus a postconciliar synod confessed "one divinity, power, or essence (*ousia*)" in "three most perfect *hypostasesin*, that is, in three perfect *prosopois*."[3] Basil, Gregory of Nazianzus, and, even more, St. Gregory of Nyssa (d. ca. 395), the three leading Cappadocian writers, had been using interchangeably *hypostasis* and *prosopon* (i.e., the "face" or visible manifestation and characteristics of the *hypostasis*). Although ready to talk of three *hypostaseis* in God (*Tomus ad Antiochenos*, 5–6), Athanasius preferred *prosopon* to *hypostasis*. Building on Origen, the Cappadocians, and Athanasius, a synod that met a year after Constantinople I put trinitarian language firmly in place: three *hypostaseis* or *prosopa*, and one divinity, power, *ousia*, or *physis* (nature) in God. Origen, Athanasius, the Cappadocians, and the postconciliar synod of 382 (in its letter to Pope Damasus) spoke of God's nature or *physis* (the essence seen as a principle of activity) interchangeably with the divine *ousia*.

Besides reaffirming in a fresh way the Nicene confession of Jesus' divinity, Constantinople I also upheld the divine identity of the Holy Spirit. This defense came in the face of the Pneumatomachians ("fighters against the Spirit"), the Macedonians (a sect that took its name from Macedonius, a bishop condemned at Constantinople I[4]), and others who rejected the divinity of the Holy Spirit. Whatever their names, various groups emerged during the fourth century to question and deny the divine identity of the Spirit. The Arians and Anomeans, holding the Son to be creature and radically inferior to the Father, argued even more for the creaturely, inferior status of the Spirit. In his letter to Serapion, Athanasius wrote of others ("Tropici") who accepted the divinity of the Son but held the Spirit to be a creature, who shares the nature of the ministering spirits or angels, even if of a higher rank than they.

Comparing the Creeds

Conciliar teaching on the Holy Trinity comes predominantly from Nicaea I and Constantinople I. Hence, comparing and contrasting their credal confessions will clarify further the way trinitarian doctrine became stabilized in the course of the fourth century. Let us follow J. N. D. Kelly by naming as *N* and *C* the Nicene Creed and its fuller form from Constantinople I, respectively. The reader will find the text of *C* (with its differences from *N* indicated) at the beginning of this chapter.

Both *N* and *C* started, not with one divine substance that was then said to subsist in three persons, but with the Father, the source of unity from whom we can then move and confess the Son and the Spirit. Both

N and *C* confessed the "ONE God, the Father almighty" and the "ONE Lord Jesus Christ," but neither Nicaea I nor Constantinople I apparently felt the need to specify their faith "in the Holy Spirit" as faith "in the ONE Holy Spirit."[5] Paul had felt this need, repeating "the same" with reference to the Spirit, the Lord (Jesus), and God (the Father): "There are diversities of charisms, but the *same* Spirit. There are diversities of service, and the *same* Lord. There are diversities of activities, but the *same* God, who effects all things in everyone" (1 Cor 12:4–6). *N* and *C*, with their "one God, the Father almighty" and the "one Lord Jesus Christ," paralleled more closely what Paul had written earlier in 1 Corinthians of "one God the Father" and "one Lord Jesus Christ" when offering a christological monotheism (1 Cor 8:6), to which the apostle did not add a further pneumatological qualification: "and one Holy Spirit who gives us life." Whatever we make of Paul not supplying there a model of one/one/one, *N* and *C* might have taken a cue from a late first-century figure, Clement of Rome. In his Letter to the Corinthians he had applied *one* to all three persons: "Have we not one God and one Christ and *one* Spirit of grace poured upon us?" (56.6).

What *N* and *C* provide is a "genetic" approach to the tripersonal God, with the divinity streaming from the Father to the Son and to the Holy Spirit. In *N, the Father* appears four times (once in the first article and three times in the second), and in C six times (once in the first article, three times in the second, and twice in the third). In the second and third articles of *C*, the Son and the Holy Spirit are presented in a variety of ways as being "from" and "with" the Father.

Let me refer back now to the text provided at the start of this chapter and comment on some additions made by *C*, inasmuch as they bear on trinitarian faith. *C* specifies that the Son was begotten from the Father *before all ages.* When read today, this phrase, which has its antecedents and equivalents in some Eastern baptismal creeds,[6] strengthens the notion of the Son's personal and eternal preexistence. At Nicaea I, however, the composers of *N*, in the face of Arian misinterpretations, may have been reluctant to use such language because *before*, by suggesting *after,* could carry the kind of false temporal connotations that Origen remarked on (see Chapter 5) and that the Arians could have exploited. Constantinople I presumably took over the phrase from Eastern antecedents to produce a more balanced flow to their confession.

The next addition, *from the heavens*, has trinitarian relevance in that it points to the divine origin of Jesus. He comes from God the Father, as well as being incarnated *from the Holy Spirit and the Virgin Mary*, another addition, this time one that bears on his earthly origin in history. The idea of the Son's double generation, which we noted in Irenaeus's writings, is hinted at here: the eternal generation from the Father ("begotten from the Father *before all ages*") and the generation in time from the Virgin Mary. We meet for the first time in *C* a reference to the Holy Spirit's existence, expressed in terms of the Spirit's activity and relationship to the Son. The reference to the virginal conception, witnessed to by Matthew and Luke, reinforces here in an anti-adoptionist way the sense of Jesus' divinity: He came from God and was not simply adopted by God at baptism.

Among other things, the impact of three further additions made by *C* (the Son who *sits on the right hand of the Father*, who will come *again with glory*, and *of whose kingdom there will be no end*) is to underline the divine identity of Jesus. He sits neither near nor under the divine throne but on a par with and alongside the Father. His future coming in judgment will be accompanied by divine glory. In the historical context of the late fourth century, the affirmation of his endless kingdom goes beyond Luke 1:33 and is directed against the Sabellian-style heterodoxy of Marcellus of Ancyra (d. 374), for whom the Word was not a distinct *hypostasis* and for whom the divine Monad, after unfolding itself into a triad, would reverse at the end to an original unity as the divine Monad. As regards the second person of the Trinity, Marcellus had limited the existence of the Son to the period of the incarnation; the divine Monad will no longer manifest the relationship of sonship, once the purposes of the incarnation have been accomplished. Hence, seven years after the death of Marcellus, *C*'s affirmation that the Son's kingdom will have no end carries a strong anti-Sabellian, trinitarian impact.

Next we come to the most substantive additions made by *C*, those in the third article that augmented *N*'s simple confession of faith "in the

Holy Spirit." *C* confesses the Spirit as (divine) *Lord* (see 2 Cor 3:17–18) and *Life-giver* (Rom 8:2; Jn 6:63; 14:6; 2 Cor 3:6), who *proceeds from the Father*. Naming the Holy Spirit as derived *from* the Father, *C* used *ek* rather than *para,* both of which we find in John 15:26: "the Spirit of truth who proceeds (*ek-poreuestai*) from (*para*) the Father."[7] Paul uses *ek* when speaking of "the Spirit that is from (*ek*) from God" (1 Cor 2:12). By confessing that the Spirit proceeds from, but is not begotten by, the Father, *C* makes it clear that the Father is *not* Father to the Spirit but Father only to the Son. (Otherwise we would find ourselves worshiping two divine siblings: two Sons and Brothers, or one Son and one Daughter.) In terms of later theology the Father can be called Breather of the Spirit.

The next addition in *C, who with the Father and the Son is together worshiped and together glorified,* expresses an equality in divinity that extends to the Spirit the kind of adoration due only to God. Besides having abundant biblical antecedents (e.g., Dt 6:13; Mt 4:10) and being used in the NT of the Father and the Son (e.g., Rv 5:10–14; 7:10–12), the language of "worshiping" and "glorifying" echoes the usage of Athanasius and especially that of Basil about "giving glory to the Father and the Son and the Holy Spirit" (*De Spiritu Sancto,* 27.68). The activity of the Spirit, *who spoke through the prophets,* has its background in the OT (e.g., Is 61:1; Ez 2:1–2; Mi 3:8), the NT (1 Pt 1:10–11; 2 Pt 1:21), and pre-Nicene writers (e.g., see in Chapter 5 Justin on "the Spirit of prophecy" and "the prophetic Spirit," and Irenaeus on the Holy Spirit "who through the prophets proclaimed the saving dispensations"). What comes through the first half of *C*'s third article is an affirmation of the Holy Spirit's divine identity, but, unlike the case of the Son, the Spirit is neither said to proceed from the Father "before all ages" nor to be of "one essence/substance with the Father." Clearly the Spirit is acknowledged to be eternally preexistent "before" speaking (in a divine way) through the prophets and effecting the incarnation (through the virginal conception). But *C* seems to avoid calling the Spirit "God" (as the Son is called "true God from true God") and "of one substance with the Father."

In its letter to Pope Damasus, the postconciliar synod of 382 confessed "the uncreated, consubstantial (*homoousios*) and coeternal Trinity." Later Constantinople II was to speak likewise of the entire Trinity as *homoousios* (DH, 421; ND, 620/1), but *C* shows how Constantinople I remained a little circumspect by not confessing the Spirit's divinity and divine consubstantiality in the full way that it did in the case of the Son. J. N. D. Kelly puts his finger on the probable motive for this caution. The Emperor Theodosius encouraged somewhat guarded speech about the Spirit's divinity in the hope of winning over some of the less intransigent Macedonians.[8]

Finally, a word about the two major omissions in *C*'s adaptation and expansion of *N:* the first bearing on the origin of the Son ("that is from the essence/substance of the Father, God from God") and the second on the Son's creative work (in bringing into existence "things in heaven and things on earth"). Some have interpreted these omissions as good evidence for denying that *C* is a modified version of *N*. But, given the liturgical scope and more careful composition of *C*, one can understand how these omissions do not tamper with Nicene teaching. *C* drops "God from God" but maintains *N*'s "true God from true God"; likewise it drops "from the substance of the Father" but maintains "of one substance with the Father." In both cases, mere doublets are avoided. Omitting "things in heaven and things on earth" takes nothing away from the confession that *C* retains: through the Son "all things came into existence." The fact that *C* has already in its first article specified with "heaven and earth" what the creation of "all things" covers makes it superfluous to add this specification again in the second article. In *Early Christian Creeds,* Kelly argues effectively in favor of the tradition that existed universally from A.D. 451: at Constantinople I, the Nicene faith was ratified in the form of *C*, the greatest of all Christian creeds which entered into its own after 451 but whose impact had been delayed, among other things, by the fact that Constantinople I was slow in acquiring ecumenical status.

After investigating the biblical witness, the pre-Nicene testimony, and then *N* and *C*, we are in a position to follow the development in trinitarian doctrine that has led up to the end of the second millennium.

But any progress that was to take place would do so in the light of the convictions enshrined in the Nicene-Constantinopolitan Creed.

That credal confession presents a divine communication in creation and salvation history that presupposes an eternal communion within God: the Father, the only begotten Son, and the "proceeding" Holy Spirit. In particular, God's self-communication *ad extra* through the missions of the Son (who "came down from heaven" and "became man") and the Spirit (who "spoke through the prophets" and effected the incarnation) in the history or "economy" of salvation presupposes and reflects the self-communication *ad intra:* the eternal generation of the Son and procession of the Spirit. Thus the "economic" Trinity or Trinity in creation and history on which the Creed largely focuses reveals the immanent Trinity and is identical with it.

7.
FROM ATHANASIUS TO AQUINAS

"We see, rather than believe, the trinity which is in ourselves; whereas we believe rather than see that God is Trinity."

St. Augustine, *De Trinitate*

"Firmly I believe and truly
God is Three, and God is One."

John Henry Newman, *The Dream of Gerontius*

No less than Christian believers in other ages, fourth-century theologians tried to explore faithfully the unity, diversity, and relationships within the Trinity. They knew that the tripersonal God is present in the entire cosmos and in all human history—not least in the history of Jesus and his church. They felt the obligation to reflect on the divine mystery, inasmuch as their reflections could serve worship and discipleship. Yet, what Basil the Great admitted about the generation of the Son from the Father qualified their wrestling with the whole trinitarian mystery: "Thought and reflection are utterly unable to penetrate the begetting of the Lord" (*De Spiritu Sancto*, 6.14). With something of that reverential attitude, this chapter aims to retrieve certain Christian reflections on the Trinity from the fourth to the thirteenth centuries, in particular, those reflections and questions that enjoy an enduring value for believers of all times. We look first at some writers who headed the development during the fourth century, from Nicaea I to Constantinople I.

St. Athanasius

With Athanasius, an older contemporary of the Cappadocians, the fatherhood of God became an issue of sustained and systematic analysis. Fatherhood, he repeated, belongs eternally to God and defines the being of God. For later trinitarian thought, Athanasius developed the fundamental principle that the Father-Son relationship partially but necessarily defines the word *God.* When he wrote of God being inherently relational and generative, in the footsteps of Nicaea I ("begotten, not made") he distinguished clearly between generation and creation as distinct modes of operation. Thus he could speak of that "reciprocal delight" between Father and Son that existed "prior" to creation (*Contra Arianos*, 2.64). To deny the eternal existence of the Son would be to deny the eternal fatherhood of God.[1]

A challenge from the "Tropici" led Athanasius to reflect also on the Holy Spirit. The name of this heterodox group, which anticipated the subsequent deviations of the Eunomians, Macedonians, and other "Pneumatomachians," came from their habit of explaining away uncomfortable scriptural texts as mere figures of speech or tropes. In his *Letter to Serapion,* Athanasius wrote of the Tropici: "As the Arians in denying the Son deny also the Father, so also these men in speaking evil of the Holy Spirit speak evil also of the Son" (1.1). They misunderstood the Spirit to be an angelic creature who differed from the other angels only in rank and not in nature. To call the Spirit a creature was, for Athanasius, to be "guilty of a direct impiety against the Son himself" (ibid., 1.31). In positive terms, this meant that a true doctrine of the Spirit stood or fell with a true doctrine of the Son, and vice versa. According to Athanasius, being truly divine, the Spirit "proceeds" from the Father and is "given" by the Son. What then does the Spirit receive from the Son? Apparently Athanasius held that, while deriving the whole divine nature and existence from the Father, the Spirit is sent on mission by the Son. This seems to imply that it is through the Son that the Spirit is in and from the Father.

The Spirit is then "in the Son,"[2] as the Son is "in the Father" (ibid., 1.20). This way of putting the inner-trinitarian relations obviously raised two difficulties. If derived from the Father, the Spirit should also be a Son; hence, the Spirit and the Word would be "two brothers." If the Spirit is such a brother, "how is the Word the only begotten?" Second, Athanasius's talk about the Spirit being "in the Son" and the Spirit as image of the Son bearing "the same relation to the Son as the Son to the Father" (ibid., 1.21) triggered the objection: "If the Spirit is of the Son, then the Father is the Spirit's grandfather." Athanasius's retort, that we should not "dare to ask" such "human questions" about God and think in a merely human way where obviously a son can be a father to another son (ibid., 1.15,16), hardly seems satisfactory. Nevertheless, in a graphic way he brought up here the summons to speak about the derivation of the Son and the Spirit in ways that do not make it seem either that they are both "Sons and Brothers" or that the Son begets the Spirit and so makes the Father a divine grandfather.

A few years later, when defending orthodox trinitarian faith against the Eunomians and Macedonians, Gregory of Nazianzus responded to this same style of objection (*Orationes,* 31.7). Against the Tropici and subsequent heterodox groups it was necessary to insist on the uniqueness of the Son as *only* begotten and, therefore, without a "brother." The Spirit cannot be thought of as a second Son; similarly, the Son cannot be a father to the Spirit, who would then be a kind of divine grandson—to suppose this would be postulate within the divine being two "fathers" and hence two "gods." Only the "unbegotten" Father *qua* Father enjoys the distinctive characteristic of being principle (*arche*) of the divine life that is in the Son and the Spirit.

Besides meeting objections to orthodox trinitarian faith, what Athanasius (and his contemporaries) helped to establish was the conviction that believers can neither know nor say anything of the Son, apart from the relationship with the Father and the Spirit. The Father and the Spirit are necessarily involved in any reference to the Son. What applies to the Son holds true also of the Father and the Holy

Spirit. One knows nothing of the Father apart from the relationship to the Son[3] and the Spirit and nothing of the Spirit apart from the relationship to the Father and the Son.

Apropos of the divine status of the Spirit, Athanasius argues in a way that parallels his argument for the divinity of the Son. Just as the creative activity of the Word/Son shows that he cannot be a mere creature, so it is with the "re-creating" activity of the Spirit: It is "through the Spirit" that we become "partakers of God" (*Letter to Serapion,* 1.9,24).[4] Here Athanasius attributed to the Son the work of creation (with the Word remaining perpetually present to sustain all created reality), and that of sanctification and divinization to the Spirit. This was to bring up the question: What kind of distinction can be drawn between the work of creation and that of sanctification? How distinct are the Son and the Spirit in their "outside (*ad extra*)" activities?

Where Irenaeus's image of the Son and Spirit as "the two hands of God" might encourage the notion that the Son and Spirit could operate separately, if not independently, the former in the work of creation and the latter in that of divinization or re-creation, Athanasius underlined the unity in trinitarian activity: "The Father does all things through the Word in the Holy Spirit. Thus the unity of the holy Triad is preserved" (ibid., 1.27). This led him to comment on some Pauline texts about divine gifts (which we recalled in Chapter 3) that might suggest separate divine activities: "The Apostle does not mean that the things which are given are given differently and separately by each person, but that what is given is given in [by?] the Triad, and that all [gifts] are from the one God" (ibid., 1.31). Yet the more Athanasius or others were to insist on the unity of divine operations *ad extra,* the more problematic it becomes for us to distinguish the eternal existence of three distinct divine persons *ad intra* (within the godhead). While maintaining the unity in divine activity, we need to ask: What distinct elements emerge in that divine activity so that believers rightly discern three distinct divine persons "behind" that activity?[5] A unilateral emphasis on unity in divine action could seem like a high road back to rigid, monopersonal monotheism and the modalist "monarchianism" opposed by Tertullian and others (see Chapter 5).

Besides his central support for the reception of Nicene faith in Jesus' divine consubstantiality with the Father, Athanasius expounded the fatherhood of God and, consequently, the inner-trinitarian relations between the Father, the Son, and the Holy Spirit. That involved him both in defending the truly divine status of the Spirit and in endeavoring to say something coherent about the external operations of the tripersonal God.

The Cappadocians

Without pretending that the Cappadocian writers (in particular, Basil, Gregory of Nazianzus, and Gregory of Nyssa) formed a monolithic school of theology, we can find in them enough similarities and links to justify dealing with them together. Like Athanasius, they wrestled with the central mystery of the tripersonal God: How can we grasp, even marginally, the differentiated unity of God or the divine unity in distinction? They too reflected and wrote in a polemical situation, refuting various denials of the divinity of the Spirit and of the Son. Like Athanasius, in his *De Spiritu Sancto,* Basil argued from what the Holy Spirit does. The sanctifying work of the Spirit reveals a divine identity. Because only God is holy by nature, only a divine agent can make us creatures holy. In the same work, Basil also rejects the Arians and Eunomians, who denied the divinity of the Son by their misinterpretations of John's Gospel (ibid., 8.20). Like Athanasius, the Cappadocians insisted that the Holy Spirit "proceeds from" but is not "begotten by" the Father (ibid., 18.46), answering thus the objection that trinitarian faith makes the Spirit a second Son. Perhaps even more than Athanasius, the Cappadocians vindicated orthodox doctrine by appealing to the profession of trinitarian faith at baptism (ibid., 10.26; 11.27; 12.28).[6]

Where they clearly went beyond Athanasius was in developing their language of three coequal and coeternal *hypostaseis* or persons/subjects sharing the one divine *ousia* or essence/being/substance.[7] At the heart of God, the Cappadocians saw an interpersonal communion or *koinonia,* with communion as the function of all three divine persons and not simply of the Holy Spirit. For this interpersonal model of the Trinity, God's inner being is relational, with each of the three persons totally related to the other two in "reciprocal delight"—to borrow an Athanasian expression quoted above. What Basil said of the Father and the Son applied to relationships among all three persons: "We cannot conceive of either [Father or Son] apart from their relationship with each other" (ibid., 6.14). Even if the term and the full deployment of the associated theology came later with St. John Damascene (d. ca. 749), we find in the Cappadocian theology an early intimation of the *perichoresis,* or "cyclical movement," the being-in-one-another of the Trinity. In a unique "coinherence" or mutual interpenetration, each of the trinitarian persons is transparent to and permeated by the other two.

Such trinitarian theology "saves" the divine threeness but might seem to sacrifice the unity and even lapse into tritheism—a danger not lost on the Cappadocians. In his treatise *Ad Ablabium,* Gregory of Nyssa took pains to argue that "there are not three gods," or as we might say today "not three separate divine subjects." Father, Son, and Holy Spirit are each truly God, but in this "three-in-one," there are not three gods. Enjoying a unique unity, one infinitely closer than that between any three human persons, the Trinity is not to be reduced to the social analogy of even a perfect human family (father, mother, and child) or, still less, to that of thoroughly harmonious committee of three.[8]

The subjectivity of Father, Son, and Holy Spirit is always an infinitely radical *inter*subjectivity. To account for the unity within the Trinity, Gregory of Nyssa and the other Cappadocians pointed to the fact that one of the persons (the Father) relates to the other two as the source or "cause" of their divinity—something that the Nicene Creed had already hinted at by starting with the Father, even if it did not explicitly call him the source of the other two divine persons. There is one God because there is one Father. This "mon-archy" of the Father could be seen, however, to favor a descending view of the Trinity and even an unacceptable subordination of the Son and Spirit to the Father, the sole unoriginated fountainhead of divinity. But, properly understood, the "mon-archy" of the Father does not mean superiority (let alone any exclusive superiority) or a false subordination, but both unity and distinction.

Basil, along with the other Cappadocians, maintained the order that had been drawn from Matthew 28:19 and had long ago become traditional in the baptismal liturgy: Father, Son, and Holy Spirit.[9] This led Basil to offer explanations for other trinitarian sequences found in the New Testament. Apropos of the sequence found in 1 Corinthians 12:4–6 (discussed in Chapter 3), he assured his readers: "Just because the Apostle…mentions the Spirit first, and the Son second, and God the Father third, do not assume that he has reversed the rank. Notice that he is speaking in the same way that we do when we receive gifts: first we thank the messenger who brought the gift; next we remember him who sent it, and finally we raise our thoughts to the fountain and source of all gifts" (*De Spiritu Sancto,* 16.37). Thus Basil maintained the sequence: the Father as source and fountain, the Son as sender, and the Spirit as messenger. This descending order in the story of salvation accounted for the distinctions and unity within the eternal life of the Trinity: One of the persons (the Father) stood in the relation of "cause" to the other two. Yet, all three persons rank as genuinely divine.

As regards the traditional doxology, "Glory to the Father through (*dia*) the Son in (*en*) the Holy Spirit," Basil observed: "We are not describing the Spirit's rank, but confessing our own weakness." He added: "We are incapable of glorifying God on our own; only *in* the Spirit is this made possible" (ibid., 26.63). This doxology echoed the grace that we are given through the Holy Spirit. Basil found it, however, more appropriate to the Spirit's dignity and the Trinity's inner communion to use a doxology that had already existed in the third century and which he helped to promote: "Glory to the Father with (*meta*) the Son, together with (*sun*) the Holy Spirit." In this doxology, Basil believed the opposite errors of (1) the Sabellians and of (2) the Arians and "Pneumatomachians" were met and overcome. Praising Father, Son, and Holy Spirit who are "with" one another responded to the Sabellian error in denying any personal distinctions within God. Praising the Son and the Holy Spirit equally "with" the Father acknowledged their divinity against those who denied it to the second or the third person of the Trinity. This latter doxology has prevailed in general liturgical use as: "Glory be to the Father *and* to the Son *and* to the Holy Spirit."

Before leaving the Cappadocian contributions, let me add a word on trinitarian actions in the story of creation and redemption. Centuries later an ecumenical, or general, council of the church, the Third Council of Constantinople (681), was to speak, in the context of Christ's two "wills" and "energies" or operational powers, of the divine "will and energy" (DH 556–58; ND 635–36). At about the very same time, in the West, several local councils held at Toledo (in 638, 675, and 693) emphasized that the actions of the Trinity are "inseparable" (DH 491, 531, 535, 538, 571; ND 315, 630, 633). Without anticipating this language of a later age, the Cappadocians taught that, although the three persons of the Trinity always work together, yet something distinct is contributed by each. Each act of God, as Basil put it, is "initiated by the Father, effected by the Son, and perfected by the Spirit" (*De Spiritu Sancto,* 16.38). In his short treatise *Ad Ablabium* or *Quod Non Sint Tres Dei,* Gregory of Nyssa said something similar: "We are not told that the Father does anything by himself in which the Son does not cooperate or that the Son has any isolated activity apart from the Holy Spirit." Yet, after this affirmation of the inseparable character of trinitarian operations, Gregory added: "Every activity originates from the Father, proceeds through the Son, and is brought to perfection in the Holy Spirit" (47.21–48.2). St. Augustine of Hippo (d. 430) was to struggle with this theme of unity in the Trinity's operations. Granted that the divine actions *ad extra* are common, does that mean that they are undifferentiated and indistinguishable? If not, on what grounds may we distinguish the divine persons and appreciate their threefold particularity that is implied by the diversity of the verbs (*originates, proceeds,* and *is brought to perfection*)?[10]

St. Augustine

Where Athanasius and the Cappadocians to some extent developed their trinitarian thinking in polemical opposition to denials of the divinity of the Son and of the Spirit coming, respectively, from Arians and Pneumatomachians, Augustine wrote his *De Trinitate* slowly and arguably in a somewhat less polemical way. He took at least 17 years to complete the work, which—one must add—is neither his last nor his only work on the Trinity. Often and to a considerable extent misleadingly, Augustine has been contrasted with Cappadocians on the grounds that whereas they started their trinitarian theology with the three persons (and then moved to the one shared essence), he began with the unity of the divine being in one essence or substance and moved to the three persons. This stereotype has frequently been expressed by the captions of "Eastern" and "Western" trinitarian doctrine. The truth here is somewhat different.

(a) Two Analogies

After dedicating the early books of *De Trinitate* to what the scriptures witness about the divine persons, Augustine takes up the interpersonal relationship of paternity and filiation to develop the model of trinitarian love (*De Trinitate,* 8.8.12). The Father is the Lover, the Son the Beloved, and the Holy Spirit the mutual Love that passes between Father and Son. Eastern Christians have criticized this analogy (which such medieval theologians as Richard of St. Victor [d. 1173] were to develop in the West) for depersonalizing the Holy Spirit or at least for not allowing the identity of a distinct person to come through clearly. After all, in the I-Thou relationship, the mutual gift of love that two persons bestow on each other is not a third person or at least does not emerge as an activity that defines a person distinct from the I and the Thou. What limits the mutual love that finite creatures *have* for one another is not true at the divine level. God *is* love (1 Jn 4:8,16). Within the divine life the Holy Spirit is the Love (uppercase) that the Father and the Son bestow on each other.

Eastern Christians can have a further problem with the love analogy in that it leads to holding that the Spirit proceeds from the Father *and* the Son. The Son receives from the Father both love and the capacity to love reciprocally. The Spirit also proceeds from (or through?) the Son by being this reciprocal Love (uppercase).

In the *De Trinitate,* Augustine himself went on to exploit the human soul and its faculties as the best mirror of the Trinity that is available. He was justified in doing so by the biblical faith that human beings are made in God's image and likeness (Gn 1:26–27). From the NT revelation of the Trinity, one could expect to find in human beings and their highest faculties some analogy to God as tripersonal. In particular, Augustine's trinitarian theology drew support from the way the NT hints that the generation of the Son (e.g., Mt 11:27—"No one knows the Son except the Father") and the procession of the Spirit (e.g., Rom 5:5—"God's love has been poured into our hearts through the Holy Spirit that has been given us") are somehow mirrored in or paralleled by the two basic activities of the human spirit: knowing and loving.[11] By interpreting the Son as the Word coming from the divine Mind, as we have seen in Chapter 5, Irenaeus, Tertullian, Athanasius, and others[12] prepared the way to expound the generation of the Son in terms of the Father's act of thought. Augustine himself contributed the theme of the Holy Spirit as the fruit and reality of mutual love. In the scheme of *mens/notitia/amor,* Augustine found in the mind's being, the mind's knowledge of itself, and the mind's love for itself an image of the Trinity: the Father as Being, the Son as Consciousness, and the Spirit as Love (*De Trinitate,* 9.2.2). He brought further refinements into this trinitarian model with the scheme that he preferred of the human memory (with knowledge coming through memory), intelligence (or understanding), and willing (*memoria/intelligentia/voluntas*): (*De Trinitate,* 9.8; 10.10,14–16; 11.11,17–19). The psychological analogy[13] attends to the way in which the interior word (*verbum mentale*) arises through an act that can be compared with generation. The eternal Word or Son of God is distinct from and yet identical with the generating Father. Similarly, the divine act of love gives rise to its eternal, immanent fruit (*impressio amati in amato*), the Holy Spirit. Augustine's psychological (and very influential) analogy of self-presence, self-knowledge, and self-love preemptively avoids any risk of tritheism but might seem to encourage a monopersonal, modalist view of God. Does this intrapersonal analogy, taken from a human being's cognitive and affective powers, "save" the divine unity (and so avoid any suspicion of tritheism) but "lose" the personal threeness of God and so risk falling back into modalism? Furthermore, because knowing and loving are identical in God's being, what room is there to explain through these activities the generation of the Son and the procession of the Spirit? How can the divine knowing and willing illuminate the existence in God of three persons and not be taken to be merely the interior soliloquy of only one person?[14]

One should repeat here that Augustine's reflections on the Holy Trinity are by no means confined to *De Trinitate,* an impression that could be given by a widely used textbook, Henry Bettenson's generally valuable *The Later Christian Fathers.*[15] All the extracts from Augustine's trinitarian writing provided by Bettenson (pp. 230–36) are taken from *De Trinitate*. This is to slip over what one finds in other works by Augustine. In *The City of God* he remarks, for instance, that "God is everything that he has except for the relations through which each person is referred to each other" (11.10.1). The remark not only anticipates the trinitarian theology of God as "subsistent relations" (i.e., that mutual ordering of the three divine persons who exist in relationship) developed by St. Thomas Aquinas (d. 1274) but also parallels a passage in *De Trinitate* (5.5–6) that discusses innertrinitarian relations and that Bettenson does not quote. Among Augustine's enduring legacies was his sense of the divine persons being reciprocally relational realities.

One should also add that in Book 15 of *De Trinitate,* Augustine highlighted again the love analogy to interpret the Trinity. The Holy Spirit is the Gift of mutual love between Father and Son—a theme already developed much earlier in *De Trinitate* (5.11–12). Centuries later, Richard of St. Victor held that mutual love, to be perfect, must be love shared with a third person. In God, we find not just an I-Thou relationship or reciprocal love but also the Holy Spirit as the "Co-beloved (*Condilectus*)." There is a "movement" from self-love (the Father) to mutual love (the Father and Son) to shared love (the Father, Son, and

Holy Spirit). This interpretation of God as absolute communion of love takes a little further Augustine's trinitarian theology of love.

(b) The Procession of the Spirit

Before reviewing Augustine's reflections on the procession of the Spirit, it could be useful once again to jump ahead in time. When he wrote, the Western church had not yet unilaterally added to the Nicene-Constantinopolitan Creed the words about the Spirit proceeding from the Father "and the Son"—the *Filioque* addition that since the time of Patriarch Photius of Constantinople (d. ca. 895) has contributed to the separation between Eastern and Western Christianity. I say "contributed"—the division arose and continued also because of a wide range of political, cultural, and ecclesial factors; theological differences over the *Filioque* and its interpretation never operated alone, as the only cause.

The *Filioque,* a term expressing the double procession of the Holy Spirit, may have been already interpolated into the text of the creed at the Third Synod of Toledo in 589. It was undoubtedly added in 675 by the Fourth Synod of Braga, also in Spain. After being widely used in the West from ca. 800 when the creed began to be chanted at Mass, the addition was eventually adopted also in Rome soon after 1000.[16] In the Spanish setting of Toledo III and Braga IV, the *Filioque* addition appears to have been introduced to support orthodox trinitarian doctrine against Priscillianism, a heresy that included a deep strain of Sabellianism. A strong view on the Son's role in the procession of the Spirit helped shut out Sabellian denials of true personal distinctions within the godhead.

Before summarizing Augustine's thoughts on the origin of the Holy Spirit, we should recall a few important elements in the prior tradition. Much of the difficulty will relate to the question: How are the Father and Son related in and to the emergence of the Spirit? In his *Adversus Praxean,* along the lines of his image of the spring/river/canal, Tertullian wrote of the Spirit being "from the Father through the Son" (4). In the following century, where Hilary of Poitiers repeated "from the Father through the Son,"[17] Marius Victorinus drew on such NT passages as Jesus' words in John 16:14 ("He [the Spirit of truth] will glorify me because he will take what is mine and declare it to you") to reach the conclusion that the Son, together with the Father, "produced" the Holy Spirit. Victorinus's conversion to Christianity and resignation of his post as a famous rhetor in 362 (after which he dedicated himself to theological writing) played a role in Augustine's own conversion to Christianity in 386.

Subsequently, Augustine himself wrote of the Father endowing the Son with the *capacity* to produce the Spirit. Hence, it is in a primordial or "original" sense (*principaliter*) that the Spirit proceeds from the Father (*de Patre principaliter*). For Augustine, any denial of this procession from the Father and the Son, "as from one principle (*tanquam ab uno principio*)," would violate the divine unity (*De Trinitate*, 5.14). Often, Christian art in the West was to violate the divine unity by representing the Spirit being breathed equally and simultaneously from the *separate* mouths of the Father and the Son. But, in Augustine's view, the Spirit proceeds from the Father through the Son, the Son being considered the agent of the Father in this procession by equally producing the divine Spirit. (The Son's being equal in the production of the Spirit was and is important when facing Arian challenges to the Son's true and equal divinity.) What the Son does here, according to Augustine, happens "through the gift of the Father" and not independently, just as his divinity is derived from the Father. Being and acting in such a "derivative" way does not exclude being equal in divinity and in the production of the Spirit.

In general, the Greek theologians found no difficulty in saying that the Spirit proceeds *from* the Father through the Son, the Son being considered the Father's instrument or agent, but it remained axiomatic that the *Father alone* is the ultimate source or fountainhead of deity and that both the Son and Spirit derive from him, the former by generation and the latter by procession. For Eastern theologians, however, the *Filioque* suggested a fundamental difference of view over the mystery of the triune divinity—an unacceptable view of the Son being equal in the production of the Spirit. Hence, they normally rejected the Augustinian idea of the Son forming with the Father a single co-principle for the procession of the Spirit. Such a double origin for the Spirit contradicts the divine unity.

Distinguishing between the (economic) mission and the (immanent) procession of the Spirit, Eastern theologians have continued to appeal to John 15:26: "When the Advocate comes, whom *I will send* to you *from the Father,* the Spirit of truth *who proceeds from the Father,* he will testify on my behalf." This perspective insists that only the Father is the ultimate source and fountainhead of divinity, from whom the Son and the Spirit derive—the former by generation and the latter by procession. Yet, it is worth remarking here that the original, unexpanded form of the Nicene-Constantinopolitan Creed did not state that the Spirit proceeds from the Father *alone*. In confessing that the Spirit proceeds from *the Father,* it refers to One who has this name precisely because of the generation of the Son. In effect, the creed confesses that the Spirit proceeds "from the Father of the Son."

Here one can undoubtedly indulge unsubtle polarities and even downright caricatures, whether it be about the procession of the Holy Spirit in particular or about the whole doctrine of the Trinity in general—as if all the problems and differences were to go back, for instance, to the Greeks beginning with the reality of the divine persons and the Latins with the unity of the divine nature. But one should respect the fear that Eastern Christians have of neglecting or subordinating the Spirit. They remain strongly trinitarian in their faith because they experience the life and living witness of the Spirit in the church. We need to ask: How trinitarian have Western Christians been? The Eastern problems with the Western understanding (from Augustine on) of the procession of the Holy Spirit spring from concerns about the subordination of the Spirit to the Son (in the life of Christians) and of Pneumatology to Christology (in the work of theologians). In the Christocentric theology of the West, which at times seems to indulge Christomonism or a unilateral stress on Christ's being and work,[18] the Spirit becomes the Spirit of Christ rather than the Spirit of (God) the Father.

Before leaving Augustine, we should pay tribute to his reverent sense of the ultimately unknowable mystery of the tripersonal God. Respecting the very finite limits of our thought and language, he wrote:

> Because the Father is not the Son, and the Son is not the Father, and the Holy Spirit, who is also called the Gift of God, is neither the Father nor the Son, then certainly there are three. Therefore, it was said in the plural number: "I and my Father are One" (Jn 10:30). But when it is asked "Three what?" then the great poverty from which our language suffers becomes apparent. But the formula "three persons" has been coined, not in order to give a complete explanation by means of it, but in order that we might not be obliged to remain silent. (*De Trinitate,* 5.10)

At the end, Augustine concludes with a humble prayer to God: "O Lord, the One God, God the Trinity, whatever I have said in these books as coming from you, may they acknowledge who are yours. But for anything coming from myself, may you and they who are yours forgive me" (ibid., 15.28). Within a century of Augustine's death in 430, trinitarian theology enjoyed a significant development when moves toward a little more precision in the language of persons began.

Boethius and Beyond

By the middle of the fifth century, mainline believers had organized certain inferences that had been drawn from the founding experiences of Christianity, witnessed to by the NT, and shared by those who accepted the good news about salvation through Jesus and his Spirit. The divine action in delivering them from sin and sharing with them a new life as well as challenges coming from such heterodox groups as the Sabellians, Arians, and Pneumatomachians had led them to explicitate further what the NT authors had begun to indicate about the intradivine existence of the tripersonal God (the immanent Trinity). The divine action in the whole story or "economy" of salvation that reached its climax with the missions of Jesus and the Holy Spirit, while leaving intact the monotheistic faith (inherited from Judaism) that everything in the orders of creation and redemption came from a single divine source,[19] nevertheless, made some differences and distinctions within the inner life of God show through.[20]

From the trinitarian pattern in "outward" divine activity, Christians grasped a little of the intradivine life; they moved from the "economic" to the "immanent" Trinity or tripersonal God.

From their experience of the specific missions of the Son and the Spirit, believers understood that these specific missions mirrored distinct derivations from the Origin (uppercase) within the godhead, from the God whom Jesus named *Abba*[21] and who was understood to be unoriginated or without origin from either the Son or the Spirit. The one divine essence, substance, or nature belongs to three realities, who—while they cannot be conceived of independently or one without the other[22]—nevertheless, are to be distinguished. In a letter to Pope Damasus, a synod that met after Constantinople I confessed "one divinity, power, or substance (*ousia*)" in "three most perfect subsistences (*hypostaseis*), that is in three perfect persons (*prosopois*)."[23] Basil, Gregory of Nazianzus, and, even more, Gregory of Nyssa had been using interchangeably *hypostasis* and *prosopon* (i.e., the "face" or visible manifestation and characteristics of the *hypostasis*).

(a) Boethius

In the next century the Council of Chalcedon (451) defined Christ to be one "subsistence (*hypostasis*)" or "person (*prosopon*)" in two "natures (*physeis*)," without turning aside to describe in detail what any of these three terms meant (DH 302; ND 615). Here, as elsewhere, Chalcedon left some unfinished business. Karl Rahner's classical observation about Chalcedon being more a beginning than an end,[24] if it holds true about anything, bears on the notion of person. In any case, rather than being the proper work of an ecumenical council, the analysis and definition of such terms belong rather to philosophers and theologians.

More than a half-century after Chalcedon, such analysis moved some steps forward through the insights of Boethius (d. ca. 524). Let me sketch his contribution to trinitarian theology and then examine what came subsequently with Richard of St. Victor and Thomas Aquinas. Boethius affected all subsequent trinitarian (and christological) doctrine in the West by his definitions. In his *Contra Eutuchen et*

Nestorium (also called *Liber de persona et duabus naturis Christi*), he defined *nature* as "the specific difference informing anything" and *person* as "an individual substance of a rational nature" (nr. 3). This influential account of *person* highlighted the individuality and rationality of the reality that is the center of action and attribution. It had nothing as such to say about the freedom, history and interrelatedness of persons, let alone about the way *person* functions analogically. Human, angelic, and divine persons may be all persons, but they realize their personhood variously and not exactly in the same way. Even, or one should say especially, within the Trinity, Father, Son, and Holy Spirit realize their personhood in different ways because they have distinct positions within the whole structure of the tripersonal, divine life.

It may be better to say here that the divine persons are persons in different ways because of distinct atemporal events within the divine life, with the Father eternally "generating" the Son and "breathing" the Spirit, the Son being "generated" (and in some sense being involved in the "breathing" of the Spirit), and the Spirit being "breathed." Loosely based on John 3:8 ("The wind/spirit blows where it wills"), *breathing*, or *spiration*, was introduced into trinitarian doctrine to speak of the way the Spirit who proceeds from the Father (or is breathed by the Father) and/or through the Son. Latin theology distinguished, as we will see below, between active and passive spiration. While common to the Father and the Son, active spiration does not constitute a new person, whereas passive spiration is another name for the Holy Spirit, as being breathed by the Father and the Son.

(b) Richard of St. Victor

Medieval theology modified Boethius's definition by introducing *existence* and adding the characteristic of incommunicability. Persons exist as their unique and incommunicable selves. Richard of St. Victor defined *person* as "the incommunicable existence of an intelligent nature" (*De Trinitate*, 4.22.24). Rationality, as before, remained dominant among the characteristics of a person. Existence seems a clear improvement. The divine persons are three incommunicable existents. The Father exists but is not the Son or the Spirit; the Son exists but is not the Father or the Spirit; the Spirit exists but is not the Father or the Son. The earlier definition from Boethius could be wrongly taken to imply three substances in God rather than affirm three distinct (but inseparable) persons sharing equally and completely the one rational substance or nature. Boethius's definition applies reasonably well to all cases of created persons, where one individual substance coincides with one person.[25] But it may not be so adequate in the context of trinitarian theology. Modern times, especially after the "turn to the subject" effected by René Descartes (d. 1650), have brought new or at least partially new elements in the accounts given of what it is to be person. We will examine these changes later.

We saw earlier how Richard of St. Victor pushed the analogy of love when expounding the tripersonal God in the light of St. John's lapidary confession: "God is love" (1 Jn 4:8,16). Self-love is not the truest and highest form of love. As gift and exchange, love is plural and requires fellowship with others. To be perfect, the human dialogue of mutual love must be open and, in fact, shared with a third person; the love of two persons is thus fused by a third. This version of love at its highest and best, if true of human beings, must be true also of God and in an infinitely greater way.

Thomas Aquinas

Aquinas did not, however, accept this move from human love to what we can say about God's tripersonal life. He found in this version of love something of Plato's account of eros, or love as combining need (or desire) and resourcefulness. To complete ourselves, we human beings need to love, but God must be understood to be utterly complete and beyond all such need. Moreover, Richard's trinitarian theology moves from love—from the reciprocal love between the Father and the Son to identify the Spirit as the Co-Beloved or Bond of love. But Thomas normally acknowledged the priority of knowing over willing; hence, he preferred the analogy of the Son's generation being like our thinking and that of the Spirit being like the inner fruit of love. Thomas followed Augustine in holding the priority of knowing (*nihil amatum nisi praecognitum* or "nothing is loved unless it is already known"), even if sometimes he espoused the principle of *per amorem ad veritatem* ("through love to the truth").

On any showing, Augustine's *De Trinitate* was the most sustained attempt in the patristic period to develop a helpful human analogy to the Trinity. In maintaining Augustine's psychological model and developing the classic medieval theology of the Trinity, Aquinas elaborated several items: first, the event-like attributes of Father, Son, and Holy Spirit, to be named in the scholastic tradition as trinitarian *notions* or *properties*. Through the innertrinitarian events of begetting and spiration (or breathing), atemporal events that have no beginning and no end, God is constituted tripersonal. These necessary events in the divine life, of generation and spiration, do not either divide an existing substance or produce a new (divine) substance, as is the case, for example, with generation in the human sphere. But this eternal generating and spirating causes the existence of three divine persons, who are relatively distinct from each other. They are distinct inasmuch as paternity or fathering and filiation (and breathing and being breathed in the case of the Holy Spirit) are distinct.

At the same time, personal being in God is totally relational; in Aquinas's terms, the divine persons are the relations expressed by generation and spiration (ST 1a 40. 2 ad 1). They are subsistent relations, that is to say, relations that exist in themselves and are not mere "accidental" relations that are added to already existing substances (such as a business relationship that a human person takes on).[26] Thus through the eventlike attributes of generation and spiration, clarified by his language of subsistent relations, Aquinas worked out further the second part of what we quoted above from Augustine: "God is everything that he has except for the relations through which each person is referred to each other."

As regards the first part of the statement, "God is everything he has," Aquinas (ST 1.40.2) totally concurs by using a principle definitively enunciated by St. Anselm of Canterbury (d. 1109) in *De processione Spiritus Sancti* (nr. 1): "Everything in God is one where there is no opposition of relationship."[27] Hence God *is* the divine knowing, willing, and acting, a knowing-willing-acting shared equally by the three divine persons. To put this in the modern terms, there is only one mental state in God, a mental state that has a plural subject (the Father, the Son, and the Holy Spirit). Talk of a group mind or group will slips dangerously toward three divine substances, whose collaboration is so harmonious that one can speak of their group mind and group will. Apart from two events in God's life (generation and spiration) that cause the opposition of relationship, every perfection is simply one in God.

What then of trinitarian operations *ad extra*? Are the divine persons so totally one that nothing whatsoever distinguishes them in their common action? Arguing for distinctive roles and making such activity collaborative (with Father, Son, and Holy Spirit each doing a part that adds up to a joint effort) rather than accepting strictly common action leads not only to tritheism but to an inadequate picture of divinity. Instead of being together all-powerful, the three divine persons would have only their limited specialties. But, rather than postulating distinctive roles, why not think of distinctive *terms* for the divine activity? Aquinas distinguished between a divine action *ad extra* and the term of such action.[28] He pointed to the example of the incarnation. All three divine persons are jointly involved in bringing it about, but the term or visible point of arrival, the Incarnate Son of God with his mission, is irreducibly special to the Word (ST 3a. 3. 1–4). Only the Son assumes a human existence and actualizes—or rather is—the personal being of Jesus. To put this point in terms of the eventlike attribute that constitute the tripersonal life of God, just one event in the divine life (the generation of the Son) and not others (e.g., the spiration of the Spirit) is connected through hypostatic or personal union with the term of the incarnating action, the human life of Jesus and the events that constitute it.

The enduring legacy of Thomas's trinitarian theology can be summed up as follows. There is one divine nature, substance, or essence. There are two processions, although it is preferable to speak of the generation of the Son and the spiration/breathing of the Spirit. There are three persons, *hypostaseis* or subjects. There are four (subsistent) relations, or orderings of the divine persons among themselves that constitute them three persons in one God: paternity, filiation, active spiration, and passive spiration. Paternity constitutes the Father, filiation the Son, and passive spiration the Spirit. Active spiration, which belongs to the Father and is somehow shared by the Son, does not form a new person. There are five notions or properties of the Trinity, eventlike attributes that ground the relative identities of the three persons. The Father is unoriginated, generative and breathing; the Son is generated and breathing; the Spirit is breathed. Thus we have a fivefold scheme for trinitarian theology, to which respect for this ultimate divine mystery added no proof: "There are five notions, four relations, three persons, two processions, one nature, and no proof (*Sunt quinque notiones, quattuor relationes, tres personae, duae processiones, una natura, nulla probatio*)."

Despite the way he distanced himself from Richard of St. Victor's particular trinitarian model of love, Thomas along with other medieval theologians endorsed the radical, loving interconnectedness (*circumincessio*) of the three divine persons, something better expressed in Greek as their *perichoresis*, or reciprocal presence and interpenetration. Their innermost life is infinitely close relationship with one another in the utter reciprocity of love.

Beyond Aquinas

To complete this attempt to retrieve medieval trinitarian reflections that retain their importance, I wish to highlight two issues.[29] The first had emerged before the time of Thomas: the question of divine attributes. How should we fill out the content for what we would consider the *right* concept of deity? What makes God to be God? Where and how does "God" get its meaning for those in the Christian tradition? The question comes up clearly for any well thought out trinitarian theology that affirms that deifying attributes exist equally in all three divine persons.

From the second century, strains of Platonic, Stoic, and Aristotelian thought left their impact on essential ways for describing divinity. In a style that is more conceptual than experiential and historical, the God of philosophers has turned up in theological writing, especially from the time of Anselm and his notion of the greatest possible/conceivable, thinking Being. Philosophical versions of God highlighted all "omni-properties" and "total" characteristics as being essential for divinity: The tripersonal God is omnipotent, omniscient, omnipresent (yet beyond all space and time with their limits), the creator and sustainer of everything, perfectly free and perfectly good. The triune God is subsistent Being itself, the uncaused cause, the one necessary, infinite Being who is utterly self-sustaining, self-determining, and therefore totally self-explanatory. In every way complete, ultimate, and unconditioned, God is infinitely simple and profoundly uncomplicated—unlike spatial and temporal beings who are divided or separated into parts. Such philosophical analysis, even before Aquinas had also left his mark on official church teaching about the tripersonal God and the divine attributes! Thus the Fourth Lateran Council in 1215 defined faith in God as follows: "We firmly believe and confess without reservation that there is only one true God, eternal, infinite (*immensus*) and unchangeable, incomprehensible, almighty and ineffable, the Father, the Son, and the Holy Spirit: three persons indeed but one essence, substance, or nature entirely simple" (DH, 800; ND, 19).

Undoubtedly these ways of putting matters can help to clarify and explicitate biblical attributes of God. The struggle to explicitate the divine attributes continues. Almost every issue of such journals as *Religious Studies* reflects contemporary attempts to explore what God's being involves. At the same time, whether we listen to the voices of the past or of the present, we always need to lead God-talk back to the scriptures and their account of divine self-communication in the history of revelation and salvation. Doing that reminds us that we need to hear the voice of God when we ask: What makes God to be God? We may never attempt to define the divine attributes independently of the tripersonal God made known in the biblical story of revelation. Any account of God depends primarily on God, the tripersonal God definitively revealed in the history of Jesus. It could be that modern developments in biblical study have made some theologians a little more sensitive to the need to root in the scriptural record their reflections on the Trinity and on trinitarian attributes. Gains in intellectual clarity about the divine perfections should not be allowed to entail a loss, a muted disregard for the fact that knowledge of the tripersonal God must always be rooted in the biblical revelation.

The other medieval development that deserves recalling here came at the level of liturgical and popular devotion. From the time of Anselm, devotion to Jesus underwent a sea-change as it became more personal and mystical. Devotion to the human Jesus (as sufferer, friend, lover, and mother) grew stronger through the impact of St. Bernard of Clairvaux (d. 1153), Cistercian writing, St. Hildegard of Bingen (d. 1179), St. Francis of Assisi (d. 1226), Julian of Norwich (d. ca. 1423), and many others. Fresh developments in liturgy, painting, sculpture, and architecture furthered a deep sense of Jesus in his suffering, loving, human existence. After nearly a thousand years of depicting Jesus as untouched by pain, bypassing death, and already reigning in triumph from the cross, Christian artists finally found the courage to represent more directly the crucifixion and Jesus' agonizing death. Parallel to this fresh sense of the human, suffering Jesus, one also finds a new sensibility to his divinity and place in the Trinity. The strong Christ of trinitarian life belongs to a renewed appreciation of the tripersonal God that began in the tenth century and reached its climax with the institution of the Feast of the Holy Trinity in 1334.

The greatest of all medieval poets, Dante Alighieri (d. 1321), lent his weight to this popular appreciation of faith in the tripersonal God. At the end of his *Paradiso,* Dante envisions God as utterly active, with "spinning" or "circling" symbolizing the completely actualized divine perfection; in the divine spinnings, the Holy Spirit proceeds from or is breathed by both Father and Son: "In the profound and clear ground of the lofty light there appeared to me three spinnings (circlings) of three colors and of the same extent. The One seemed reflected by the Other as rainbow by rainbow, and the Third seemed fire breathed forth equally from the One and the Other" (Canto 33.115–20). As elsewhere in the *Paradiso,* spinning symbolizes completely actualized intellection and perfection.

A key text for this popular and liturgical appreciation of the Trinity was the Athanasian Creed, sometimes called *Quicumque* from its opening word. Composed in Latin, probably in Southern Gaul and certainly in the fifth century, this creed, if falsely attributed to Athanasius, found wide liturgical use in the Middle Ages (and beyond). What the *Quicumque* stated in precise and rhythmic formulations was frequently translated into trinitarian images.[30] While coming from the fifth century, this creed shaped the heart of Western trinitarian faith in the medieval period. Let me close the chapter by quoting its trinitarian confession:

> We worship one God in the Trinity and the Trinity in unity, without either confusing the persons or dividing the substance; for the person of the Father is one, the Son's is another, the Holy Spirit's another, but the Godhead of Father, Son and Holy Spirit is one, their glory equal, their majesty equally eternal. Such as the Father is, such is the Son, such also the Holy Spirit; uncreated is the Father, uncreated the Son, uncreated the Holy Spirit; infinite (*immensus*) is the Father, infinite the Son, infinite the Holy Spirit; eternal is the Father, eternal the Son, eternal the Holy Spirit; yet they are not three eternals but one eternal, just as they are not three uncreated beings or three infinite beings but one uncreated and one infinite. In the same way, almighty is the Father, almighty the Son, almighty the Holy Spirit; yet they are not three almighty beings but one almighty. Thus, the Father is God, the Son is God, the Holy Spirit is God; yet they are not three gods but one God. Thus the Father is Lord, the Son is Lord, the Holy Spirit is Lord; yet they are not three lords but one Lord. For, as the Christian truth compels us to acknowledge each person distinctly as God and Lord, so too the Catholic religion forbids us to speak of three gods or lords.
>
> The Father has neither been made by anyone, nor is he created or begotten; the Son is from the Father alone, not made nor created but begotten; the Holy Spirit is from the Father and the Son (*Spiritus Sanctus [est] a Patre et Filio*), not made nor created nor begotten, but proceeding (*procedens*).[31]
>
> So there is one Father, not three Fathers; one Son, not three

Sons, one Holy Spirit, not three Holy Spirits. And in this Trinity there is no before or after, no greater or lesser, but all three persons are equally eternal with each other and fully equal. Thus in all things, as has already been stated above, both unity in the Trinity and Trinity in the unity must be worshiped. Let him therefore who wishes to be saved think this of the Trinity. (ND 16; DH 75)

8.
Our Modern Setting

"Eternal Trinity, you are like a deep sea, in which the more I seek, the more I find; and the more I find, the more I seek you... You feed the hungry in your sweetness, because you are gentle, without a trace of bitterness. O eternal Trinity!"

St. Catherine of Siena, *On Divine Revelation*

"Our pen is on the watch for the sophistries of those who consider it beneath their dignity to begin with faith, and who thus are led into error by their immature and perverted love of reason."

St. Augustine, *De Trinitate*

Beyond question, the Reformation in the sixteenth century and, even more, the Enlightenment, which began in Europe in the seventeenth century and spread to North America and elsewhere, have deeply shaped the context for reflecting on trinitarian faith at the end of the second millennium. But other factors, such as the rise of the human sciences and personalist philosophies have helped to shape that context. Let us look at matters chronologically with a view to identifying questions that must be faced in the systematic section that follows.

The Reformation

Mainline Protestant and Anglican reformers left in place the inherited faith in Christ's divinity and the Trinity. In his two catechisms of 1529, Martin Luther (1483–1546) took over from the Nicene-Constantinopolitan Creed the three-article structure that explicitates a faith that is clearly historical and primarily trinitarian. The Apostles' Creed, by moving straight from "I believe in the Holy Spirit" to "the holy Catholic Church," may let the centrality of trinitarian faith slip slightly out of the picture. Of course, "the holy Catholic Church, the communion of saints, the forgiveness of sins, the resurrection of the body, and the life everlasting" are all brought about through the Holy Spirit, but the trinitarian shape of Christian belief comes through more clearly in the Nicene-Constantinopolitan Creed. Luther did well in following it and in moving back from the diffusion of a 12-article catechesis based on the Apostles' Creed to a tightly trinitarian, three-article catechesis.

At a time when many radical reformers went to excess in claiming direct guidance from the Holy Spirit, John Calvin (1509–1564) championed mainline teaching on the internal testimony of the Holy Spirit.[1] A leader of the Catholic reformation, St. Ignatius Loyola (1491–1556), recorded in his spiritual diary an astonishing trinitarian mysticism. A century later, Blaise Pascal (1623–1662) deeply experienced and championed "the God of Abraham, Isaac and Jacob, the God of Jesus Christ." Great mathematician and physicist that he was, Pascal refused to raise the question of God except in terms of that history that climaxed with Jesus' life, death, and resurrection: "We know God only through Jesus Christ."[2] The Enlightenment debates about God and trinitarian faith that began in the seventeenth century left behind the proper setting endorsed by Luther, Calvin, Ignatius, Pascal and others: the biblical history of revelation and salvation.

Luther's thinking about the Trinity raises difficulties, however, when he pictures Christ as the one who carries the sins of the world and is the object of divine anger on the cross. A penal substitute for sinners, the Son of God suffered the rightful punishment imposed on human misdeeds. Luther even wrote of a war between God (the Father) and God (the Son). He understood Christ to have literally taken upon himself the guilt of human sin, just as if he had personally committed all those sins himself. He suffered as our substitute on the cross, and his atrociously cruel death placated the divine anger and so made justification available for us. Not a few Catholic preachers, not least in France, shared this view of God's vengeance and anger being appeased at the expense of his Son. The victim of the divine justice, Christ was even "credited" with having suffered the pains of the damned—a terrible view of the redemption allegedly supported by some verses from St. Paul (e.g., Gal 3:13), the scapegoat in Leviticus 16, and Christ's cry of abandonment on the cross (Mk 15:34). Misplaced eloquence from Catholic and Protestant pulpits turned God into a murderer who carried out an implacable vendetta before being appeased and exercising the divine mercy.[3]

In the twentieth century, notable theologians such as Jürgen Moltmann in *The Crucified God*[4] have given fresh currency to the language of Luther and others of a kind of war taking place on Calvary within the Trinity—a war that pits the Father against the Son, with the Holy Spirit playing a reconciling role. After the trinitarian philosophy-theology of G. W. F. Hegel (1770–1831), modern theologians who develop the notion of an inner-trinitarian war do so in historical terms. We will come later to Hegel, who has encouraged his successors to think of the Trinity in a historical way. But he encouraged them to replace the God of history with the history of God.

Sixteenth-century religious turmoil also gave rise to two challenges to trinitarian faith that proved similar and joined forces: Socinianism and Unitarianism. A religious system that denied the divinity of Christ and the existence of the Trinity, Socinianism drew its name from the Italians, Lelio Francesco Maria Sozini (1525–1562) and his nephew Fausto Paolo Sozzini (1539–1604; his name was spelled differently from that of his uncle). Eventually, many Socinians joined other forces to form the Unitarian Church. In rejecting the divinity of the Son and of the Holy Spirit and defending a strict monotheism, Unitarians accepted only one divine person. Developed by Martin Cellarius

(1499–1564), Michael Servetus (1511–1553), and Fausto Sozzini, Unitarianism eventually drew its intellectual prestige from such figures in the United States as William Ellery Channing (1780–1842), Ralph Waldo Emerson (1803–1882), and Charles William Eliot (1834–1926), who was president of Harvard University for 40 years and, among other achievements, reformed the Harvard Divinity School. In terms of official membership, Unitarianism has dwindled in numbers.

But its antitrinitarianism lives on among modern exponents of liberal Christology, who present Jesus as differing from other human beings in degree and not in kind. He goes beyond us, they say, only because of his higher degree of holiness but not because, as a divine person, he belongs to an infinitely different kind of being, God. John Hick, for example, invites his readers to accept such a Jesus, who is not the Son of God but only one who embodies "the ideal of human life lived in faithful response to God."[5] Such a low Christology inevitably brings down the doctrine of the Trinity and issues in a latter-day version of Unitarianism (which in a modern guise echoes Sabellianism). Hick is no exception here. He writes: "God is humanly known—as creator, as transformer, and as inner spirit [lowercase]. We do not need to reify these ways as three distinct persons."[6]

The Enlightenment

A brilliant contemporary of Pascal, René Descartes (1596–1650) furthered the notion of person as a unique subject of consciousness and self-consciousness. More than a century later, a concern for freedom and morality prompted Immanuel Kant (1726–1804) to stress person as the subject of freedom, a moral end in itself and never a means to an end. The philosophical input from Descartes, Kant, and John Locke (1632–1704) led to the emergence of a (but not *the*) typically modern notion of person as the subject of self-awareness and freedom—in brief, person as a conscious and autonomous self ("I think and am free; therefore I am person"). This notion, when applied to the doctrine of the Trinity, readily produces what looks suspiciously like tritheism:

three autonomous subjects living and working together in a quasi-social unity.

In aiming to eliminate everything except certain "clear and distinct ideas," Descartes began with his own existence, which could not be denied because the very act of denial asserted his own existence: "*Cogito ergo sum* (I think, therefore I am)." Rationality rather than any relationship ("*Amor ergo sum;* I am loved, therefore I am") provided the Cartesian point of departure. The intellectual ground was laid for the birth and spread of the Enlightenment, that movement which resisted authority and tradition, defended human rights and freedom, encouraged empirical methods in scientific research, and aimed at deciding issues through the use of reason alone. Along with Kant and Locke, prominent figures of the Enlightenment included Denis Diderot (1713–1784), Benjamin Franklin (1706–1790), David Hume (1711–1776), Gotthold Ephraim Lessing (1729–1781), Jean-Jacques Rousseau (1712–1778) and François-Marie Arouet (better known as Voltaire) (1694–1778).

Many members of this movement rejected special divine actions (such as miracles and Jesus' resurrection from the dead) and special divine revelation in history. In religious matters, as elsewhere, human reason was to be decisive. This approach obviously ruled out faith in a tripersonal God revealed in the special history of the people of God and Jesus Christ. Trinitarian belief had no place in *Religion within the Limits of Reason Alone,* to quote the title of Kant's classic work from 1793. In any case Kant could see no practical importance for such faith. In *Conflict of Faculties* he wrote: "The doctrine of the Trinity, taken literally, has *no practical relevance at all,* even if we think we understand it; and it is even more clearly irrelevant if we realize that it transcends all our concepts. Whether we are to worship three or ten persons in the Deity makes no difference."[7] The rational worldview and method of Enlightenment thinkers reversed the Augustinian axiom of "believe in order to understand (*crede ut intelligas*)," and made it read: "If you believe, you will not understand." Belief in the tripersonal God revealed definitively in Jesus' death and resurrection was put aside as an obstacle to honest thought and true understanding.

Where Kant's form of idealism (transcendental idealism) showed the extent to which the human mind constructs what we call external reality, Hegel went even further by identifying the rational and the real. What is thought is reality, and reality is what is thought. In Hegel's philosophy, all history and nature become the evolutionary manifestation of the Absolute Spirit. A necessary dialectic constitutes this dynamic and progressive manifestation. There is identity or oneness (of the Absolute in itself), difference or estrangement, and reconciliation or reunification. In this cosmic drama, the Absolute Spirit is necessarily manifested in the dialectical progression of history: from the kingdom of the Father (the Absolute in itself), to the kingdom of the Son (or self-expression of the Spirit toward the other), and the kingdom of the Spirit, where the Spirit reaches its completion and enters general consciousness. Hegel produced here the richest treatment of the Spirit ever found in Western philosophy.

Much of Hegel's thought can put the nerves of mainline Christian theologians on red alert. For those who examine the centrality of history in Hegelianism, the question arises: Is it the Absolute (uppercase) that is historical, or the Historical (uppercase) that is absolute?[8] Does Hegel's "monism" of the Spirit leave any room for a redemptive difference *and* free interpersonal community between God and the world? If God *is* (of necessity) the world, God can no longer offer salvation *to* the world; the one absolute subject cannot redeem human subjects and bring them to share in the life of intratrinitarian dialogue. Nevertheless, Hegel encouraged notable theologians to think of the Trinity in historical terms.

Hans Urs von Balthasar (1905–1988) elaborated a trinitarian theology in which the Father, the Son, and the Holy Spirit as dramatic persons receive from and act on one another, giving and receiving their identity within these relationships. When reflecting on the history of Good Friday and Holy Saturday, von Balthasar interpreted this history as an inner-trinitarian drama, but unlike Luther he rooted his interpretation in the Trinity's "prior," eternal life: even "before" the incarnation, the eternal generation of the Son already expresses the "kenosis" of the Father's heart.[9]

Directly or indirectly Hegelian thought has its impact also on Jürgen

Moltmann's "social" theology of the Trinity (which verges on tritheism) to be found in *The Trinity and the Kingdom of God*.[10] Moltmann approaches the death of Jesus as primarily an intratrinitarian drama or "the inner history of the Trinity." Many fear that Moltmann's insistence on the crucifixion and resurrection as an inner-trinitarian event (with a rupture in the divine life and the Father "ceasing" to be the Father) may be confusing the intradivine life with the story of human salvation even to the point of "imprisoning" God in the world's becoming. It is one thing to uphold a strong link between the theology of the cross and the doctrine of the Trinity and to emphasize that it was the Son of God who died and was raised by the Father through the power of the Holy Spirit, but it is another thing to expound the crucifixion as affecting and even shaping the inner life of the tripersonal God. If one pushes matters to an extreme and argues that the paschal mystery "constitutes" or "creates" the Trinity, as if God somehow needed such a historical process to become trinitarian, then—paradoxically—the divine persons cannot share in that mystery inasmuch as they are not "present" prior to the event. Nevertheless, in *The Crucified God*[11] and subsequent publications, however one evaluates the particular shape of his arguments, Moltmann has rightly urged the need to think through in a trinitarian way the center of Christology: Jesus' crucifixion and resurrection. Moltmann's colleague on the Protestant theological faculty of Tübingen, Eberhard Jüngel, has also developed his theology of the Trinity and theology of the cross in strict relationship with one another. Once again the idealist legacy is clear, and so too is the risk of lapsing into Hegelian speculations about the inner history of God that have no firm roots either in the witness of the Bible and the great tradition or in the experience of Christians at worship.

Twentieth-Century Influences

Various other forces, both beyond Christianity and within Christian scholarship and life, have exercised their impact on the latest developments in trinitarian theology. Let us review some of them.

The emergence of personalist philosophies, for instance, should be mentioned. These philosophies conceive human persons as existing in and constituted by their relations to other self-aware subjects. The work of Martin Buber (1878–1965) and others has offered theologians the language of "I, Thou, and We" when speaking about the relational reality of God. When the I relates to the Thou, another person who addresses me and responds to me in love, a We emerges to unite us. This homely experience hints at the I of the Father, the Thou of the Son, and the We of the Holy Spirit.

Modern times have brought further possibilities for portraying the eternal life of the Trinity. C. G. Jung (1875–1961), for example, drew on the human experience of psychological growth. In the child's state of consciousness, the Father is the authority figure who provides a ready-made pattern of existence, the parent to whose laws one submits. The Son is represented by the process of self-individuation and self-assertion when a growing human being seeks autonomy. The third phase, when an individual surrenders independence to share in some larger reality, symbolizes the Spirit. Jung associated trinitarian belief with this threefold account of human development: submission, self-assertion, and then self-surrender.

The transcendental therapy of K. Graf Dürckheim studies the situations in which human beings can feel threatened by death in its various forms. They can be overwhelmed by a sense of injustice and meaningless absurdity. They can be abandoned, cruelly treated, and hated. Then they can be given life, they can experience a deeper order and meaning in things, and they can know themselves to be the objects of loving goodness. These experiences can make people long even more for some experience of life, meaning, and love that will change everything. These experiences and longings studied by Dürckheim and his school may be seen to point to a tripersonal God, who is total Life, Meaning and Love (all in uppercase). This view of the Trinity may be more compelling in a world that in some ways seems to be becoming more deadly, more absurd, and more cruel.

Nineteenth- and twentieth-century emancipatory movements have had their impact on trinitarian reflection. In promoting liberation from oppressive sexism, feminism, for example, has raised as never before the question: Is there something inherently sexist in the way the Trinity has been traditionally named and understood as *Father, Son, and Holy Spirit?* Does such naming encourage androcentric patriarchy, or—properly understood—could it and does it rather subvert an oppressive, male-dominated system? Furthermore, what might trinitarian faith and theology "supply" for liberation from the scourges of racism, unbridled nationalism, and destruction of the environment? At least here and there, moral thinkers point to trinitarian faith as ultimate encouragement for those who cherish a true unity in diversity. The loving interrelatedness of the divine persons can vitalize human beings who seek the grounds for respecting one another and the natural world in a healing and "wholesome" way.

Almost since the origins of Christianity, believers have looked for "*vestigia Trinitatis* (traces of the Trinity)" or hints of the tripersonal God to be found in the created world and, especially, in human beings. Augustine of Hippo saw the Trinity mirrored in human knowing and loving. Buber's philosophy encourages those who find hints of the Trinity in the I-Thou-We of interpersonal relationships. Such openness to *vestigia Trinitatis* has a peculiar significance in contemporary interreligious dialogue. Some find in Hindu thought a kind of trinitarian triad in the scheme of "being, awareness of being, and consciousness of being."

Finally, we should mention the impact of modern biblical and patristic studies. To be sure, one should not indulge a false faith in modern scholarship. Technical advances can encourage a kind of scholarship that studies biblical and patristic philology, while doing almost anything to avoid confronting the content of the Bible (and of the patristic works) and their important messages. Nevertheless, trinitarian theology can take advantage of some progress in fresh methods and approaches. Liturgical studies, however, have enjoyed little impact on trinitarian theology, at least in western theology. It is still rare to find anyone drawing on liturgical scholarship when expounding faith in the tripersonal God.

The yield from the biblical and historical chapters of this book leaves us many possible systematic issues to pursue in the third and final part of this book. Let me single out for special attention the personal existence of the Holy Spirit (Chapter 9), the use of personal language for all three divine persons (Chapter 10), naming the Trinity as *Father, Son, and Holy Spirit* (Chapter 11), and possible images of the Trinity (Chapter 12). Right through these chapters, I will keep in mind trinitarian implications for Christian worship and life. These concluding chapters, if they are to be argued well, must take up again and apply some conclusions already established earlier on the basis of the biblical and traditional witness.

Contemporary Thinking

9.
THE PERSONAL EXISTENCE OF THE HOLY SPIRIT

"Every authentic prayer is prompted by the Holy Spirit, who is mysteriously present in every human heart."
John Paul II, an address to Cardinals, December 1986

"...the Holy Ghost over the bent
World broods with warm breast and ah! bright wings."
Gerard Manley Hopkins, *"God's Grandeur"*

Before reflecting on the personhood, actions, names, and images for the trinitarian persons, we need to be quite sure that we are dealing with *three* persons. That entails looking hard at the personal existence of the Holy Spirit—something that may not be so obvious. In Paul's letters and beyond, is the "Spirit" still only a (Jewish) personification of God's activity and disclosure? If "wisdom" in the OT has striking personal characteristics (see Chapter 1) and yet is not a distinct person, why find a distinct person in what may seem to have less striking personal characteristics, Paul's "Spirit"? The case of wisdom in the OT shows us that personal characteristics do not necessarily signal the presence of a distinct person; we may be dealing, or may so far be dealing, only with a "mere" personification. The question remains: What kind or amount of personal characteristics should lead to the conclusion that we face an ontologically distinct person? What indicates that we encounter not simply a new *mode* of divine action in salvation history but a distinct, *personal* presence? Do we meet in Paul's letters and subsequent Christian writings at least a latent trinitarianism—that is to say, their witness to a threefold religious experience that leads believers to move beyond Jewish ideas and recognize within God not only a distinct divine Son but also a distinct divine Spirit?

A Distinct Existence

The two major creeds of Christianity have little to say about the Holy Spirit and the person of the Spirit. More than 50 years after the cryptic statement from the First Council of Nicaea ("we believe in the Holy Spirit"), the First Council of Constantinople (381) needed to say more, not least because of the Pneumatomachian denials of the Spirit's genuine divinity. Hence it added: "We believe in the Holy Spirit, the Lord and Life-giver, who proceeds from the Father, who with the Father and the Son is together worshiped and glorified, who spoke through the prophets." Constantinople I also added a reference to the virginal conception as affirmed by Matthew and Luke. The incarnation took place through the Holy Spirit and the Virgin Mary.[1] The Nicene-Constantinopolitan Creed confesses a minimum about the identity and work of the Spirit: the Spirit is divine Lord and to be worshiped; the Spirit gave voice to the prophets and human existence to Jesus. The Apostles' Creed has even less to say. It professes that the power of the Spirit effected the conception of Jesus, and that the Spirit is the object of faith ("I believe in the Holy Spirit"). Even that minimum, however, intimates a lot. To be, along with the Father and the Son, the object of our faith implies that the Spirit is personal.

Patristic theology on the Spirit took things a little further; for instance, in Augustine's reflection on the Spirit as the Love that the Father and the Son bestow on each other. Despite its attractions, this way of interpreting the Father/Son relationship leaves the Spirit somewhat passive and seemingly without any person-defining activity. The

Love that the Father and Son bestow on one other may not seem to allow for a clear identity to emerge for the Spirit. Why and how does this gift of mutual love (of both, from both, and to both divine persons) give rise to a distinct divine person? It is the economy of salvation as witnessed to and interpreted by the NT that can help us here.

From the OT personification of the Spirit of God, which is active in creation and the work of prophets, we pass to the NT where the relationship to Jesus and his followers brings out the personal role and status of the Holy Spirit. Through the Holy Spirit, God creates and sanctifies the human existence of Jesus, uniting that humanity to the person of the Son. In effecting the conception and sanctification of Jesus, along with the assumption of his humanity into the "hypostatic" or personal union with the Son of God, the Spirit brings about eminently personal results. The ministry of Jesus, particularly as interpreted by Luke, will see the Spirit causing conspicuously personal effects by announcing good news to the oppressed, liberating those imprisoned by evil, and curing the sick (Lk 4:18–21). The results point to a personal agent, rather than some "mere" supernatural force, at work.

The resurrection of Jesus reveals a personal power (rather than an unspecified power) to be in action (Rom 8:11). This resurrection, the life-giving action *par excellence,* is accomplished by the Spirit who is the Giver of life. For repentant sinners, the life-giving Spirit offers deliverance from the state of death (Rom 7:24) and entry into life and peace (Rom 8:6). It requires such a personal agent to open human hearts to hear the message of Jesus. John's Gospel makes this point both in terms of the Father enabling people to come to Jesus (Jn 6:44,65) or being given life by the Spirit (Jn 6:63; 3:6). The Spirit witnesses to Jesus and reminds the disciples of all they have been taught by Jesus (Jn 14:26; 15:26). According to the Book of Revelation, the Spirit instructs Christians by "speaking" to the seven churches (Rv 2:7,11,17,29; 3:6,13,22). In Paul's terms, the Spirit makes it possible to acclaim Jesus as divine Lord (1 Cor 12:3) and writes Christ's image on human hearts (2 Cor 3:2–3)—sanctifying operations that are manifestly the work of a personal agent. In the life of the church, the personal Spirit imparts a whole range of gifts for the building up of the body of Christ (1 Cor 12:4–13). In empowering the baptized to join Jesus in prayer to the Father and in bringing suffering human beings and all creation to their final liberation and transformation (Rom 8:14–30), the Holy Spirit has already begun the eschatological work that obviously implies a personal (divine) agent. By fashioning relationships between Jesus and human beings, among human beings, and between the whole created world and God, the Spirit achieves effects that demand the presence of a personal power. We can sum up much of this activity of the Spirit as bringing Jesus to be "with us, for us, and in us." Through empowering the whole Jesus story, the Spirit makes him with us through the incarnation, for us in his life and ministry, and in us as risen from the dead.

The difference between the strikingly vivid "face" of Lady Wisdom in the OT and the more discreet appearance of the Holy Spirit in Paul's letters and subsequent Christian writing (that we remarked on above) should not be allowed to exaggerate the impact of the question: How can we call the former a "mere" personification of God's activity and the latter a distinct divine person? In the OT, the impact of Wisdom is not normally specified in a way that touches particular people here and now. As we saw in Chapter 1, Wisdom shared long ago in the original work of creation, was powerfully there in the historical exodus, is linked with King Solomon and Jerusalem, but is scarcely ever associated with some specific, contemporary person. Almost the only exception is Ben Sirach, who reflects in his closing poem on the role of Wisdom in his own life (Sir 51:1–27). In the case of the Holy Spirit, however, Paul writes at length of the way that very specific communities of Christians receive and experience the Spirit right there in Paul's own world (1 Cor 12:1–31; Gal 3:2–5). For the apostle, the Spirit is not "back there and then" but is powerfully at work in the here and now on namable communities and individuals.

What can be more easily appreciated within Christian history, however, may not seem so obvious at the world level. Here perhaps it could be the universal quality of the activity that stands in the way of acknowledging easily the Spirit's personal status. It is one thing to credit a personal agency with effecting what happens to the centurion

Cornelius, his relatives, and friends (Acts 10:24,44–48). After all, the Spirit descends on this group of Gentiles when they hear Peter's witness to the life, death, and resurrection of Jesus and then accept baptism into the Christian community. The whole Cornelius story enjoys a deeply personal and interpersonal feel from beginning to end. Likewise, it is easy to identify the personal Spirit behind the prophetic utterances of such later charismatic leaders as St. Brigitta of Sweden (d. 1373) and St. Catherine of Siena (d. 1380).

But it can be another thing to interpret personally a worldwide activity that crosses both the boundaries of cultures and many centuries of history. There it can be tempting to think of a less-than-personal force, a divine wind that blows unpredictably (Jn 3:8), a vague graciousness that shows up everywhere, or the common spiritual interdependence of all peoples and things. Yet, the personal quality of that universal activity of the Spirit constantly shows through in both a vertical and a horizontal way. First, wherever the Spirit succeeds in opening human hearts to the divine, it brings about some kind of personal encounter with the personal God and not just a hazy religious consciousness. Second, at the horizontal level, the Holy Spirit works against alienation, injustice, and violence to spread solidarity, justice, and peace. However we describe these "fruits" of the Spirit (Gal 5:22–23), these interpersonal and social realities signal a personal cause, the Holy Spirit.

Chapter 10 will propose a distinction between God's *actions* (which are common to all three divine persons) and those actions' visible *terms,* which allow us to distinguish between the three persons. Apropos of the Spirit's action in the world beyond the Christian community, one must also (or even primarily) think of the term as eschatological. It will take the end of all things and all history to let us discern the visible term of the Spirit's full activity on the world and the cosmic scene.

In the order both of salvation and creation, the wide functions of the Spirit are person defining, and they let a distinct identity come through. The Spirit shows the personlike characteristics of loving, purposeful activity, being the origin and sustainer of all the activity that binds us together vertically (through Jesus and toward the Father), horizontally (toward one another), and eschatologically (toward the transformed future of the whole cosmos). "One Spirit" (Eph 4:4) is operating rather than many "divine" angels or spirits, as some latter-day Tropici (see Chapter 7) might allege.

Championing the Spirit

Back in Chapter 3, we examined briefly the Pauline phrase "the Spirit of God" (e.g., 1 Cor 2:11,14). If taken as a defining or appositional genitive ("the Spirit that is God") and pushed to an extreme, it might bewitch us into joining Georg Hegel in his way of interpreting *Spirit* as the most adequate term for God. For Hegel, this term expressed the immanent divine presence that permeates all creation, especially rational human beings. In the Hegelian version of consciousness, the Absolute Spirit is the Mind that creatively moves history forward. In the total event of universal history, the Mind posits its own other and achieves itself (or its own free personal identity) by knowing and willing itself in this object. The Absolute Spirit, with its threefold dynamic, is symbolized by the triune God of Christian faith.[2] The triunity here described seems close to a pantheistic blurring of God (the Absolute Spirit) with the created world. In this Hegelian scheme, so far from being overshadowed by or even swallowed up by the Father and Son, the Absolute Spirit takes over and becomes "all in all" (1 Cor 15:28).

The Spirit, besides being philosophically "championed" in an idealistic (and even pantheistic) fashion, is expounded at times in a unitarian fashion that takes up unilaterally the Johannine "God is Spirit" (Jn 4:24) and does away with personal distinctions within God.[3] Ways of putting this view vary, but they can be profiled together. Jesus, in the "high" or proper sense of these titles, is not the Word of God or the Son of God. Along the lines of classical adoptionism, he is understood as a mere man in whom God as Spirit came to be redemptively present and at work in the world. The divine energy continues to work for the creation of a new humanity and a new world. Thus the "Divine Spirit" amounts simply to a way of speaking of the one God being redemptively present in and through the man Jesus. Within the godhead, there is neither a distinct Son nor a distinct Spirit. *Spirit* becomes simply a term for God's outreach to the world, with Jesus as the highest embodiment of this outreach. This Pneumatology remains not too far from the OT personification of *Spirit* as divine action in the world and God's being in relation to the world.

A third vindication of the Spirit may have much more in its favor: taking the Holy Spirit as the feminine principle within the Trinity. Encouraged by Jungian theory with its images of the feminine as transforming, Donald Gelpi follows others in retrieving an ancient, at times Gnostic, idea about the Holy Spirit as Divine Mother.[4] In some forms of Gnosticism, the Spirit is a lower mother figure that emits Sophia-Prunicos, who descends below and takes on a material body. Yet, Gnostic and other extravagant ideas should not obscure the maternal tradition of the Spirit articulated by St. Ephrem the Syrian (d. 373), especially in his reflections on baptism. From the medieval period, we have the witness of St. Catherine of Siena (ca. 1347–1380) who in some passages understood the Holy Spirit to be feminine. Yves Congar has documented some voices from the great tradition who appreciate the Spirit's maternal role in our growth toward God.[5] Through the ages, Christians have (often? only sometimes?) experienced the Spirit in a feminine/motherly role as the One who forms them and gives them birth (Jn 3:5).

Yet, it may be important here to recall some relevant variants that occur outside the trinitarian formula of *Father, Son, and Holy Spirit* used in baptism and other traditional settings. On the basis of an image from Jesus about his acting like a mother hen (Mt 23:37 par.) and other NT passages, St. Anselm of Canterbury (ca. 1033–1109), St. Bernard of Clairvaux (1090–1153), Julian of Norwich (d. ca. 1423), and other medieval writers at times called Jesus our "Mother." In earlier centuries, such figures as Clement of Alexandria, Origen, St. John Chrysostom, St. Ambrose of Milan, and St. Augustine of Hippo had written of Jesus feeding and instructing his followers like a mother. Where the Son could be called Mother, occasional voices from the tradition named the

Holy Spirit as Father: an Archbishop of Canterbury, Stephen Langton (d. 1128), in a hymn attributed to him, *Veni, Sancte Spiritus,* gave the Spirit the title of *Father of the poor* (*Pater pauperum*).

The Spirit of the Future

One might have expected that some major writer would have called the Spirit "the Father of the world to come." Instead, we find that title applied to Jesus in *Catholicum Hymnologium Germanicum* (in the translation by Edward Caswall (1814–1878): "To Christ, the prince of peace, And Son of God most high, The Father of the world to come, Sing we with holy joy." This hymn echoes what is said in Isaiah 9:6 about the "child born to us," who will be named "Everlasting Father and Prince of Peace."

Yet those who appreciate the linkage of the Spirit with the future consummation of all things would have been happy to have found "Father of the world to come" ascribed to the Spirit. As we saw in Chapter 3 above, the NT does not explicitly follow the OT in representing the Spirit as operative in the creation and conservation of the world. Normally, when it introduces the theme, the NT claims the creative and conserving power of God for Christ (e.g., Jn 1:3; Col 1:16–17). By not attributing such power in the first creation to the divine Spirit, the NT allows the Holy Spirit's place in the fashioning of the new and final creation to shine forth more clearly (e.g., Rom 8:18–30). Through the liberating impact of the Holy Spirit, they experience and will experience the tripersonal God. The whole material world yearns in the painful convulsions of cosmic birth pangs (Rom 8:22), and the gift of the Spirit makes Christians in particular groan for their full transformation to come (Rom 8:23). Without being as obviously cosmic as Paul, Luke highlights the way the Spirit is *the* eschatological gift and power.

The time of the church, the interim time between the resurrection of the crucified Jesus and his final coming in glory, is the time of the Holy Spirit. Through the Spirit human history begins to take an even clearer shape as the trinitarian history of God. The Spirit sends Philip to join the Ethiopian official (Acts 8:29), directs Peter to meet the messengers from the centurion Cornelius (Acts 10:19—a point repeated in 11:12), and sets Barnabas and Paul apart for the decisive work among the Gentiles (Acts 13:2). The key to this worldwide mission, the Spirit guides in a special way the Christian leaders, who are to proclaim boldly the good news to all people. Their words form an *epiclesis* which calls down the Spirit to change the human race and its cosmos to become the final kingdom of God (Acts 28:31). We are all now in the time of the Spirit, the time of the ultimate consummation.

10.
Trinitarian Persons and Actions

"The three subjects are aware of each other through one consciousness which is possessed in a different way by the three of them."

Bernard Lonergan, *A Second Collection*

"When it is asked 'Three what?' then the great poverty from which our language suffers becomes apparent."

St. Augustine of Hippo, *De Trinitate*

Problems can be solved, but divine (and human) mysteries are to be pondered. When we ponder a mystery and refuse to dismiss it as either an irrational contradiction or a "mere" problem, it inevitably deepens. Nowhere else does such deepening happen more dramatically than in the case of the mystery of the divine Trinity. Is the trinitarian God one in mind, will, and action? If so, how can this be so? If the Father, the Son, and the Holy Spirit are one in mind, will, and action, in what sense can they be three persons? If the three act as one and so are one in nature, what room is left to distinguish three persons? Let us begin with the trinitarian persons.

Three Persons

How does our finite language of personhood fare when applied to God?[1] Do we conceive God as personal by using some finite model of personhood? Will we end up picturing God too much like created persons of our own experience? Such finite picturing can involve individuating the divine persons by distinguishing their separate bodies, which may be three angelic bodies at the home of Abraham and Sarah (the OT Trinity of Roublev and others) or two human bodies (along with the body of a dove) involved in the "throne of grace" compositions (see Chapters 1 and 3). If, however, we refuse to describe God in personal language and insist on other such language as *ground, source,* or *principle of creativity*, do we risk understanding God to be less and not more than personal? Principles and sources cannot love one another in the way persons can. Surely personal language is the best and highest language we have for speaking of and to the God revealed in Jesus Christ?

(a) Challenges

Applying to God our language for persons is not a straightforward affair. Ancient Christian thinkers had already become aware of the challenge. In *De Trinitate,* Augustine wrote:

> For, in truth, because the Father is not the Son, and the Son is not the Father, and the Holy Spirit, who is also called the Gift of God, is neither the Father nor the Son, then certainly there are three. Therefore, it was said in the plural number: "I and my Father are One" (Jn 10:30). But when it is asked "Three what?" then the great poverty from which our language suffers becomes apparent. But the formula "three persons" has been coined, not in order to give a complete explanation by means of it, but in order that we might not be obliged to remain silent. (5.10)

Augustine might also have appealed here to prayer: Personal language for God makes our prayer and deep relationship to God possible. How could one adore and glorify Rahner's "three distinct manners of subsisting"[2] or Barth's "the Revealer, the Revelation, and the Revealedness" (i.e., three modes of being)?[3] The somewhat modalistic language of Rahner and Barth is not well adapted for private prayer and public worship. One should add that they themselves did not propose these particular expressions as adapted for prayer and worship.

Those who insist on personal language for the Trinity must give some account of what they mean by *person.* From an original, almost Sabellian meaning of *public mask,* or the mask that an actor wore on the stage, *person* enjoyed a further history after the Council of Chalcedon built on the Council of Ephesus to introduce the notion (along with *hypostasis*) into the doctrine of the church (see Chapter 7) and was to evolve, for example, to the existential meaning of an *Ego* that was opposed to every other person in an autonomous and distinct freedom. A trajectory of development that led from Boethius to the Middle Ages arrived at Thomas Aquinas's classical description of *person* in his *Summa theologiae* as a "distinct subsistent in a rational nature (*subsistens distinctum in natura rationali*)" (1a.30.3 ad 4). Obviously *person* here goes beyond *hypostasis* because individual dogs and oak trees rank as hypostases or distinct subsistents.

Chapter 8 recalled the impact of Descartes, Locke, and others on subsequent versions of *person.* A psychological overlay stresses self-consciousness and freedom. Here we must beware, however, of those who talk glibly of "*the* modern concept of person," as if we had kept the word *person* from the patristic period but had simply changed its meaning.[4] This is to forget that psychological characteristics were not lacking in the fourth and fifth century, as we see very clearly in the case of Augustine of Hippo. This is also to ignore modern debates over the concept of *person.* Alongside those who interpret persons as conscious, autonomous selves, postmodern thinkers emphasize the opposite: the decentered and fragmented self, whose weak identity becomes the victim of powerful forces. But those believers who share such a postmodern outlook will almost certainly refrain from representing the three divine persons as three decentered, fragmented selves.

(b) Trinitarian Persons

However the contemporary debates go, certain themes, nevertheless, recur: Persons are conscious (or minded), free, and relational (or persons-in-community). The last characteristic has its special importance in curbing any desire to picture persons as autonomous, self-sufficient centers of consciousness and free activity, or even as self-absorbed individuals. Those who aspire to live as self-contained subjects and even as isolated individuals (who are "auto-nomous" almost in the sense of being a law unto themselves) become thereby less of a person in the sense that such a policy of shunning serious relationships and interdependence will not contribute to their lasting human growth and well-being. Authentic personhood does not spring out of one's private experience but is given and received within relationships. To be a person is to be an interpersonal subject, sharing love and giving oneself in love. True personal individuality comes by existing in and for other persons. We need each other in order to be ourselves.[5] Being a person does not precede interpersonal relations, as if we were first persons and only then in relationship. A newborn baby (and even more an unborn baby) never exists without being related to its mother, its father, and others. What I am saying here about the relational aspect of being a person and of personhood being interpersonhood commands, I believe, a fairly wide degree of acceptance.[6]

In the case of the Trinity, the relational aspect is both unique *and* crucial; otherwise one can slip into talk of three distinct centers of consciousness and decision making, an interpretation of the divine persons that seems to abandon monotheism and finish up with three gods in perfect dialogue among themselves. In other words, an individualistic conception of the fully personal, when applied to the tripersonal God, leads one to picture three independent, fully divine minds and wills, which could even slip into inadvertent conflict. Such a conception can hardly ward off tritheism or the idea of three self-sufficient subjects who enjoy a separate existence, always act together as a closely meshed community of divine individuals, but do not constitute one God. Of course, apart from the Trinity, all other cases of the multiplication of persons does mean a multiplication of minds and wills or a multiplication of individual instances of a rational nature.

Here, the distinction between divine and human persons (and the distinction between divine and human interrelationships) comes into sharp focus. In the case of the tripersonal God, the distinctness of interrelated persons is not constituted by a separation of conscious and free subjectivities. A threefold subsistence does not entail three consciousnesses and three wills, as if the three persons, each with their own separate characteristics, constituted a kind of divine committee. One consciousness subsists in a threefold way and is shared by all three persons, albeit by each of them distinctively. It is as if God realizes the dream expressed by the saying about persons very much in love with each other: "They are of one mind and heart." Unless we accept that all the divine essential or natural properties (like knowing, willing, and acting) are identical and shared in common by the three persons of the Trinity, it is very difficult to see how we can salvage monotheism. Each person must be seen to be identical with the divine nature or the substance of the godhead. Otherwise, the distinction between the three persons will be upheld at the expense of the real divine oneness; the divine unity will be something recognized only after the distinct and even separate constitution of the three persons.

How then are the divine relationships crucial and unique? They are just that because being person in God is defined *only* through relationship to the other persons. (Here the finite model of personhood does call for adjustment.) The three divine persons are mutually distinct only in and through their relations of origin. The internal relations between the three persons form their sole distinguishing feature. We can and should, for instance, follow Athanasius in holding that whatever we can say about the Father we can also say about the Son except that he is the Father. The Son retains his own particular, irreducible identity in relationship, as being begotten of the Father and not as being the unoriginate origin of divinity (and all reality). Thus the (subsistent) relations account for what differentiates (and unites) the one trinitarian reality. The three persons are who they distinctly are because of their relations to each other. The relational ordering, not subordination, within the Trinity answers the question: How does the Son get to be the Son and the Spirit get to be the Spirit? To use the classical language, in the Trinity there are three person-constituting relations: generating, being generated, "being spirated"—and a fourth, nonperson-constituting relation, the active spiration of the Spirit as a common peculiarity of the Father and the Son, something that belongs to the Son as deriving from the Father.[7]

The relational quality of personhood in God entails acknowledging that the three persons are persons in different ways. Because of the intradivine order of origin (in that the Son and the Holy Spirit are not the origin of the Father), there is an asymmetry between them. They are ordered to one another in an asymmetrical way. The self-giving of the Father, which is the condition for the self-giving of the Son, for example, happens in a way that cannot be reversed.

To say something about this relational, differentiated unity that is the divine life of unity-in-distinction and distinction-in-unity, the ideas of *koinonia*, or perfect communion, and *perichoresis* have often been pressed into service, as we saw in Chapter 7. In the trinitarian communion, the oneness does not happen at the expense of the true distinction between the persons or vice versa. The *perichoresis,* or mutual indwelling, means a supremely intense and blissful mutual presence, a reciprocal coinherence and participation in each other that, however, stops short of the three persons being swallowed up by each other or disappearing into each other. This trinitarian situation can recall the language of the Council of Chalcedon about the two natures of Christ existing in his one person "without confusion or division" (DH 302; ND 615). Nevertheless, we deal here with an analogy about irreducible identity and inseparable unity, not a strict parallel. Where Chalcedon addressed the relationship between the two *natures* of the one person (Christ), trinitarian doctrine faces the interpersonal relationships of three divine persons in a situation of only one divine nature.

The Trinity's *koinonia* or absolutely blissful communion of love presents itself as the ultimate ground and goal of all other such relations-in-communion. In a world where sharing and community have often tragically broken down, the *perichoretic* existence of the tripersonal God invites us to live in communion with each other and with our God. Because the divine life is one of total self-giving and unconditional sharing, human beings, because they are made in the divine image and likeness (Gn 1:26), are invited to exist in a communion and loving solidarity with each other and with the divine persons—an invitation and grace classically expressed by the climax of Jesus' high-priestly prayer (Jn 17:26). Wherever human beings struggle to preserve the unity of families and communities and the unity between societies and nations and do so in a way that does not suppress personal distinction, they are in fact transcribing the Trinity's life into their moral commitment.

The Trinity's Actions

This last paragraph has brought us to the second major theme of this chapter: our relationship with the Trinity and the divine actions in the world. In Chapter 7, we recalled what Athanasius and the Cappadocians proposed about the inseparable character of trinitarian operations—a teaching that became normal doctrine.[8] We may not allocate to the three persons different activities, as if the Father, the Son, and the Holy Spirit were separately Creator, Redeemer, and Sanctifier, respectively. In reflecting on the immanent Trinity, we should avoid the similar mistake of misusing Augustine's psychological analogy so as to identify the divine act of knowing with the person of the Son and the divine act of willing with the person of the Spirit. Yet, is there a threefold particularity that we can distinguish and appreciate in the divine operations *ad extra*? Granted that the divine actions *ad extra* are common and inseparable, does that mean that they are quite undifferentiated and indistinguishable?

A distinction suggested by Augustine and made by Thomas Aquinas will help us here: the distinction between a divine "action *ad extra*" and the "term" of such an action. Aquinas pointed to the case of the incarnation: All three divine persons are jointly involved in bringing it about, but the term or visible point of arrival, the Incarnate Son of God with his mission, is irreducibly special to the Word (ST 3a.3.1–4).[9]

Only the Son assumes a human existence and actualizes—or rather is—the personal being of Jesus. As regards the first person of the Trinity, only the Father eternally generates the Son, a life-giving act *ad intra* that finds its parallel *ad extra* in the Father raising the dead Jesus (see Paul's language about the resurrection in Chapter 3). The term of that action *ad extra* is also specific and distinct: the new, glorified life of Jesus, who with the Father sends the Spirit into the world.

We should also remember here the specificity of the Spirit's functional mission and ontological presence—a divine self-communication that is strictly related to the Son's mission, visibly expresses itself in the life of the church from the time of the first Pentecost, but does not take the form of a hypostatic or personal union.[10] Both (1) at the community level and (2) at that of individuals, the sending/coming of the Spirit, like the incarnation, is an action common to all three divine persons. But the Spirit is distinguishable and indirectly visible in the term of that action: the church and the lives of individuals in whom the Spirit dwells; in the Temple (upper case) and the temples (lowercase) of the Spirit (1 Cor 3:16–17; 6:9). The Spirit and the "bride" (i.e., the church) speak with one voice in calling for the final manifestation of the Son (Rv 22:17), but not the church and the Father (nor the church and the Son). In the lives of the baptized, the Spirit works to transform them into the image of Christ or "christify" them visibly, even as during the earthly life of Jesus the Spirit anointed him (Acts 10:38) and worked powerfully through him.

Apropos of creation, Aquinas also argued for a kind of order in that "the divine persons, according to the nature of their processions, have a causality respecting the creation of things." The "processions of the persons are the type of the production of creatures" (ST 1a.45.6).

A major iconographical counterpart to Aquinas's view of the three divine persons sharing in actions *ad extra* but doing so differently has to be the throne of grace, which the opening lines of Chapter 3 recalled. In that composition, the Father, the Son, and the Holy Spirit share in the crucifixion (and coming resurrection) but do so differently. Common activity is not automatically indistinguishable activity. A trinitarian "face" is to be seen both in the "economic" missions of the

Son and the Spirit and in creation itself. God's self-communication *ad extra* always assumes a threefold form because God is tripersonal *ad intra*. In creation and OT history, the Father spoke/acted both through the Word/Wisdom about to be incarnated and in the Spirit about to be poured out. Whether in the order of redemption or that of creation, God always speaks and acts through his Word and in the Spirit, even if we must add that what is hinted at in the created order is clearly revealed only in the total history of Jesus and his Spirit.

We can sum all this up by saying that the divine persons are communicated (gratuitously in human history), each in their own personal particularity and with a diversity that stems from and reveals their mutual relations. Thus the incarnation of the Logos reveals something proper about the Logos. The grace that makes us God's adopted sons and daughters comes from and points to the Son's eternal relationship to the Father, who gives himself to us precisely as the Father. Christian experience, while it recognizes the unity of divine action that directs us to the unity of the divine nature, also testifies to the impact of the Spirit who sets us with Son and allows us to pray: "Abba, Father" (Rom 8:14–17).

The tripersonal God, precisely as tripersonal, is intimately present to us and responsive to us but is never conditioned or changed by anything or anyone outside the Trinity. The relationship of God to the created world is uniquely asymmetrical. At every moment, creatures necessarily depend on God but not vice versa. The relationship that links the world to God is determinative for the world but not for God. The divine action totally shapes the world, but the world does not shape God. No work has caught better this asymmetrical relationship than *The Cloud of Unknowing:* "He [God] is thy being and thou not his."[11]

In struggling with the questions of personhood in God and the divine actions *ad extra,* this chapter has aimed at drawing on the biblical and traditional witness to propose positions that seem at least not to be flagrantly incoherent. Unless one boldly wants to defy the divine mystery, there is simply no possibility here of any positive and probative arguments. The next chapter will investigate a somewhat easier question: How should we name the three divine persons?

John 13: 12-15

Renewal of our enthusiasm —
rediscovering the joy of our call
to serve.

How that translates into our
deacon group. — mutual
support — commitment to
enhance each other's

11.
Naming the Trinity

"Jesus' striking use of Abba expressed his intimate experience of God as his own father and this usage made a lasting impression on his disciples."

Raymond Brown, *The Death of the Messiah*

"With the sweetly melodious harp of your divine heart, through the power of the Holy Spirit, the Paraclete, I sing to you, Lord God, adorable Father, songs of praise and thanksgiving on behalf of all creatures in heaven, on earth and under the earth; all which are, were, and shall be."

St. Gertrude of Helfta, *The Herald of Divine Love*

The naming of the three persons of the Trinity has been proving a divisive issue in parts of the Western world. Are *Father, Son, and Holy Spirit* truly proper names and even strictly personal names for God?[1] If they are, like *Helmut Kohl* or *Maria Montessori,* they cannot be replaced. But if we maintain that the trinitarian names only act in this way but are not as such proper names,[2] can they be replaced or should they be retained with the assurance of Basil of Caesarea: "We are bound to be baptized in the terms we have received and to profess faith in the terms in which we are baptized, and as we have professed faith in, so to give glory to the Father, Son, and Holy Spirit" (*Epistle,* 125.3)?

Current proposals for renaming the Trinity include: *Source, Word, and Spirit; Creator, Christ, and Spirit; Creator, Liberator, and Comforter; Creator, Redeemer, and Sanctifier; God, Christ, and Spirit; Parent, Child, and Paraclete; Mother, Daughter, and Spirit; Mother, Lover, and Friend; Spirit-Sophia, Jesus-Sophia, and Mother-Sophia;* and *Father, Child, and Mother.* With terms for sovereignty now played down in some or even many cultures, such names for God as *Lord, King*, and *Ruler* seem threatened. Pressure for inclusive God-language would rule out the first two names. What future should the more personal but gender-specific name of *Father* enjoy? Has the language of divine fatherhood, by fostering a male-related image of God, legitimated male domination, underpinned the power structure of patriarchal Christianity, supported idolatrous androcentrism, helped to produce a false fixing of roles between the sexes, and proved a major (if not the major) cause of women being oppressed in the Western world (and beyond)? Did biblical traditions by naming God *Father* presuppose an antiwoman orientation that should not be tolerated any more, because calling the first person of the Trinity by that name inevitably encourages sexist disvalues and chauvinist attitudes? Let us first recall some biblical data.

Biblical Witness

Jesus compared God's saving activity to a woman searching for lost money (Lk 15:8–10) or baking bread (Lk 13:20–21; par. in Mt 13:33). Jesus applied to God such images associated with women of his time and did not depict God in terms that would have been associated exclusively with male activities. John's Gospel pictures "the hour" of Christ's death and resurrection as birth pangs (Jn 16:21; 17:1). Patristic authors such as St. John Chrysostom (*Catecheses,* 3.19) have seen in the piercing of Jesus' body on the cross and the outpouring of the blood and water (Jn 7:37–39; 19:34) a double image. Christ not only gives rise to the Church like Adam giving rise to Eve but also nurtures his offspring like a mother. Reclaiming biblical (and traditional) language for God also entails recognizing that the Holy Spirit can be linked with giving birth (Jn 3:6; Rom 8:18–27). Thus, attention to the full scope of the NT and the tradition shows that the experience of God that led to the formulated doctrine of the Holy Trinity was by no means solely associated with male activities.

When we move from activities to naming, we find God identified as *Father* 254 times in the NT (with four other possible cases). Jesus' own experience and example gave rise to this development. As Raymond Brown puts it, "One is justified in claiming that Jesus' striking use of *Abba* did express his intimate experience of God as his own father and that this usage did make a lasting impression on his disciples."[3] Far from being One whose supreme quality is power and only concern is to dominate, the compassionate Father of whom Jesus spoke knows our needs before we ask, cares for all, and forgives all, even the wickedly unjust and sinful. Jesus' Father-image subverted any oppressive, patriarchal notions of God as primarily or even exclusively an authoritarian figure. Jesus also revealed the ultimate divine reality as the Father to whom he stood in a unique relationship as the Son; acting with filial consciousness he manifested the Father.

Then Jesus' resurrection (with the outpouring of the Holy Spirit) made him the eldest Son of the Father's new, eschatological family (Rom 8:29), a family now empowered to share intimately in Jesus' relationship to the Father in the Spirit. Matthew's Gospel ends with the command to baptize "in the name of the Father, and of the Son, and of the Holy Spirit" (Mt 28:19), a point of arrival for the NT that becomes a point of departure for the rites of initiation and creeds that will take their structure around the confession of faith in the Father, the Son, and the Holy Spirit. The voices of the NT and the Christian tradition harmonize in presenting Father, Son, and Holy Spirit as the primary (not exclusive) way of speaking about the tripersonal God. In particular, the early centuries of Christianity show how faith in Jesus as Son of God coincided with faith in God as Father. Thus Hilary of Poitiers called "the very center of a saving faith" the belief "not merely in God, but in God as Father, and not merely in Christ, but in Christ as the Son of God" (*De Trinitate*, 1.17).[4]

When the Trinity is named, *God the Father* functions validly if we align ourselves with the meanings communicated in that metaphor by the biblical witnesses (above all, by Jesus himself) and refuse to literalize it.[5] It is these meanings that convey true information about the tripersonal God. *Father* names personally the God revealed in Israel's history and known relationally as the *Abba* of Jesus' life, death, and resurrection (together with the outpouring of the Holy Spirit). *Father* fixes the reference when Christians speak distinctively of the tripersonal God and what they believe the Trinity to be like. The image and language of *Abba* emerged from Jesus' specific experience of God. Once we agree that language and experience, while distinguishable, belong inseparably to each other, we would misrepresent Jesus' experience if we insisted on replacing his central language for God. Fidelity to Jesus calls on believers to name the first person of the Trinity primarily as *Father,* which entails acknowledging Jesus himself (though once again not exclusively) as the Son of God.

By not arguing for an *exclusive* use of male names, I recognize that we do and should also use other names: Such a gender-neutral name as *Creator* for the first person of the Trinity and such a female name as *Wisdom* for the second person. Once we move beyond trinitarian formulations, many possibilities open up: well over 100 distinctive names for Jesus in the NT alone[6] and "God" (in the form of *ho Theos*) as the name with which the NT often designates God the Father. The question at issue is not the use of other distinctive names but rather the primary way of naming the Trinity when we use trinitarian formulations, and—in particular—the name *Father* for the first person.

When we call God *Father,* we are clearly not making a literal statement; that is to say, one in which we mean a male parent and so use the word in its primary, matter-of-fact biological sense. Nor are we introducing a simile; that is to say, using language in its customary sense and merely comparing God with some characteristic of a male parent. Here, as elsewhere, metaphor asserts an identity that simile lacks; hence, it can create a greater impact than a mere simile because of the tension entailed and because, literally speaking, it is partly false. From what we saw previously in Chapter 1, the metaphor of God as Father conveys falsity at the primary, literal level but truth at the metaphorical level. Indisputably taking this metaphor literally—that is, forgetting it is an extended use of language—can only result in a distorted and oppressive version of the first person of the Trinity. Setting such misuse aside, we need to add something more on the positive side. This particular metaphor communicates a challenge as well as truth.

As was pointed out in Chapter 1, God is King established itself as a predominant metaphor in the OT, occurring much more often than metaphors about God as Husband and Father. In naming the divine King of Israel, the OT praises God for doing what earthly kings should do but frequently fail to do. God feeds the hungry, protects strangers, supports widows and orphans, and sees that justice is done for the oppressed (Ps 146:5–10). Far from being taken from common kingly conduct of the time, this picture of divine kingship stands in judgment over the repeated failure of Israel's human kings to secure the rights of the weak and defenseless. Similarly, the picture that Chapter 1 painted of the OT metaphor of God as Father to the whole people and to individuals, so far from being drawn from fatherhood as commonly practiced in the Ancient Middle East, reproves and criticizes the harsh way many fathers acted toward their children. The metaphor God is Father evaluates and finds wanting the standard practices of fathers in patriarchal societies. No human fathers can match the standard of compassionate love and constant care set by God. Recalling the tender providence of the divine Father, one can easily concur with the injunction: "Call no one your father on earth, for you have one Father—the one in heaven" (Mt 23:9).

Some later books of the NT may seem to tamper with the ideal portrait of divine fatherhood to be drawn from the OT and, even more, from Jesus' proclamation of *Abba,* whose nonpatriarchal behavior is illustrated by the parable of the prodigal son, and from the letters of Paul (see Chapter 3). A household code of conduct that lists domestic virtues and has much in common with popular Hellenistic philosophy turns up in various Deutero-Pauline and later letters (Eph 5:21–6:9; Col 3:18–4:1; 1 Tm 2:8–15; 6:1–2; Ti 2:1–15; 1 Pt 2:18–3:7).[7] Normally arranged according to three sets of superiors (husbands, parents, and masters) and subordinates (wives, children, and slaves), this household code calls on the first set to be responsible and the second set to be obedient.[8] The code receives a Christian perspective and motivation. Authority should be exercised with understanding and love. Thus two passages exhort fathers to protect and encourage the lives of their children: "Fathers, do not provoke your children to anger, but bring them up in the discipline and instruction of the Lord" (Eph 6:4; see Col 3:21).

Yet, we should take our distance from some aspects of these domestic rules for patriarchal society that accepted, for instance, the institution of slavery even while recognizing the idealized color given to them by faith in Christ. But—and this is relevant to the present chapter—no passage suggests that human fatherhood, even when virtuously practiced according to this domestic code of conduct, provides the source and standard for naming God *Father.* Indeed, one possible translation of Eph 3:14 would suggest the very opposite, when it speaks of adoring "the Father, from whom all fatherhood in heaven and earth takes its name."[9] Whatever exegesis we adopt here, one thing is clear: No NT example of a household code even implies the message, "You Christian fathers represent God and your example shapes our proper image of the Father in heaven."

Christians of the NT period and the following centuries experienced God as Father (e.g., Rom 8:15; Gal 4:6) and did not draw their sense of *Abba* from the patriarchal system of Greco-Roman culture, let alone from pagan images of the divine. Justin Martyr, for instance, found the father image of Zeus revolting: "A parricide and son of a parricide, being overcome by the love of evil and shameful pleasures, he came into Ganymede and those many women he seduced" (*First Apology,* 21). Far from being a Christianized version of such an unscrupulous, exploitative tyrant, "The heavenly Father desires the repentance of sinners, rather than their punishment" (ibid., 15).

Renaming the Trinity

Having recalled some relevant data, let us return to the question of names for the Trinity. Suppressing the traditional naming of the Trinity would mean loss rather than gain. Such alternate proposals for the first person as *Source* and *Parent* sound remote, even impersonal, and nowhere near as directly relational as *Father.* Unquestionably, these alternatives contain or imply some personal and relational elements and are not intended to subvert Christian belief in a personal God. But if we try using (exclusively?) *Source, Parent,* and so forth as forms of address to God, we will perceive the superiority of *Father.* Some of the alternative triads (e.g., *Creator, Christ, and Spirit*) have a strong Arian flavor about them, as if only the first person of the Trinity were properly divine, possessed the power of creation, and had in fact freely created out of nothing Christ and the Spirit. One might object here that Hilary of Poitiers said something similar when he wrote of faith "in the Creator, the Only-Begotten, and the Gift." Yet, he used such language immediately after recalling Jesus' mandate to baptize "in the name of the Father, and of the Son, and of the Holy Spirit" (*De Trinitate,* 2.1.33). The context for Hilary's alternate triad removed any sense of Arian ambiguity.

Although it may claim some kind of NT pedigree (perhaps in Acts 3:13,26; 4:27,30), "Child" (as in *Parent, Child, and Paraclete* and *Father, Child, and Mother*) seems to depreciate the second person of the Trinity, as if the Son were not yet properly mature. Moreover, to use *Father, Child, and Mother* could seem a little like a rerun of a Gnostic myth summarized by Irenaeus as *Father, Mother, and Son* (*Adversus Haereses,* 1.29). Renaming the first person of the Trinity in different ways could well mean saying something different and changing basic belief. A certain crypto-modalism comes through some of the alternate proposals I listed: *Creator, Liberator, and Comforter,* for instance, can readily suggest a monopersonal God who behaves toward us in creative, liberating, and comforting ways but whose inner life is not differentiated into three divine persons. Another triad, *Creator, Redeemer, and Sanctifier,* can claim considerable background in

Christian tradition. But if used by itself, it fails to distinguish Christianity from other religions in a way that naming *Father, Son, and Holy Spirit* does. After all, other religions can and do profess faith in deities who create (or in some lesser way make), redeem, and sanctify human beings. The names *Father, Son,* and *Holy Spirit* tie Christian faith firmly into the revealing and saving history that culminated in the events of the first Good Friday and Easter Sunday. Once again, let me insist that I am speaking about the primary way of naming the Trinity, the three names used in the Nicene-Constantinopolitan Creed. This does not mean that such formal trinitarian language is the only way of speaking about and addressing God. In these days, we may need more than ever some alternatives to prevent our "Father" language from collapsing into crass literalism.

All in all, I would maintain that a persuasive case can be made for maintaining *Father, Son, and Holy Spirit* as the principal (but not, I repeat, exclusive) way for naming the Christian God. What Basil of Caesarea says about *the Holy Spirit* being the "chief and distinguishing name" for the third person of the Trinity (*De Spiritu Sancto,* 9.22) applies also to the traditional names of *Father* and its correlative, *Son*. These names fix historical references, convey insights, and preserve the core of Christian identity. Alongside the name *Jesus,* nothing else so expresses our continuity with the faith of first Christians and their successors down through the ages. It seems to me to be no accident that the familiar and frequent practice of "the sign of the cross" draws together both items: the historical crucifixion of Jesus and the invocation of the Trinity.

In arguing at fuller length for the traditional naming of the tripersonal God, one would need to go back to earlier centuries, examining—for instance—the trinitarian language of Richard of St. Victor about the Lover, the Beloved, and the Co-Beloved. Does Richard's language, despite his intentions, encourage a tritheistic picture of the "Best of Friends," three gods whose utterly unselfish love for each other keeps them eternally "friends together?" Then in the twentieth century, how should one evaluate the proposals of Karl Barth (1886–1968) about the one God who subsists in three divine "modes of being" (the Revealer, the Revelation, and the Revealedness) and the reflections of Karl Rahner (1904–1984) on three divine "manners of subsistence"? Certainly the concerns of Johann Gottlieb Fichte (1762–1814) about the finite nature of our talk of personhood should be heard. Nevertheless, if we do not use personal language when speaking of and to God, will we finish up saying less rather than more about God?

Admittedly no language is adequate when we talk about and name God. We know so little of God; revelation, so far from making God less mysterious, lets the divine mystery come through even more powerfully. Nevertheless, the experience of Jesus and of his first followers helps us discern and decide what to say about God. There is some truth status in the three names, the *Father,* the *Son,* and the *Holy Spirit.* These are names we can use when speaking to God in the setting of trinitarian prayer. Our language of devotion should guide the language of "scientific," theological explanation. The next chapter will complete this exploration of trinitarian faith by examining possible analogies for the God who is Father, Son, and Holy Spirit.

12.
IMAGES OF THE TRINITY

"Those who have not believed will not experience; and those who have not experienced will not know."
St. Anselm of Canterbury, *Epistola de Incarnatione Verbi*

"An absolute, eternal, and infinite Self-existence, Self-awareness, Self-delight of being that secretly supports and pervades the universe even while it is also beyond it, is then the first truth of spiritual experience."
Sri Aurobindo, *The Life Divine*

Earlier chapters reported analogies used by Tertullian, Augustine, Richard of St. Victor, and others in their attempts to articulate something of their trinitarian faith. Wonderful trinitarian images were developed by Hildegard of Bingen, Gertrude of Helfta, and other women mystics in the Middle Ages.[1] Some of these analogies and images came from the physical world, as was the case of Tertullian's appeal to the model of a "fountain" that gives rise to a river and a canal, or with Hildegard's vision of a bright human figure (the Son) surrounded by light that is both white (the Father) and red (the Spirit) (*Scivias,* 2.2). Human life supplied analogies, as with Augustine's psychological model of the Trinity or Richard of St. Victor's appeal to true human love that involves the lover, the beloved, and the co-beloved. While this appeal could find only a general support in the NT (e.g., 1 Jn 4:8,16), other analogies might claim a firmer starting point in the NT; for instance, in Paul's comparison between the Holy Spirit and the human spirit (1 Cor 2:10–11).

In this concluding chapter, I want to serve the readers by pulling together the whole book. My way for doing this is through reflecting on some major analogies (or comparisons) and images (or pictures) that trinitarian theology has taken up from the beginning of Christianity. Obviously, not all analogies can be classed as images (i.e., mental, visual, or verbal pictures) because some analogies (e.g., A is to B as X is to Y) remain quite abstract. I take models to be elaborated analogies and/or images, such as the model of the body used at times to describe the church.

But first a word about the search for analogies or likenesses. A desire to place something or to relate it to our other beliefs and pieces of knowledge fuels the quest for comparisons. Those who compare things and look for analogies between them, should ask: What features do they have in common? What features are not shared? In what respects do they correspond or fail to correspond? The act of comparing may allow us to detect many close similarities or only a few, slight similarities. The extent to which a correspondence shows up firmly will determine the strength and usefulness of an analogy—that is to say, its power to explain and illuminate. Undoubtedly, when we face the ultimate mystery of the tripersonal God, we cannot hope to come up with anything like a successful analogy that displays many common elements. As the Fourth Lateran Council insisted in 1215 (DH 806; ND 320), any similarity between God and creatures will always be characterized by an even greater dissimilarity. We should be properly humble and negative in our theologizing, remembering the infinite differences and acknowledging that here, if anywhere, all analogies end in apophatic silence. That said, what are some analogies and images that are available?

Top-Down Models

The story of Jesus being virginally conceived, especially as we read it in Luke 1:26–38, could encourage us to express vertically and from above the order of the trinitarian persons as Father, Holy Spirit, and Son. Through the Spirit (who proceeds from the Father), the Father (who is the ultimate fountainhead of deity and all reality) generates the Son; the Spirit is not the Father of Jesus. In his human existence, Jesus is created through the power of the Spirit but obviously not from the divine substance of the Spirit. For his "economic" mission, Jesus is conceived through the Spirit but is sent by the Father and not by the Spirit (e.g., Mk 9:36–37; 12:6 parr.; Rom 8:3).

This picture that can be drawn from the annunciation scene corresponds to the way in which Mark, followed closely by Matthew and Luke, images the baptism: from heaven the voice of the Father, the descent of the Spirit under the form of a dove, and right at the bottom the Son coming out of the water (Mk 1:9–11). Thus the annunciation and baptism scenes yield a similar spatial ordering and top-down picture. Both scenes have inspired Christian artists, who at times have added above the descending dove a divine hand or even the figure of the bearded, kingly Father (inspired by the "Ancient of Days" in Dn 7:9). Whatever one says about these additions, the artists have rightly glimpsed in the baptism story the most vivid trinitarian event in the whole NT, one event in which the three persons all share, albeit differently. In the case of the transfiguration scene (Mk 9:2–8), they have taken the cloud on the mountaintop to symbolize the Holy Spirit or else have added a field of light to include the Spirit. Yet, the fact remains that the NT texts are less explicitly trinitarian for the transfiguration than they are for the baptism of Jesus.

In the baptism, the ordering of the three persons corresponds to that which we find expressed in a Deutero-Pauline prayer for wisdom (Eph 3:14–17). It also corresponds to a theme mentioned in the introduction to this book: the *epiclesis* or eucharistic invocation of the Holy Spirit, which asks that the Spirit descend upon the gifts to change them into the body and blood of Christ for the spiritual profit of those who receive them. Through the presence of the Spirit, the eucharistic presence of Christ is actualized.

At the end of his Gospel and in Acts, Luke changes the order of Father-Spirit-Son into Father-Son-Spirit. At Pentecost the ordering takes the shape of the Father raising and setting the Son at his right hand so that he might receive and pour out the Spirit upon the world (Acts 2:32–33). In this "mon-archical" (one *arche,* or principle) and top-down scheme, with the Spirit sent from the enthroned Father through the Son, the Father also remains the sole fountainhead of all divinity and reality. This holds good of the second-century picture from Irenaeus that we introduced in Chapter 5: the Son and the Holy Spirit being and functioning as the "two hands" of God. This particular version of the top-down model clearly shows that the Father is not from another and does not owe his being to any other cause. The Son is generated by the Father; the Spirit, in coming "after" the Son, owes its substance to the Father. One is left wondering as to what distinguishes the Son and the Spirit and how they are connected. Because Irenaeus himself (while probably thinking of the two hands of the divine potter) says very little, one might expound the image in the language of later times. Should we think of the two hands of God functioning beautifully together like the two hands of a master pianist, or like the two hands of a champion golfer? In either case, the two hands belong so intimately to the player that we hardly distinguish them from the pianist or the golfer. From that point of view, the Irenaean analogy saves the unity but may lose the threeness.

In both the Lukan Pentecost scheme and Irenaeus's two-hands analogy, some other difficulties can recur that Chapter 7 showed Athanasius to have faced. The Pentecost pattern of the Spirit being from the Father through the Son could suggest to the unwary that the Father is a divine grandfather and the Spirit the grandchild in question. Irenaeus's picture might make the Son and the Spirit look like siblings. In both the Pentecost and the Irenaean picture, one risks subordinationism or making the Son and the Spirit look less, even much less, than the Father.

Serial Models

Hints of subordinationism seem less apparent in Augustine's model of love (see Chapter 7), in which the Spirit is the Bond (uppercase) of mutual love between the Father and the Son. A speculative difficulty here is that the distinct personality of the Spirit may not come through. In an I-Thou relationship, the love that two persons bestow on each other is not a third person or at least does not easily emerge as an activity that defines a person distinct from the I and the Thou. Nevertheless, what is not true at the human level (where we only *have* love) could be true at the divine level (where God *is* love). Moreover, this model resonates well with the Christian experience of trinitarian prayer, grounded in the Son's new presence in the history of salvation and then recorded and encouraged by St. Paul (e.g., Rom 8:9–27; 1 Cor 2:9–16). Those who pray are taken by the Spirit into the divine conversation, the exchange of ongoing love between the Father and the Son. This claim can be tested, both in public worship and private prayer, by deliberately aligning oneself with the experience expressed by these two Pauline passages. Moreover, Richard of St. Victor's interpretation of God as absolute communion of love (in a movement from self-love, to mutual love, and on to shared love) develops attractively the love analogy in trinitarian theology.

Chapter 7 sketched the way Augustine himself explored the highest human activities of knowing and loving as the best analogy for the Trinity's life. He expounded the generation of the Son in terms of the Father's act of thought, with the Holy Spirit as the fruit and reality of their mutual love. Some have criticized this psychological analogy, drawn from the mind's knowledge of itself and love of itself, for encouraging a monopersonal, even modalist, view of God. Does this intrapersonal analogy "save" the divine unity but "lose" the threeness of God? How can the divine knowing and willing illuminate the existence in God of more than one person?

Augustine held, as Chapter 7 pointed out, that the Father endows the Son with the capacity to produce the Spirit. In the original sense (*principaliter*), the Spirit proceeds from the Father; hence, Augustine argued for the procession of the Spirit taking place from the Father and the Son, "as from one principle (*tanquam ab uno principio*)" and not independently from the Son. Thus the Son forms with the Father a single co-principle for the breathing of the Spirit and is in no way an independent source for the Spirit. Even then, as we saw, Eastern theologians fear that this subordinates the Spirit to the Son, as well as tampers with belief in the Father as the ultimate fountainhead of deity.

Christian Art

In recalling some of the top-down and serial models used to express trinitarian faith, we have already here and there mentioned some contributions of Christian art. A circle represents perfection, and, in the symbolism of numbers, a triangle is equivalent to the number three. To express trinity in unity, some artists have been content with such abstract versions of the trinitarian mystery, expressing the tripersonal God as three concentric circles, as a triangle, as a triangle that contains a circle (or is surrounded by a circle), or as three overlapping circles contained within a triangle. Gothic art, which lasted from the twelfth to the sixteenth century, found the triangle representing the Trinity to be essential. Taking up the theme of radiant light (e.g., Heb 1:3; the Nicene Creed; Justin; and Tertullian), other artists have represented the Trinity as three torches, with the second and third lit from the first but not diminishing its brightness. In a representational vein that follows the NT image of the risen Christ sitting at the right hand of the Father, artists have sometimes portrayed the Father and the Son sitting side by side, with the Holy Spirit above and between them. Much more often artists, or at least Western artists such as El Greco, have presented the Father holding the cross with the Son dead on it (or the Father simply holding the dead body of the Son) with the Holy Spirit as dove hovering between them.

Generally, artists have been content with the NT symbol of the Spirit as a dove, but not always.[2] A fresco in the Gothic Church of St. James in Urschalling (near Chiemsee in Bavaria) depicts the Spirit as a lovely woman embraced by the Father (on her left) and by the Son (on her right). This fresco gives the Spirit more visual weight than the frequent symbol of the dove. Occasionally, art has symbolized the Trinity as three men, side by side. In a somewhat grotesque mood that may betray anxiety about maintaining the unity in triunity, it has pictured three human faces on one head and even three heads emerging out of one neck. Leaving symbols drawn from human life behind, a fifteenth-century window in Paderborn Cathedral presents three hares that share their ears—a motif that can also be found elsewhere, in an English church of Long Melford.

Trinitarian icons based on the three angels who visit Abraham and Sarah (Gn 18:1–15) have the notable advantage not only of bringing out God's spiritual nature but also of firmly locating trinitarian faith in the story of salvation history. Even if the famous Roublev version of this Genesis scene expresses the majestic beauty and grace of the tripersonal God and (through the table, the chalice, and the tree in the background) hints at the climax of the divine self-communication in Jesus' passion, death, and resurrection, other icons that represent this scene bring out more emphatically the story of salvation. They introduce the figures of Abraham and Sarah, as well as that of the servant who prefigures Christ's death by slaying the tender calf.

Other Analogies

In attempting to give some explanation of how God can be both one and three, some have turned to impersonal analogies; for instance, one flag with three distinct bands of color, or one plant (like the Irish shamrock) with trifoliate leaves. The latter analogy looks slightly better than the first, inasmuch as it involves a living being and not simply pieces of cloth. Tertullian introduced material images for the Trinity, for example, that of the spring, the river, and the canal. Undeniably the continuity of water can point to the unity in the divine substance. Yet, there are limits here. For instance, a canal flows very slowly, if at all, and necessarily much slower than a river. A canal does not come across as a good image for the Holy Spirit. In the twentieth century, G. L. Prestige offered a comparison that could please those who love mountains: the Matterhorn. Its three faces (the northern, the eastern, and the Italian) present completely one identical object. Likewise, one and the same divine substance has three "presentations," which/who are nevertheless distinct.[3] This analogy, however, implies the modalist sense of a monopersonal deity presented in three ways. Besides, like the analogies of the tricolor flag and the shamrock, it does not allow for God's being immaterial and nonspatial, and it lacks the dynamic movement and sense of the Father's being the source of divinity conveyed by Tertullian's spring-river-canal image. That image also has some merit by suggesting the relations of origin. But, all in all, material analogies for the Trinity run into problems over the spiritual nature of God and the personal distinctions within the deity.

Inspired by fourth-century writer Marius Victorinus, others have turned to the world of sound for their comparisons: One and the same sound can involve a speaker, the word spoken, and the breath or voice that carries the sound to us. Besides highlighting the dynamic unity of the Trinity, this analogy has the advantage of drawing on the personal world, even if it remains blatantly "monopersonal" in character.

The same is true of a further analogy for the Trinity that was developed by C. G. Jung and that we recalled in Chapter 8. He drew on the human experience of psychological growth. In the child's state of consciousness, the Father is the authority figure who provides a ready-made pattern of existence, the parent to whose laws one submits. The Son is represented by the process of self-individuation and conflict when a growing human being painfully seeks autonomy. The third phase, when an adult individual surrenders independence to share in some larger reality, symbolizes the Spirit.[4] An obvious drawback to this comparison is that it may be personal, but it remains monopersonal.

Further threefold patterns of common human experience have been pressed into trinitarian service. Hindu mysticism contributes the *saccidananda* triad: being, awareness of being, and enjoyment of being.[5] The personalist philosophy of Martin Buber and others has offered theologians the language of I, Thou, and We when talking about the ultimate, relational reality of God. This scheme has been associated with Plato's Family Triad of father, mother, and child (*Timaeus,* 50d). The mutual knowledge and love of the parents gives rise to and is completed by the child. However, besides the sense of a certain inferiority of the third person (the child), this scheme seems to produce the order of Father, Holy Spirit, and Son.

These images of the tripersonal God—that come, respectively, from psychological development, a mystical philosophy of being, and the language of community—offer help toward grasping just a little the "immanent" Trinity. But they are all taken from created reality and general human experience and are not immediately rooted in that particular history of God's revealing and saving self-communication that came to its climax in the dying and rising of Jesus, along with the sending of the Spirit. Christian reflection on God begins with the economic Trinity, the story that revealed Father, Son, and Holy Spirit and gave rise to the worshiping community. Our language about the immanent Trinity must not lose its link to the special experience of salvation in biblical and postbiblical times. Once we forget the divine presence in that history and our lives, we may be merely manipulating concepts in our minds.

The special history of God's self-communication reached its peak with the events of the first Good Friday and Easter Sunday. The paschal mystery revealed God as the Giver, the Given, and the Self-Giving. For us all and for our salvation, the Father gave up the Son (Rom 8:32). The Son was given up (1 Cor 11:23) or gave himself up (Gal 2:20). The Spirit, who is the process of Self-giving, gave Christ the new life in the resurrection in which we too can share (Rom 8:11). To put things thus is to retrieve a sense of how the original Christian belief in the tripersonal God was clearly founded in the resurrection of the crucified Jesus. Whenever Christians make the sign of the cross "in the name of the Father, and of the Son, and of the Holy Spirit," their invocation and gesture associate belief in the tripersonal God with the Easter mystery. Even without realizing it, they link their faith in the Trinity with the events of the first Good Friday and Easter Sunday.

In and through all their sufferings, the destiny of human beings depends on the tripersonal God. No one put this more emphatically than Masaccio in his version of the throne of grace in the church of Santa Maria Novella in Florence. He presents a trinitarian revelation of the cross as answering the radical perplexities of our salvation and future. Below Masaccio's trinitarian image, you see a skeleton with its message: "I was what you are, and what I am you will be." Our longings are infinite, but our human experiences remain finite, and all experiences end with the silence of death. Trinitarian faith, so our introduction insisted, expresses itself in and as (1) knowledge, (2) worship, and (3) action. We speak *of* the tripersonal God in our theological knowledge, *to* God in our prayer, and *for* God through our prophetic action. But knowing will drift off into empty speculation, while action will either lose its energy or lapse into self-protective ideology, unless both our knowing and acting draw life from worship. Apart from prayer before the trinitarian throne of grace, which reveals a divine love that totally gives and receives, there is no answer to the ultimate question of our death.

Right here and now, we live and move and have our being (Acts 17:28) in the embrace of the tripersonal God, who is known through faith and prayer. Enfolded by the Trinity, we can replicate in worship Paul's experience of the divine persons that anticipates the final communion with them and the glorious consummation to come (Rom 8:9–30). Communing with the tripersonal God is, or should be, our most natural activity. In his glorified humanity, the crucified and risen Jesus has gone ahead of us all into the life of God. In our turn, we are called to share forever his presence and to enter the infinitely communicative divine love. Both here and hereafter, we can say: "Outside the Trinity there is no salvation (*extra Trinitatem nulla salus*)." Far from being an abstract speculation or a doctrine to which Christians are called to pay lip service, belief in the Trinity is a matter of our human life, death, and life forever.

EPILOGUE
A CODA

The God in whom we all live and move and have our being (Acts 17:28) is tripersonal. Closer to us than we are to ourselves, God is Father, Son, and Holy Spirit—with each person communicated to us and present to us in a unique way. We experience here, and hereafter we will look upon, the tripersonal God. Where words fall away into silence, music may help. After all my words, I want to close with a hymn to the Trinity. Brian Wren wrote the text and Marty Haugen made a popular arrangement of the music (as found in the *Gather* hymnal published by G.I.A.). Wherever and whenever this book of mine is used for a course, I hope that teachers and students will end by singing together "How Wonderful the Three-in-One."

Wren has drawn on Richard of St. Victor for his trinitarian language of Lover, Beloved, and Equal Friend. He highlights the tripersonal being of God right from the title and the opening line, "the Three-in-One," rather than "the One-in-Three." "Communing love in shared delight" leads us to the infinite happiness that is the shared life of the Trinity, a theme treasured by Richard but often ignored by later, over-solemn studies of the Trinity. "Energies of dancing light" recalls the "activities" (in Greek "energies") of the Holy Spirit (e.g., 1 Cor 12:6,10), the biblical image of God as Light, the Creed's confession of the Son relating to the Father as *Light from Light,* and the patristic theme of *perichoresis,* or interpenetration of the three persons.

Wren's first verse (just as the fifth verse will do) praises the "immanent Trinity" or three persons in their eternal life together. He then follows the Creed's pattern and order: from the Creator conceiving and bringing all things to birth (verse 2), to the Son coming in time "to heal our brokenness and loss" (verse 3), and on to the Spirit calling us to share in "Love's communing life" (verse 4). The final verse switches the order to "Divine Belov'd" (the Son) and "Empow'ring Friend" (the Spirit) to "Eternal Lover" (the Father)—the trinitarian sequence found in Ephesians 2:18.

The whole hymn blends beautifully praise of the tripersonal God (or doxology) with gratitude for the divine work of creation and redemption (or soteriology). The title and the opening words of the first and last verses put the emphasis on the wonderful glory of God. Please join me, Brian Wren, and Marty Haugen now in singing our trinitarian theology.

"How Wonderful the Three-in-One."

"How wonderful the Three-in-One, / Whose energies of dancing light / Are undivided, pure and good, / Communing love in shared delight.

Before the flow of dawn and dark, / Creation's Lover dreamed of earth, / And with a caring deep and wise, / All things conceived and brought to birth.

The Lover's own Belov'd in time, / Between the cradle and a cross, / At home in flesh, gave love and life / To heal our brokenness and loss.

Their Equal Friend all life sustains / With greening pow'r and loving care, / And calls us born again by grace, / In Love's communing life to share.

How wonderful the Living God: / Divine Belov'd, Empow'ring Friend, / Eternal Lover, Three-in-One, / Our hope's beginning, way and end."

GLOSSARY

Ad extra. The actions and relations of the Trinity "outside" or toward creatures.

Ad intra. The life and relations of the Trinity "within" or between the divine persons.

Adoptionists. All those in the ancient world and in modern times who hold that Christ was a mere man who was adopted by God at the baptism or the resurrection.

Arians. Those who followed Arius of Alexandria in asserting that God's Son did not always exist and hence was not divine by nature but only the first among creatures.

Cappadocians. The fourth-century saints from Cappadocia, a region of modern Turkey—above all, Basil the Great, Gregory of Nyssa (Basil's brother), and Gregory of Nazianzus (Basil's friend).

Consubstantial. Of one and the same substance or essence.

Deists. Those in modern times who accept the existence of the Creator but reject in principle any special divine revelation or activity. The Deist "God" leaves nature and human history to unfold according to their own laws.

Demiurge. A name used by Plato for the divine architect of the world and by Gnostics for an inferior deity who made the material universe that they despised.

Economic Trinity. The Trinity as active and revealed in the plan ("economy") for creating and saving human beings and their world.

Eschatology. The study of the "last things" or God's final kingdom.

Essence. The indispensable properties that together characterize whatever exists and that are needed for its existence; often called in Greek *ousia* and in Latin *substantia*.

Filioque. "And from the Son"; a word added to the Nicene-Constantinopolitan Creed by a Spanish synod in 675 to affirm that the Holy Spirit "proceeds" from the Father *and* the Son.

Generation. The origin from a living being of another living being that shares the same nature; numerically the same nature in the case of God's Son and generically the same in the case of human offspring.

Gnosticism. A movement emerging in the second century A.D. that promised salvation through *gnosis,* or esoteric knowledge of spirit, being freed from matter.

Homoousios. Of one and the same substance (i.e., consubstantial), as opposed to *homoiousios,* or of a similar substance.

Hypostasis. That which "stands under" an individual existing being; a person in the case of beings of a rational nature.

Immanence. God's presence everywhere and in everything.

Immanent Trinity. The radically mysterious existence together of the three divine persons in their eternal life.

Logos. Word: either the interior word of thought or the exterior word of speech.

Macedonians. Fourth-century heretics who denied the divinity of the Holy Spirit; they drew their name from Macedonius, a Bishop of Constantinople who was deposed in 360.

Middle Platonism. A development from the philosophy of Plato (d. 347 B.C.) that lasted from the first century B.C. until the third century A.D. To protect the absolute divine "otherness," it elaborated notions of intermediary agents.

Modalists. Those who so stress the unity of "Father, Son, and Holy Spirit" that they deny any personal distinction within God; they understand the three divine names to refer merely to the modes, or manners, in which the monopersonal God acts and is revealed.

Monarchians. Those who stressed the *one* principle (*arche*) in God, sometimes to the point of denying any personal distinctions within the divinity.

Monotheism. Belief in one (and only one) personal, all-powerful, all-knowing, and all-loving God, who is the creator and Lord of everyone and everything and yet exists distinct from and beyond the whole universe.

Nature. The essential properties that characterize some individual living being and that are expressed in its activity.

Neoplatonism. A philosophy that dominated from the third to the sixth century A.D. and that understood all beings to derive in concentric circles from a single spiritual source, identified as the One and the Good.

Ontology. The study of being and the necessary truths of all beings; frequently synonymous with metaphysics.

Ousia. Essence or substance.

Patripassians. "Father sufferers" or those early third-century monarchian modalists who elaborated the consequence of their heresy—the Father became incarnate, suffered the passion and died on the cross.

Perichoresis. The reciprocal presence and interpenetration of the three divine persons.

Person. A distinct individual with the power to know, love, and act freely in relationship with other human beings and their world.

Platonism. A philosophy that highlights the otherness of God and the higher world of ideas over against the visible, changing world.

Pneumatomachians. "Spirit fighters" or those fourth-century heretics who denied the divinity of the Holy Spirit.

Procession. The derivation of the Holy Spirit from the Father (who is not derived from another divine person) through the Son (who derives from the Father through generation).

Sabellians. Followers of Sabellius (third century A.D.); they belonged among the modalist monarchians by denying distinct persons in God.

Soteriology. The systematic study of God's "work" in saving human beings and their world through Jesus Christ.

Spiration. The "breathing" or procession of the Holy Spirit from the Father through the Son.

Stoicism. A school of philosophy called after the *stoa* or porch in Athens, where its founder, Zeno (d. 263 B.C.), taught; it understood God and the divine energy to pervade everything.

Subordinationists. Those who assigned an inferior status to the Son and the Holy Spirit as being "under" and derived from the Father. The

Arians went to the extreme of declaring the Son and the Spirit to be creatures, and so infinitely inferior.

Substance. That which "stands under," or the essential characteristics shared in common with those of the same nature.

Transcendence. The otherness of God who goes beyond the created world and is not to be identified with it.

Tritheism. The belief in three separate gods who choose to exist and function together. This belief differs sharply from orthodox trinitarian faith in three divine persons who constitute one God.

Unitarians. Those who accept only one divine person. In practice, they converge with Adoptionists, Arians, Deists, Modalists and Sabellians.

Vestigia Trinitatis. Traces of the Trinity; hints of the tripersonal God to be found in the created world and especially in human existence.

NOTES

1. The Old Testament Background

1. On monotheism, see A. Schenker, "Le monothéisme israélite: un dieu qui transcende le monde e les dieux," *Biblica* 78 (1997), 436–48; A. V. Ström et al., "Monotheismus," *Theologische Realenzyklopädie,* vol. 23. 233–62; J. J. Scullion, "God (OT)," ABD vol. 2, 1041–48.

2. See G. O'Collins and D. Kendall, *The Bible for Theology* (Mahwah, NJ: Paulist Press, 1997), 83–86.

3. M. Rose, "Names of God in the OT," ABD, vol. 4, 1001–11.

4. Sheffield: JSOT Press, 1989, 160.

5. This reproach fits into an OT context, which highly treasures reverence for parents (Dt 5:16; 21:18–21).

6. G. Vermes, *The Dead Sea Scrolls in English* (Harmondsworth: Penguin Books, 3d ed., 1987), 192 (i.e., IQH 9.34–35).

7. See J. L. Crenshaw, *Old Testament Wisdom: An Introduction* (London: SCM Press, 1982); D. F. Morgan, *Wisdom in Old Testament Traditions* (Oxford: Blackwell, 1987); R. E. Murphy, "Wisdom in the OT," ABD, vol. 6, 920–31; Idem., *The Tree of Life: An Exploration of Biblical Wisdom Literature* (New York: Doubleday, 1990).

8. See M. Scott, *Sophia and the Johannine Jesus* (Sheffield: JSOT Press, 1992), 50.

9. See C. V. Camp, *Wisdom and the Feminine in the Book of Proverbs* (Sheffield: Almond Press, 1985).

10. See P. W. Skehan and A. A. Di Lella, *The Wisdom of Ben Sira,* Anchor Bible 39 (New York: Doubleday, 1987).

11. See M. Scott, *Sophia and the Johannine Jesus,* 54.

12. See C. Larcher, *Le Livre de la Sagesse ou la Sagesse de Salomon,* 3 vols. (Paris: Librairie Lecoffre, 1983–1985).

13. Her role in mediating immortality anticipates the Patristic theme:

Eternal and hence divine by nature, Jesus can grant the gift of immortality (e.g., St Irenaeus, *Adversus Haereses* 3.18.7).

14. Another OT book expresses succinctly her accessibility: "Wisdom appeared upon earth and lived among human beings" (Bar 3:37).

15. R. E. Murphy, *The Tree of Life,* 144.

16. See T. E. Fretheim, "Word of God," ABD, vol. 6, 961–68.

17. See F. W. Horn, "Holy Spirit," ABD, vol. 3, 260–80, at 260–65. On the diverse Jewish conceptions of "spirit" when the Christian era came, see J. R. Levison, *The Spirit in First Century Judaism* (Leiden: Brill, 1997). The Jewish scriptures speak of "the Holy Spirit" only in Ps 51:13; Is 63:10–11; and Wis 1:5; 9:17.

18. The prophetic books refer to empowerment by the "spirit" but not very frequently (Is 61:1; Ez 2:1–2; Mi 3:8; Zec 7:12; see also Neh 9:30).

19. G. von Rad, *Old Testament Theology,* trans. D. M. G. Stalker, vol. 1 (London: Oliver & Boyd, 1962), 444; trans. corrected.

2. The History of Jesus and Its Trinitarian Face

1. G. O'Collins, *Interpreting Jesus* (Ramsey, NJ: Paulist Press, 1983), 195–99; idem., *Christology* (Oxford & New York: Oxford University Press, 1995), 273–78. See R. E. Brown's *Birth of the Messiah,* (Garden City, NY: Doubleday, 2d rev. ed., 1993), 122–64, 298–308, 517–33, 697–712.

2. R. E. Brown, *Birth of the Messiah,* 706–07. See J. J. Kilgallen, "The Conception of Jesus (Luke 1,35)," *Biblica* 78 (1997), 225–46.

3. On the baptism of Jesus, see J. P. Meier, *A Marginal Jew: Rethinking the Historical Jesus,* vol. 2 (New York: Doubleday, 1994), 100–16, 182–91. On Mark's version of the baptism, see R. A. Guelich, *Mark 1–8:26,* Word Biblical Commentary, vol. 34a (Dallas: Word Books, 1989), 29–36; on Matthew's version, see D. A. Hagner, *Matthew 1–13,* Word Biblical Commentary, vol. 33a (Dallas: Word Books, 1993), 53–60. On Luke's version of the baptism, see J. A. Fitzmyer, *The Gospel according to Luke I–IX,* Anchor Bible 28 (Garden City, NY.: Doubleday, 1981), 479–87; J. Nolland, *Luke 1–9:20,* Word Biblical Commentary, vol. 35a (Dallas: Word Books, 1989), 157–65.

4. Matthew depicts Jesus' baptism as a public manifestation for others, even if it is only Jesus who sees or experiences the descent of the Spirit (Mt 3:16).

5. In their call-visions, Moses, Isaiah, and Jeremiah all have something to say in response to the divine voice. The inaugural vision of Ezekiel takes place on the banks of a river (Kebar) with the heavens opening (Ez 1:1), but the rest of that symbolic vision differs strikingly in its content and length from what we read in Mark 1: 10–11.

6. On baptism with "Spirit and fire" see J. Nolland, *Luke 1–9:20,* 152–53, and R. A. Guelich, *Mark 1–8:26,* 27–28.

7. For a helpful discussion of this Lukan passage, see J. A. Fitzmyer, *The Gospel according to Luke (X–XXIV),* Anchor Bible 28a (Garden City, NY: Doubleday, 1985), 864–76.

8. Apropos of the baptism, Raymond Brown writes with due caution: "The chief intention of the three [synoptic] Gospel accounts is to tell *readers* who Jesus is, not whether they are to think that John the Baptist or the bystanders saw or heard anything. John 1:32 describes a vision (internal or external?) of John Baptist, without implying that anyone else was present. One may *suspect* that Jesus' decision to accept baptism from John the Baptist was for him a moment of unique perception about the direction his life should then take. We need not suppose, however, that the perception was phrased by him in the christological language used to describe the baptism in the Gospels" (*Birth of the Messiah,* 710, n. 335).

9. J. P. Meier, *A Marginal Jew,* vol. 2, 108–09. Right here, however, one has to wonder how Meier can rightly speak of these two insights being "developed intellectually and experienced existentially" by Jesus and at the same time refuse to say anything about Jesus' psychological state. To say something about Jesus' psychological state, as Meier himself rightly does here, is not the same as (mistakenly) pretending to offer a full "clinical report" and so to "pyschoanalyze" Jesus.

10. See J. P. Meier, *A Marginal Jew,* vol. 2, 407–23.

11. St. Thomas Aquinas, ST 3, a. 45, art. 4, ad 2.

12. On Luke's version of the Transfiguration, see J. A. Fitzmyer, *The Gospel according to Luke (I–IX),* 791–804; for Matthew's version, see D. A. Hagner, *Matthew 14–28,* Word Biblical Commentary, vol. 33b (Dallas: Word Books, 1995), 488–95.

13. See the helpful discussion of Matthew 11:25–30 in D. A. Hagner, *Matthew 1–13,* 315–21; on the parallel in Luke 10:21–22, see J. A. Fitzmyer, *The Gospel according to Luke (X–XXIV),* 864–76.

14. See G. D. Fee, *God's Empowering Presence: The Holy Spirit in the*

Letters of Paul (Peabody, MA: Hendrickson, 1994), 410–12; J. P. Meier, *A Marginal Jew,* vol. 2, 358–59.

15. When reporting Jesus' prayer in Gethsemane, Matthew and Luke do not reproduce the Markan *Abba*, just as they drop other Aramaic expressions Mark records (Mk 3:17; 5:41; 7:11; 11:34; 15:34). The only Markan Aramaisms that survive in either Matthew or Luke are *Hosanna* (Mk 11:9–10; par. in Mt 21:9) and *Golgotha* (Mk 15:22; par. in Mt 27:33).

16. J. D. G. Dunn, *Christology in the Making* (London: SCM Press, 2nd ed., 1989), 27.

17. On the Lord's Prayer, see J. A. Fitzmyer, *The Gospel according to Luke X–XXIV,* 896–908; and J. Nolland, *Luke 9:21–18:34,* Word Biblical Commentary, vol. 35b (Dallas: Word Books, 1993), 607–21; J. P. Meier, *A Marginal Jew,* vol. 2, 291–302, 353–60, 363–64.

18. One should also observe here that ancient Judaism displays no uniform system of messianic expectation. Along with the dominant notion of a Davidic Messiah or king who would restore the kingdom of Israel, there were minor messianic strands that included a priestly messiah, an anointed prophet, and a heavenly Son of Man. One should also observe that figures promised in ancient Judaism are not necessarily anointed and so "messianic"; conversely, someone who is anointed and so "messianic" is not necessarily an eschatological figure (e.g., Ps 45:7). In particular, pre-Christian Judaism offers no evidence that "a/the Son of God" or "son of God" was ever regarded as *messianic,* in the sense of being expected as the future, anointed agent of YHWH. On the evidence for "Son of God" emerging as a messianic title at the time of Jesus, see my *Christology,* 115–18.

3. The Trinity According to St. Paul

1. R. Bultmann, *Theology of the New Testament,* vol. 1 (London: SCM Press, 1952), 81.

2. Some, like the so-called Macedonians (from around A.D. 360) would, however, deny the true divinity of the Spirit. While recognizing a distinct subject or an acting individual, they took the Holy Spirit to be a higher angel or some creature made by the (truly divine) Son.

3. On the divine implications of Jesus' self-presentation, see C. A. Evans, "Jesus' Self-Designation 'The Son of Man' and the Origins of His

Deification," in S. Davis, D. Kendall, and G. O'Collins (eds.), *The Trinity* (Oxford: Oxford University Press, 1999), 29–47.

4. See N. T. Wright, *The Climax of the Covenant* (Edinburgh: T. & T. Clark, 1991), 120–36.

5. That *Lord* in Romans 10:13 means the risen Jesus is made clear by the context, in particular by Romans 10:9. J. A. Fitzmyer calls Romans 10:12–13 "an eloquent witness to the early church's worship of Christ as *Kyrios*" (*Romans,* Anchor Bible 33 [New York: Doubleday, 1993]), 593. The OT passage that Paul echoes and applies to Jesus in Philippians 2:10–11 includes an adamantly monotheistic oracle. YHWH is the one God to be adored by all nations: "Turn to me and be safe, all you ends of the earth, for I am God; there is no other" (Is 45:22).

6. A possessive genitive ("the Spirit that belongs to God or Christ") would largely coincide with the second possibility. Some call a genitive of identity a defining, appositional, or epexegetical genitive.

7. *Christology in the Making* (London: SCM Press, 2d ed., 1989), 146. Some writers misuse 2 Corinthians 3:17 to identify the risen Christ with the Holy Spirit; on this see J. D. G. Dunn, *The Theology of the Apostle Paul* (Grand Rapids, MI: Eerdmans, 1998), 422–23; and G. O'Collins & D. Kendall, *The Bible for Theology* (Mahwah, NJ: Paulist Press, 1997), 93, 183.

8. For helpful analyses of the Pauline passages this chapter has mentioned, see G. D. Fee, *God's Empowering Presence: The Holy Spirit in the Letters of Paul* (Peabody, MA: Hendrickson, 1994). In *The Theology of Paul the Apostle,* J. D. G. Dunn differs at times from Fee; for instance, in not attending much to the "triadic" texts found in Paul's letters; see also Dunn's remarks (263).

4. The Trinity in the Witness of Luke, Matthew, Hebrews, and John

1. This Q-saying seems to have been modified by Matthew in favor of his preferred language ("my Father in heaven" [twice], in place of the original "the angels of God") and of a more straightforward reference to Jesus ("me" [twice], in place of "me" and "the Son of man"): "Everyone therefore who acknowledges me before others, I also will acknowledge before my Father in heaven; but whoever denies me before others, I also will deny before my Father in heaven" (Mt 10:32–33). On these verses in Matthew, see D. A.

Hagner, *Matthew 1–13,* Word Biblical Commentary, vol. 33a (Dallas: Word Books, 1993), 287–89. On Luke 12:8–9 see J. A. Fitzmyer, *The Gospel according to Luke X–XXIV*, Anchor Bible 28a (Garden City, NY: Doubleday, 1985), 958, 960–61.

2. On the three parables of Luke 15, see J. A. Fitzmyer, *The Gospel according to Luke X–XXIV,* 1071–94.

3. On the Spirit, see F. W. Horn, "Holy Spirit," ABD, vol. 3, 260–80; E. Kamlah et al., "Spirit, Holy Spirit," in C. Brown (ed.), *The New International Dictionary of the New Testament* (Grand Rapids: Zondervan, 1986), 689–709; R. Menzies, *The Development of Early Christian Pneumatology: with special reference to Luke-Acts* (Sheffield: Sheffield Academic Press, 1991).

4. On Luke's notion(s) of the Holy Spirit, see J. A. Fitzmyer, *The Gospel according to Luke I–IX,* Anchor Bible 28 (Garden City, NY: Doubleday, 1981), 227–31.

5. See L. Hartman, *"Into the Name of the Lord Jesus": Baptism in the Early Church* (Edinburgh: T. & T. Clark, 1997). On the various passages cited from Acts, see J. A. Fitzmyer, *The Acts of the Apostles,* Anchor Bible 31 (New York: Doubleday, 1998).

6. For literature on Mt 28:16–20, see D. A. Hagner, *Matthew 14–28,* Word Biblical Commentary, vol. 33b (Dallas: Word Books, 1995), 878–80.

7. See J. N. D. Kelly, *Early Christian Creeds* (London: Longmans, 3d ed., 1972).

8. On the trinitarian implications of Hebrews see H. Hübner, *Biblische Theologie des Neuen Testaments,* vol. 3 (Göttingen: Vandenhoeck & Ruprecht, 1995), 19–34.

9. See Justin, *Dialogue with Trypho,* 43.1; see also 11.2.

10. J. D. G. Dunn, *Christology in the Making* (London: SCM Press, 2d ed., 1989), 230–39.

11. A development from the philosophy of Plato himself (d. 347 B.C.), Middle Platonism lasted from the first century B.C. till the third century A.D. To protect the absolute divine "otherness," it elaborated notions of intermediary beings and agents. Stoicism, a school of philosophy called after the *stoa,* or porch, in Athens where its founder Zeno (d. 263 B.C.) taught, highlighted harmony between human beings and the whole cosmos. Behind the regular order of nature the Stoics recognized a rational world-soul; they understood God and the divine energy to pervade everything. The Roman emperor Marcus Aurelius (d. A.D.180) was Justin's contemporary and a major figure in

the audience the Christian philosopher and theologians addressed. The Jewish philosopher and Bible scholar, Philo of Alexandria died ca. A.D. 50.

12. In this context it is worth observing that, even if the NT comes close in such Pauline phrases as *the Spirit from God* and *the Spirit of God* (1 Cor 2:11–12) no NT text ever calls the Holy Spirit *God* (*Theos*) as happens very occasionally in the case of Jesus (e.g., Jn 1:1; 20:28).

13. In the letters to the Seven Churches, the Book of Revelation passes on "the words" of Jesus who "died and came to life" (Rv 2:8). But the messages are also described as being what "the Spirit says to the churches" (Rv 2:7,11,17,29; 3:6,13,22). The visionary is "in the Spirit" (Rv 1:10) but sees the risen Lord (Rv 1:12–16) as well as hearing his words.

5. The Trinity Before Nicaea

1. For further material on the period and authors discussed in this chapter, see L. Abramowski, "Die Entstehung der dreigliedrigen Taufformel," *Zeitschrift für Theologie und Kirche* 81 (1984), 417–46; R. M. Grant, *Gods and the One God* (Philadelphia: Westminster Press, 1986); J. Grillmeier, *Christ in the Christian Tradition,* vol. 1, trans. J. Bowden (London: Mowbrays, 2d ed., 1975); A. Houssiau, "La baptème selon Irénée de Lyon, *Ephemerides Theologicae Lovanienses* 60 (1984), 45–59; J. Moingt, *Théologie trinitaire de Tertullien,* 4 vols. (Paris: Aubier, 1966–1969); E. Osborn, *The Emergence of Christian Theology* (Cambridge: Cambridge University Press, 1993); idem., *Tertullian, First Theologian of the West* (Cambridge: Cambridge University Press, 1997); W. Rordorf, "La Trinité dans les écrits de Justin Martyr," *Augustinianum* 20 (1980), 285–97.

2. One should add that *ousia* could have other meanings: e.g., individual reality; in ***Divine** Substance* (Oxford: Clarendon Press, 1977) C. Stead spelled out 28 possible meanings for *ousia*. But here in Justin's writings *ousia* seems to mean "essence."

3. The Jewish philosopher and exegete, Philo of Alexandria (d. ca. A.D. 50), when describing the divine power that creates and orders the world and through which God is made known, wrote of a second such power (*Quaestiones et Solutiones in Exodum,* 2.62). Directly or indirectly influenced by him, Justin differs, however, from Philo through the doctrine of the incarnation and the sharply drawn history of the Logos of "second God" (*First Apology,* 33). Philo's own agenda is different. To instruct people about the

human appearances of God in the Bible, while maintaining the divine immutability, the Jewish scholar allows that God may be improperly called two.

4. *Early Christian Creeds* (London: Longman, 3d ed., 1972), 148.

5. Encouraged by the Stoic idea of the world as a body, Athanasius also understood the Word to fill the universe (*Contra Arianos,* 8.1), to guide it (ibid., 1.23), and thus to make God the Father known to all (ibid., 12.3). In this work, he maintained the theme of the Word, who is the image and true glory of God, dwelling within human beings (ibid., 3.10).

6. See J. Dupuis, *Toward a Christian Theology of Religious Pluralism* (Maryknoll, NY: Orbis, 1997).

7. The architect of Neoplatonism, Plotinus (A.D. 205–269/70), taught that all modes of being derive in concentric circles from a single spiritual source, identified as the One and the Good.

8. St. Melito of Sardis (d. ca. 190), a slightly younger contemporary of Justin, insisted even more on the scandalous faith in the divine Creator of all things who died on a cross: "He who hung up the earth is himself hung up; he who fixed the heavens is himself fixed [on the cross]; he who fastened everything is fastened on the wood" ("On the Pasch," 96).

9. Referring to baptism, 1 Clement (late first century) asks: "Have we not one God, and one Christ, and one Spirit of grace which has been poured over us?" (46.5). The *Didache* (late first or early second century) writes of baptism being administered "in the name of the Father, and of the Son, and of the Holy Spirit" (7).

10. See J. Wicks, "Rule of Faith," in R. Latourelle and R. Fisichella (eds.), *Dictionary of Fundamental Theology* (New York: Crossroad, 1994), 959–61. Irenaeus's "rule of faith" could not be identical with the creed because in his day no fixed, declaratory creed had yet emerged.

11. The image of God's "two hands" leaves much to be clarified about the activity of the Trinity. Do the Son and the Holy Spirit act in harmonious tandem but separately—like the hands of a piano player, or should the image be rather that of a joint operation—like the two hands of a golfer? Irenaeus himself probably thought of the two hands of a potter working together to produce a new artifact (see Is 64:8).

12. We have here one of those subordinationist formulations that turn up sometimes in Irenaeus's writings—this time one that affects the Spirit. Whereas the Son "was always with the Father," the Spirit was with him only

"before the creation" and seems to have been brought into existence in view of creation.

13. Elsewhere, Irenaeus remarks how baptism declares the truth of God, who is Father, Son, and Holy Spirit (*Adversus Haeresus,* 3.17.1).

14. Centuries later, St. Anselm of Canterbury looked to the Nile in proposing a similar analogy for the Trinity: one body of water forming at various points the spring (he did not know about the existence of Lake Victoria), the river itself, and a lake in which the waters of the river accumulate (*Epistola de Incarnatione Verbi,* 13).

15. In *Amazing Grace: A Vocabulary of Faith* (New York: Riverhead Books, 1998) Kathleen Norris writes of Tertullian's "image of the Trinity as a plant, with the Father as a deep root, the Son as the shoot that breaks forth into the world, the Spirit as that which spreads beauty and fragrance, 'fructifying the earth with flower and fruit.'...deep down, that mystery is as real as the air we breathe, as everything that grows from the ground under our feet" (291).

16. See J. N. D. Kelly, *Early Christian Creeds,* 70–88.

17. In *De Principiis,* Origen wrote: "God is light, according to John. The beam of this light is the only Son; he proceeds inseparably from him as the beam from the light, and illumines all creation.... This beam, offering itself with more moderation and sweetness to the fragile and feeble eyes of mortals, teaches them little by little to accustom themselves to endure the brightness of the light...It makes them capable of receiving the light in all its glory" (1.27).

18. On Arius and Arianism, see D. E. Groh, "Arius, Arianism," ABD, vol. 1, 384–86; R. Williams, *Arius: Heresy and Tradition* (London: Darton, Longman & Todd, 1987).

6. From Nicaea I to Constantinople I

1. See, for example, A. Grillmeier, *Christ in Christian Tradition,* vol. 1, trans. J. Bowden (London: Mowbrays, 2d ed., 1975); R. P. C. Hanson, *The Search for the Christian Doctrine of God* (Edinburgh: T. & T. Clark, 1988); J. N. D. Kelly, *Early Christian Doctrine* (New York: Harper & Row, 2d ed., 1960; G. L. Prestige, *God in Patristic Thought* (London: SPCK, 2d ed., 1968).

2. See also Basil, *De Spiritu Sancto,* 30.77.

3. See N. Tanner, *Decrees of Ecumenical Councils,* vol. 1 (London: Sheed & Ward, 1990), 28.

4. A semi-Arian who was Bishop of Constantinople from 342 until he

was deposed by the Arian Council of Constantinople in 360, Macedonius did not found the party called after him and may not even have subscribed to the heresy that drew its name from him and that from 360 denied the true divinity of the Spirit.

5. Admittedly, in the context of the Spirit, *C* speaks of *one* Church and *one* baptism.

6. See J. N. D. Kelly, *Early Christian Creeds* (London: Longman, 3d ed., 1972), 182, 197, 217.

7. The Greek *ek* indicates in general the origin (either personal or impersonal) of someone or something, whereas *para* regularly points to a *personal* origin or source.

8. See J. N. D. Kelly, *Early Christian Creeds,* 342–44.

7. From Athanasius to Aquinas

1. See P. Widdicombe, *The Fatherhood of God from Origen to Athanasius* (Oxford: Clarendon Press, 1994).

2. Athanasius understood this "being in" reciprocally: While the Spirit is in the Son, it is also true that "the Son is in the Spirit as in his own image" (Letter to Serapion, 1.21).

3. As Hilary of Poitiers remarked, the existence of the Son is implied in the very name of "Father" (*De Trinitate,* 7.31).

4. When describing the Spirit's "re-creative" work, Athanasius appreciated the dramatic signficance of 1 Pt 1:4 (about our "becoming participants of the divine nature"), a verse that had been somewhat strangely neglected by earlier writers.

5. A century earlier, Origen had led the way in struggling with the issue of reconciling the *common* activity of the Trinity with actions *proper* to each divine person (*De Principiis,* 1.3.5–4.2).

6. Athanasius himself also supported orthodox trinitarian faith by appealing to the threefold baptismal confession: *Letter to Serapion,* 30; *Contra Arianos,* 42.

7. Here, however, one should recall that the Cappadocians rarely employ the phrase "one *ousia* (essence), three *hypostaseis* (subsistences)." They also designate what is one in God by *physis* (nature) or *theotes* (deity), and what is three in God by *idiotetes* (properties) and *prosopa* (persons). See J. T. Lienhard, "*Ousia* and *Hypostasis:* the Cappadocian Settlement and the

Theology of "One *Hypostasis*," in *The Trinity*, S. Davis, D. Kendall, and G. O'Collins (eds.) (Oxford: Oxford University Press, 1999), 99-121.

8. Such analogies could all too easily encourage tritheism, as if the Father, Son, and Holy Spirit were three separate examples of divinity—along the lines of three individual human beings. Any such belief in more than one "god" means, of course, that none of them would be truly divine. Irenaeus pointed this out trenchantly against Marcion's attempt to separate the God of the OT and the God of the NT (see Chapter 5 above).

9. See B. Sesboüé, *Saint Basile et la Trinité* (Paris: Desclée, 1998).

10. See M. R. Barnes, "Rereading Augustine's Theology of the Trinity," in *The Trinity*, Davis, Kendall and O'Collins (eds.), 145–76.

11. The scriptures also yield hints that might encourage linking the generation of the Son with loving (e.g., Jn 3:35—"The Father loves the Son and has placed all things in his hands") and the procession of the Spirit with knowing (1 Cor 2:11—"No one comprehends the thoughts of God except the Spirit of God"). Jn 3:35, however, anticipates Jn 13:3: "Jesus, knowing that the Father had given all things into his hands, and that he had come from God…" In this verse the giving/placing all things in the hands of the Son is associated with "knowing." One should add that here and elsewhere in John, "knowing" involves a positive relationship that is not too far from what is meant by "loving." Presumably the traditional liturgical order for confessing the Trinity, with the Son coming "before" the Spirit, when taken together with the normal placing of knowing/thinking "before" willing/loving, suggests linking the Son with the former and the Spirit with the latter. Yet one should recall, as Augustine himself did, the mutual conditioning that exists between knowing and loving: We know what we love, as well as loving what we know. This mutual conditioning makes it somewhat problematic to presume *tout court* that knowing comes before willing.

12. The others would include, for example, Gregory of Nyssa and his trinitarian scheme of "Mind, Logos, and Spirit."

13. Michel Barnes rightly points out that this psychological analogy for the Trinity is also found in such earlier (Greek) authors as Gregory of Nyssa: "Augustine in Contemporary Trinitarian Theology," *Theological Studies* 56 (1995), 237–50, at 238–39. In "Rhetorical and Theological Issues in the Structuring of Augustine's *De Trinitate*," *Studia Patristica,* ed. E. A. Livingstone (Leuven: Peeters Press, 1993), 356–63, Earl Muller argues that the love analogy of Book 8 is only the first step toward the *one* psychological analogy Augustine wanted to develop.

14. On some elements in the twentieth-century debate over the psychological analogy for the Trinity, see A. Hunt, "Psychological Analogy and Paschal Mystery in Trinitarian Theology," *Theological Studies* 59 (1998), 197–218.

15. Oxford: Oxford University Press, 1970.

16. When the Franks and Charlemagne (king of the Franks from 768 to 814) first tried to introduce the *Filioque* into the creed used in Rome, Pope Leo III rejected the addition. The term entered the text of the creed in Rome only when Emperor Henry II in 1013 ordered the Latin church to add the *Filioque* everywhere.

17. In the fourth century, we find this language about the Spirit proceeding "from the Father through the Son" in the writing of Gregory of Nyssa. It appears also in the works of St. Cyril of Alexandria (d. 444).

18. See Y. Congar, *I Believe in the Holy Spirit,* trans. D. Smith, vol. 1 (London: Geoffrey Chapman, 1983), 157, 159–60. Some have argued that Karl Barth (d. 1968) also reduced the work of the Spirit in favor of the Son.

19. The NT clearly affirms monotheism in statements that come from Paul (e.g., 1 Cor 8:4–6) and, very likely, from Jesus himself (e.g., Mk 12:29). In his "The Relation Between Fundamental and Systematic Theology," *Irish Theological Quarterly* 62 (1996/97), 140–69, at 154–55, Francis Schüssler Fiorenza helpfully argues against "universal" concepts of God or the notion of a "generic" God. Notions of the deity are intrinsically distinctive and drawn from specific religious traditions that have their own history. In the case of the Christian concept of God, it is related to a particular history of salvation that began with the call of Abraham and climaxed with the story of Jesus.

20. The controversies of the fourth century established the conclusion that these differences and distinctions are not to be explained by attributing to the Son and the Holy Spirit less than divine status. In his eternal generation, the Son receives himself wholly from the Father, as does the Holy Spirit who proceeds from the Father through the Son. Yet this does not mean that the Son and the Spirit are less than God. The Father who gives, the Son who receives, and the Spirit who proceeds are all coequally God. The fact that the Son and Spirit exist because of the Father does not mean that the Father is more divine or has more of what makes for divinity than the other two persons.

21. Earlier in this chapter, we saw that Athanasius, prompted by his inherited Christian faith and own experience of the missions of the Son and the Spirit, excluded their having the same origin in the Father. Otherwise, they

would be both "Sons and Brothers." Their distinct missions pointed to distinct and different origins within the divine life.

22. Earlier in this chapter, we noted Basil's insistence that "we cannot conceive of" either the Father or the Son "apart from their relationship with each other." The image used by Irenaeus about the Son and the Spirit being "the two hands" of God the Father (see Chapter 5) implies a similar kind of mutual reference, which has its roots in the NT. Paul names the Spirit both as "the Spirit of the Son/Christ" and as "the Spirit of God [the Father]" (e.g., Gal 4:6; Rom 8:9). John sets out even more clearly the mutual reference of Father, Son, and Holy Spirit. To "see" the Son is to "see" the Father (Jn 14:9), who will send the Holy Spirit in the Son's name (Jn 14:26).

23. N. P. Tanner (ed.), *Decrees of Ecumenical Councils*, vol. 1 (London: Sheed & Ward, 1990), 28.

24. K. Rahner, "Current Problems in Christology," *Theological Investigations*, trans. C. Ernst, vol. 1 (London: Darton, Longman & Todd, 1961), 149–200, at 149.

25. Further pioneering definitions of Boethius need adjustment and expansion, for instance, that of the human being as "a two-legged, reasoning animal (*homo est animal bipes rationale*)."

26. See M. Henninger, *Relations* (New York: Oxford University Press, 1989), 13–29.

27. See W. Kasper, *The God of Jesus Christ,* trans. M. J. O'Connell (New York: Crossroad, 1989), 280.

28. Centuries earlier, Augustine had distinguished the *actus* of the Trinity (which is common to all three persons) from the *terminus* (which is distinct) (*Sermo*, 52.4.8). See also the teaching of Lateran IV (DH 801; ND 20).

29. One might also expound the Augustinian tradition continued by St. Bonaventure (d. 1274). The three constitutive powers of the soul (memory, intellect, and will) correspond to the three divine persons and provide us with an illuminating trinitarian analogy.

30. See Pasquale Iacobone, *Mysterium Trinitatis: Dogma e Iconografia nell'Italia medievale* (Rome: Gregorian University Press, 1997), for rich documentation of the links between the Athanasian Creed and artistic expressions. See also J. N. D. Kelly, *The Athanasian Creed* (New York: Harper & Row, 1964).

31. One should point out that this credal statement about the Spirit proceeding "from the Father and the Son" was composed a century or more before Toledo III (589) may have introduced the "from the Son (*Filioque*)"

into the Nicene-Constantinopolitan Creed. If we accept the later date for the introduction of the *Filioque*, Braga IV in 675, then the *Quicumque* used the expression well over 200 years before it was added to the Nicene-Constantinopolitan Creed in the West.

8. Our Modern Setting

1. See J. Calvin, *The Institutes of the Christian Religion,* trans. F. L. Battles, vol. 1 (Philadelphia: Westminster Press, 1960), 1.7.4; 3.2.34–35.

2. In the Krailsheimer edition, this "pensée" is numbered 189; it is numbered 547 in the Brunschvicg edition.

3. On Luther and others who developed this thesis of Christ as a penal substitute suffering the divine anger, see B. Sesboüé, *Jésus-Christ l'unique médiateur,* vol. 1 (Paris: Desclée, 1988), 67–83, 238–47, 280–87, 360–65.

4. Trans. R. A. Wilson and J. Bowden (London: SCM Press, 1974).

5. J. Hick, *The Metaphor of God Incarnate* (London: SCM Press, 1993), ix.

6. Ibid., 153.

7. In I. Kant, *Religion and Rational Theology,* trans. A. W. Wood and G. di Giovanni, The Cambridge Edition of the Works of Immanuel Kant (Cambridge: Cambridge University Press, 1996), 264.

8. For some relevant works of Hegel, see Chapter 9, n. 2.

9. See P. Martinelli, *La morte di Cristo come rivelazione dell'amore trinitario nella teologia di Hans Urs von Balthasar* (Milan: Jaca, 1996). The dialogue with Hegel comes through von Balthasar's *A Theology of History*, translator unnamed (New York: Sheed & Ward, 1963).

10. Trans. M. Kohl (London: SCM Press, 1981); see also J. Moltmann, "The Trinitarian History of God," in his *Future of Creation* (London: SCM Press, 1979), 80–96.

11. Unfortunately, a certain ambiguity affects this book, as it switches from speaking of the suffering and death *of* God (as had Melito of Sardis, Tertullian, and other patristic writers) to speaking of suffering and death *in* God.

9. The Personal Existence of the Holy Spirit

1. Unlike the two evangelists, St. Paul writes of the preexistent Son of God being sent (Rom 8:3; Gal 4:4) or taking the initiative in coming (2 Cor

8:9; Phil 2:6–8), without mentioning (but also without denying) the operation of the Holy Spirit in effecting this mission of the Son.

2. See G. W. H. Hegel, *Hegel's Logic,* trans. W. Wallace (Oxford: Clarendon Press, 1975); id., *Lectures on the Philosophy of Religion,* trans. R. Brown et al., 3 vols. (Berkeley: University of California Press, 1984–1987); idem., *Phenomenology of Spirit,* trans. A. V. Miller (Oxford: Oxford University Press, 1977).

3. See, for example, G. W. H. Lampe, *God as Spirit* (Oxford: Oxford University Press, 1977).

4. See D. L. Gelpi, *The Divine Mother: A Trinitarian Theology of the Holy Spirit* (Lanham, MD: University Press of America, 1984), 215–38.

5. See Y. Congar, *I Believe in the Holy Spirit,* trans. D. Smith, 3 vols. (London: Geoffrey Chapman, 1983), vol. 1, 163–66; vol. 3, 155–64. See further G. O'Collins and D. Kendall, *The Bible for Theology* (Mahwah, NJ: Paulist Press, 1997), 93–94, 183–84. On the history of Pneumatology see also S. M. Burgess, *The Holy Spirit,* 3 vols. (Peabody, MA: Hendrickson, 1984–1997).

10. Trinitarian Persons and Actions

1. See C. Andresen, "Zur Entstehung und Geschichte des trinitarianischen Personenbegriff," *Zeitschrift für die neutestamentliche Wissenschaft* 52 (1961), 1–39; A. Milano, *Persona in teologia* (Naples: Dehoniane, 1984); C. Schwöbel and C. E. Gunton (eds.), *Persons, Human and Divine* (Edinburgh: T. & T. Clark, 1991).

2. K. Rahner, *The Trinity,* trans. J. Donceel and intr. C. M. LaCugna (New York: Crossroad, 1997), 103–15. At the same time, although pointing out how, when applied to the Trinity, *person* in the plural can easily imply tritheism, Rahner declares: "There is really no better word, which can be understood by all and would give rise to fewer misunderstandings" (ibid., 44; see ibid., 56–57).

3. K. Barth, *Church Dogmatics* I/1 (Edinburgh: T. & T. Clark, 2d ed., 1975), 295–347.

4. When rejecting the notion of bodiless persons in his "The Personal God and a God Who Is a Person," Adrian Thatcher at least illustrates the variety in modern approaches to personhood: see *Religious Studies* 21 (1985), 61–73.

5. Despite Jean-Paul Sartre (1905–1980) and his claim that other people are "hell," aiming to be a person by myself and simply for myself leads to nothingness—the hell of myself alone, cut off from others, and unable (or unwilling) to love anyone else.

6. See W. Kasper, *The God of Jesus Christ,* trans. M. J. O'Connell (New York: Crossroad, 1989), 289. But see also the cautionary remarks of H.A. Harris, "Should We Say that Personhood Is Relational?," *Scottish Journal of Theology* 51 (1998), 214–34.

7. In line with these four relations, classical theology of the Trinity distinguished the five "notional" properties: unoriginatedness, fatherhood, sonship, active spiration, and (passive) being spirated.

8. See H. Mühlen, "Person und Appropriation: Zum Verständnis des Axioms: In Deo omnia sunt unum, ubi non obviat relationis oppositio," *Münchener theologische Studien* 16 (1965), 37–57.

9. On the "term" of the incarnation, see E. Muller, "The Dynamic of Augustine's *De Trinitate:* A Response to a Recent Characterization," *Augustinian Studies* 26 (1995), 65–91, at 76–82.

10. On the irreducibly special activity of the Spirit, see G. O'Collins and D. Kendall, *The Bible for Theology* (Mahwah, NJ: Paulist Press, 1997), 93–100, 163–69.

11. Ed. J. McCann (London: Burns & Oates, 1924), 181.

11. Naming the Trinity

1. On names, see F. M. Denny, "Names and Naming," in *Encyclopedia of Religion,* M. Eliade (ed.), vol. 10 (New York: MacMillan, 1987), 300–07; S. A. Kripke, *Naming and Necessity* (Cambridge, MA: Harvard University Press, 1980); J. R. Searle, "Proper Names and Descriptions," in *The Encyclopedia of Philosophy,* P. Edwards (ed.), vol. 6 (New York: MacMillan, 1967), 487–91; H. Wettstein, "Causal Theory of Proper Names," in *The Cambridge Dictionary of Philosophy,* R. Audi (ed.) (Cambridge: Cambridge University Press, 1995), 109–10.

2. When commenting on 1 Corinthians, H. Conzelmann quotes P. Bachmann to state that "Father" merely acts "in the manner of a proper name" (*1 Corinthians,* Hermeneia Commentaries [Philadelphia: Fortress, 1975]), 144.

3. R. E. Brown, *The Death of the Messiah,* vol. 1 (New York: Doubleday, 1994), 174.

4. See P. Widdicombe, *The Fatherhood of God from Origen to Athanasius* (Oxford: Clarendon, 1994).

5. Here I follow what J. M. Soskice, especially in *Metaphor and Religious Language* (Oxford: Clarendon Press, 1985), and W. P. Alston, especially in *Divine Nature and Human Language* (Ithaca: Cornell University Press, 1989), have written about the use of metaphor as building on literal utterances and meanings but going beyond them. In this chapter, I talk of God as Father in the technical trinitarian sense and context, while recognizing other usages: for example (1) St. Thomas Aquinas's interpretation of *our Father* in the Lord's Prayer as referring to God *tout court,* and (2) the way *Father* may be applied to Jesus as in Edward Caswall's translation (from *Catholicum Hymnologium Germanicum*): "To Christ, the prince of peace, / And Son of God most high, /The father of the world to come, /Sing we with holy joy." Putting *father* here in lowercase and immediately after Christ being named *Son of God most high* respects the technical trinitarian sense of *Father* (uppercase). Caswall's translation also echoes what is said in Is 9:6 about "the child born to us," who will be named *Everlasting Father and Prince of Peace*.

6. See G. O'Collins, "Images of Jesus: reappropriating titular christology," *Theology Digest* 44 (1997), 303–318.

7. The synoptic Gospels witness to the way in which the message of Jesus could disrupt households by setting fathers against sons, sons against fathers, mothers against daughters, and daughters against mothers—not to mention strife between in-laws (Lk 12:51–53; par. in Mt 10 34–36). Was the same message, a generation or two later, encouraging united, if patriarchal, family life?

8. On household codes, see H. Moxnes (ed.), *Constructing Early Christian Families* (London/New York: Routledge, 1997); J. H. Neyrey, "Loss of Wealth, Loss of Family, and Loss of Honour," in P. Ester (ed.), *Modelling Early Christianity. Social-Scientific Studies of the New Testament in its Context* (London: Routledge, 1995); C. Osiek and D. L. Balch, *Families in the New Testament World: Households and Household Churches* (Louisville: Westminster/John Knox, 1997).

9. On this verse, see the standard commentaries on Ephesians listed in R. E. Brown et al. (eds.), *The New Jerome Biblical Commentary* (Englewood Cliffs, NJ: Prentice Hall, 1990), 883.

12. Images of the Trinity

1. See S. M. Burgess, *The Holy Spirit: Medieval Roman Catholic and Reformation Traditions* (Peabody, MA: Hendrickson, 1997), 87–123.

2. In *A Simple Heart* Gustave Flaubert (1821–1880) tells the life of Félicité, a person of transparent goodness who imagines the Holy Spirit as a giant parrot with rose-pink wings, an emerald body, a blue forehead, and a golden throat.

3. See G. L. Prestige, *God in Patristic Thought* (London: SPCK, 2d ed., 1952), 168.

4. See C. G. Jung, *Psychology and Religion: East and West,* Collected Works, vol. 11 (London: Routledge & Kegan Paul, 2d ed., 1969), 109–200.

5. See J. Dupuis, *Toward a Christian Theology of Religious Pluralism* (Maryknoll, NY: Orbis, 1997), 274–279.

BIBLIOGRAPHY

Bettenson, H., *The Early Christian Fathers,* New York: Oxford University Press, 1956.

———. *The Later Christian Fathers,* New York: Oxford University Press, 1970.

Brown, D., *The Divine Trinity,* London: Duckworth, 1985.

Coffey, D., *Deus Trinitas: The Doctrine of the Triune God,* New York: Oxford University Press, 1999.

Congar, Y., *I Believe in the Holy Spirit*, 3 vols., London: Geoffrey Chapman, 1983.

Courth, F., *Handbuch der Dogmengeschichte*, ed. M. Schmaus et al., vol. 2/1a-c, Freiburg: Herder, 1988–1996.

Davis, S., D. Kendall, and G. O'Collins (eds.), *The Trinity,* Oxford: Oxford University Press, 1999.

Del Colle, R., *Christ and the Spirit,* New York: Oxford University Press, 1994.

Dupuis, J., *Toward a Christian Theology of Religious Pluralism,* Maryknoll, NY: Orbis, 1997.

Fee, G. D., *God's Empowering Presence: The Holy Spirit in the Letters of Paul,* Peabody, MA: Hendrickson, 1994.

Greshake, G., *Der dreieinige Gott. Eine trinitarische Theologie,* Freiburg im Breisgau: Herder, 1997.

Gunton, C. E., *The Promise of Trinitarian Theology,* Edinburgh: T. & T. Clark, 1988.

Hill, W. J., *The Three-Personed God,* Washington, D.C.: Catholic University of America Press, 1982.

Hunt, A., *The Trinity and the Paschal Mystery,* Collegeville, MN: Michael Glazier, 1997.

Jenson, R. W., *The Triune Identity: God According to the Gospel,* Philadelphia: Fortress, 1982.

———. *Systematic Theology*, vol. 1, New York: Oxford University Press, 1997.

Johnson, E. A., *She Who Is: The Mystery of God in Feminist Theological Discourse,* New York: Crossroad, 1993.

Jüngel, E., *The Doctrine of the Trinity: God's Being Is in Becoming,* Edinburgh: Scottish Academic Press, 1966.

———. *God as the Mystery of the World,* Grand Rapids, MI: Eerdmans, 1983.

Kasper, W., *The God of Jesus Christ,* New York: Crossroad, 1989.

Kelly, A., *The Trinity of Love,* Wilmington, DE: Michael Glazier, 1989.

LaCugna, C. M., *God For Us: The Trinity and Christian Life,* San Francisco: HarperSan Francisco, 1991.

Marsh, T. A., *The Triune God,* Dublin: Columba, 1994.

Moltmann, J., *The Trinity and the Kingdom: The Doctrine of God,* London: SCM Press, 1981.

O'Collins, G., *Christology: a Biblical, Historical, and Systematic Study of Jesus,* Oxford: Oxford University Press, 1995.

O'Donnell, J., *The Mystery of the Triune God,* Mahwah, NJ: Paulist Press, 1988.

Pannenberg, W., *Systematic Theology*, vol. 1, Grand Rapids, MI: Eerdmans, 1991.

Peters, T. F., *God as Trinity: Relationality and Temporality in the Divine Life,* Louisville: Westminster/John Know, 1993.

Prokes, M. T., *Mutuality. The Human Image of Trinitarian Love,* Mahwah, NJ: Paulist Press, 1993.

Rahner, K., *The Trinity,* New York: Crossroad, 1997.

Schwöbel, C. (ed.), *Trinitarian Theology Today: Essays on Divine Being and Act,* Edinburgh: T. & T. Clark, 1995.

Studer, B., *Trinity and Incarnation: the Faith of the Early Church,* Edinburgh, T. & T. Clark, 1995.

Torrance, A. J., *Persons in Communion: Trinitarian Description and Human Participation,* Edinburgh: T. & T. Clark, 1996.

Torrance, T. F., *The Christian Doctrine of God: One Being, Three Persons,* Edinburgh: T. & T. Clark, 1996.

Volf, M., "'The Trinity Is Our Social Program': the Doctrine of the Trinity and the Shape of Social Engagement," *Modern Theology* 14 (1998), 403–23.

Welker, M., *God the Spirit,* Minneapolis: Fortress, 1994.

Zizioulas, J., *Being and Communion: Studies in Personhood and the Church,* London: Darton, Longman & Todd, 1985.

INDEX OF NAMES